BlackBerry© Pearl™
Made Simple

Written for the 8100, 8110, 8120, 8130,
and all 81xx Series BlackBerry Handhelds

The Third Book
in the BlackBerry Made Simple™
Guide Book Series

By
Martin Trautschold
Gary Mazo

BlackBerry Made Simple
www.blackberrymadesimple.com
BlackBerry Training Videos and Books

Our BlackBerry Videos are the most effective way to Learn: www.blackberrymadesimple.com

BlackBerry® Pearl™
Made Simple

This book is intended to help owners of the BlackBerry Pearl™ 8100, 8120, 8130 and related 81xx Series BlackBerry handhelds.

If you have a different BlackBerry Model, then version where you found this book. If you cannot locate this published guide, please check out our electronic versions at www.blackberrymadesimple.com

Published by
CMT Publications, Inc.
25 Forest View Way
Ormond Beach, FL 32174

Copyright © 2007 by CMT Publications, Inc., Ormond Beach, Florida, USA

ISBN-10: 1-4196-8389-6
ISBN-13: 978-1-4196-8389-3
Published Date: November 30, 2007

Published in the United States of America

10 9 8 7 6 5 4 3 2 1

Trademark Acknowledgements

Images
BlackBerry images courtesy of Research In Motion, Ltd. (www.blackberry.com)

Contact Us
Contact the authors at info@blackberrymadesimple.com
For Free Email Tips, and the Electronic Version ("E-book") in Adobe PDF format, please visit
www.blackberrymadesimple.com

Tired of reading?   Rather watch the video?

Check out our Extensive Library of BlackBerry Video Clips
We have developed more than 200 separate "Video Clips" viewable on your personal computer (and soon on your BlackBerry) that bring to life the information found in this book. Each clip will is about 3-5 minutes long and will show you on the screen exactly how to do the setup, tips and tricks! We also will add new Video Clips all the time. To learn more, please visit:
http://www.blackberrymadesimple.com

Also from

Visit our web site www.blackberrymadesimple.com
Email: info@blackberrymadesimple.com or Call +1-386-506-8224

Books:
BlackBerry Made Simple™ for Full Keyboard BlackBerries
(87xx, 77xx, 75xx, 72xx, 6xxx Series)
BlackBerry Made Simple™ for 7100 Series BlackBerries
(7100, 7130, 71xx Series)

Video Training
(Viewed On Your Computer)
We offer a full library of over 200 3-minute video training clips for:
8800 / 88xx Series, 8700 / 87xx Series, Curve™ 8300 / 83xx Series,
Pearl™ 81xx Series, 77xx / 75xx / 72xx / 6xxx Series, and
71xx Series BlackBerry Handhelds.

Custom BlackBerry or Non-BlackBerry Video Training
We develop video training to meet our client's diverse training needs.

Video Training
(Viewed On Your BlackBerry)
(Coming Soon) We are working on putting our video
Training library on the Pearl™ 8100 Series, Curve™ 8300 Series and
8800 Series BlackBerry devices.

Mobile Learning Courses & Tests
(Viewed On Your BlackBerry or Computer)
(Coming Soon) We are also using a new Mobile Learning Software and
Tracking Platform to develop a series of BlackBerry mobile learning
courses with assessment tests. Our system will automatically track each
course page viewed by a user on their BlackBerry or computer and their
test scores. And, if desired, these results can be fully integrated into a
SCORM-compliant learning management system.

What's In This Book?

Table of Contents

Search Icon -
Find Just About Anything.......198

Section 3: Communicating With Your Pearl 206

Getting Started
with Email...............................207

Advanced Email
Topics 227

Your Phone and
Voice Dialing 237

Advanced

SMS Text and

PIN, BlackBerry

and Other Instant Messengers

Connecting

Section 4: Web Browsing..... 310

Web Browsing
on the Pearl...........................311

Section 5: Multi-Media Features of the Pearl...........................331

Working with
the Camera and Pictures........ 332

Working with
Music and Videos 350

Section 6: Your Pearl as Traveling Companion..........374

Section 7: The Kitchen Sink-Troubleshooting, Backup and Utilities 412

Table of Contents

Where to Go

Authors & Acknowledgements

 **Martin Trautschold** is the Founder and CEO of BlackBerry Made Simple, a leading provider of RIM BlackBerry Training Videos and Books. He has been successful entrepreneur in the BlackBerry mobile training and software business for the past 6 years. With BlackBerry Made Simple he has been helping to train many thousands of BlackBerry users with short, to-the-point video tutorials. He has also has co-authored three BlackBerry-related "Made Simple" books. He is currently working with co-author Gary Mazo on several more books: A similar guide to the BlackBerry 8800 Series & 8300 Curve™ and a book about the "BlackBerry Addiction" phenomena. Martin's began is entrepreneurial life with a BlackBerry wireless software company which he co-founded with Ned Johnson. Together, they spent 3 years growing it and then sold it, the company's flagship product "Handheld Contact" is still being developed, marketed and sold to this day by the new owners. Martin also has 15 years experience managing complex technology and business projects for consulting, technology and energy firms in the US and Japan. He holds a Bachelor of Science in Engineering Degree from Princeton University and an MBA from the Kellogg School at Northwestern University. In his "free time" he enjoys spending time with his wife, Julie, and three children. Occasionally, he tries to sneak a few hours to ride his bicycle with friends in Ormond Beach, Florida. Martin can be reached at martin@blackberrymadesimple.com.

I would like to thank my co-author Gary Mazo for his tireless effort in helping to make this book a success. This book is much more comprehensive due to his efforts. A special thanks goes out to all the BlackBerry Made Simple customers who have asked great questions and shared their tips, many of which are in this book! I would also like to thank my wife, Julie and my daughters for their support over the many months of writing, re-writing and editing.

-- Martin Trautschold

 **Gary Mazo** is a writer, a College Professor, a gadget nut and an ordained rabbi. Currently, Gary teaches at the University of Phoenix – teaching Writing, Philosophy, Technical Writing and more. Gary is also on the Editorial staff of www.gadgetntuz.com and www.cdrinfo.com writing news and reviews of the latest in the personal/mobile electronics industry. Gary is also the Director of Kollel of Cape Cod – a cutting edge Jewish Educational institution/Congregation in Marstons Mills, Massachusetts. He holds a BA in Anthropology from Brandeis University. Gary earned his M.A.H.L (Masters in Hebrew Letters) as well as ordination as Rabbi from the Hebrew Union College-Jewish Institute of Religion in Cincinnati, Ohio. He has served congregations in Dayton, Ohio, Cherry Hill, New Jersey and Hyannis, Massachusetts.

His first book, entitled "And the Flames Did Not Consume us" achieved critical acclaim and was published by Rising Star Press in 2000.

Gary is married to Gloria Schwartz Mazo and between them, they have six children. Gary can be reached at: gary@blackberrymadesimple.com.

This book is only possible due to the support of several individuals in my life. First, I would like to thank Martin Trautschold for giving me the opportunity to join him in this project. Next, I would like to thank Kermit Woodall, Editor-in-Chief of Gadgetnutz.com for giving me my first opportunity to merge my love of writing with my love of mobile technology. Lastly, I want to thank my wife, Gloria and our kids; Ari, Dan, Sara, Bill, Elise and Jonah – without whom I would not have the support to pursue projects like this one.

                                                    -- Gary Mazo

Introduction

Congratulations on your BlackBerry Pearl!

In your hands is perhaps the smallest, most elegant, powerful and revolutionary SmartPhone available – the BlackBerry Pearl.

Do more, be more organized, have more fun!

The Pearl is the first consumer device put out by RIM (Research in Motion.) But, don't be fooled, you still have one of the most powerful business tools available – it is just a little more fun.

Unique Features on the BlackBerry Pearl

Your BlackBerry Pearl has some unique features that were new to the BlackBerry Family when it was first released. Some of the other models with trackballs on the front, including the 8800 Series and 8300 Curve™ also have some of these same features.

1. **Multimedia & Network Features** (1st for a BlackBerry)
   - Camera (1.3 or 2.0 mega pixel)
   - Media Player (Pictures, Video and Audio)
   - Video Recording (8130 and similar)
   - GPS Capable (8130 and similar)
   - Wi-Fi 80211 b/g network capable (8120 and similar)

2. **Trackball** (The "Pearl") (1st for a BlackBerry)
   - Navigate around the screen in every direction just by rolling the trackball. (This provides for more intuitive navigation compared to previous BlackBerry models

which had a trackwheel that only rolled in one direction.)

3. **SureType™ Keyboard**
    *   A 20-key keyboard laid out with the traditional keyboard "QWERTY" style but with two letters per key to minimize the size.. The BlackBerry SureType™ typing technology actually learns as your type and predicts the word for you. It even scans your Address Book to help predict hard-to-guess words like people's names and street names – simply amazing!

4. **Media Card – Expansion Memory Card** (1st for a BlackBerry)
    *   Enhance the usable memory by a factor of 30 or more on your BlackBerry with a 2.0 gigabyte ("GB") MicroSD memory card. Newer Pearl handhelds also now accept a 4.0 GB card. (This may even expand to higher capacity cards in the future.)
    *   External MicroSD slot (8130 and similar)

What Makes the Pearl so Unique?

What makes the Pearl so unique is that it can do so many things in such a "small and stylish" package. There are many SmartPhones on the market today and most are wide or bulky or both.

At the time of publication of this book, the BlackBerry Pearl is the smallest Smartphone you can buy, yet it contains all the features you could ever want.

Manage your life, organize your day and your contacts, keep in touch and have access to the industry's best email client available – all from the palm of your hand.

Beautiful chrome accents, thinner than the touted "thinnest phone" when closed, a beautiful, crisp color screen, Internet-capable and gorgeous – it is no wonder that the Pearl is taking the market by storm.

Want to "Turbo-Charge" Your Pearl?

Check out our "Software and Services Guide" chapter starting on page 503 to learn about the wide variety of amazing software and services offered for your Pearl. Consider this a good starting point to give you a feel for what you can do with you Pearl beyond all the 'standard' email, phone, web browsing. Once you see the possibilities, you can pick specific software or services to truly 'turbo-charge' your Pearl to help you be more organized and successful at both work and family life!

How This Book is Organized

Our Goal is to take you step by step through all the features of your BlackBerry Pearl. Some of the features may be already familiar to you; some are sure to be new to you.

"Must Read" Sections: These two sections will give you a jump start on your BlackBerry Pearl:

What do all the **Buttons on the Pearl** do? – Page 24

What do all the **Icons on the Pearl** do? – Pages 24 - 33

Comprehensive – Yet Simple: This seems like a paradox, but we make it happen by keeping our explanations very straight forward with plenty of screen shots to help guide you through step-by-step. It is comprehensive because we include a wealth of information about not just the basics of the Pearl, but advanced features, tips and tricks and even some third-party software and services to help you get more out of your Pearl. This book will take you through each of the features of the BlackBerry Pearl – "no pearl is left unturned – no oyster un-opened". (Sorry!) Everything that your Pearl can do will be presented for you in an informative, easy-to-understand manner.

NOTE: When we say "Everything" we mean 95%+ of all the various capabilities, we are certain there are a few things that are not in this book. If you want to let us know to add something in the next version, please email us at info@blackberrymadesimple.com.

For the New User

The BlackBerry Pearl™ is Research In Motion, Ltd. ("RIM's") first consumer product – most BlackBerries were standard issue in the business and government world, but not generally in the hands of consumers.

For new users, everything about the BlackBerry is...well....new. We will teach you how get your email up and running, manage your contacts and calendar and use all the features of your Pearl.

We even show you the fun stuff: how to take and manage pictures, use your Pearl as an MP3 player, watch videos, listen to live broadcasts and get the most up-to-date sports, stocks and weather.

For you, the book is organized to take you through, in a logical progression, the main features of your new device.

For the "Seasoned BlackBerry User"

You know the basics, but even the most basic things you are used to doing on your older BlackBerry handheld might be a little different on the Pearl.

We will also show you some of the advanced menu commands and lots of tips and tricks so you can customize your Pearl to do the things you want it to do.

You will also find a comprehensive list of web sites and 3rd party software that has been optimized to run on the Pearl. (page 503)

For All BlackBerry Pearl Users

We hope you find this resource to be a valuable tool in unlocking the potential of your BlackBerry Pearl. Whether you are a "newbie" or a "seasoned" BlackBerry user, you are now the owner of one of the most capable devices you can own. Enjoy and flaunt that!

Section 1: Getting Started With Your BlackBerry Pearl

Beginning to Use Your Pearl

Chapter Contents:
- Understanding the Keys, Buttons and Icons
- Starting and Exiting Icons
- Organizing (Moving and Hiding) Icons
- Changing Font Sizes and Types
- Different Themes ("Look and Feel")
- Setting Your Convenience Keys
- Using the Media Card
- BlackBerry Help

Learning Keys, Buttons & Icons

You will find your BlackBerry Pearl even easier to use once you learn the function of each button.

Buttons: What do they each do?

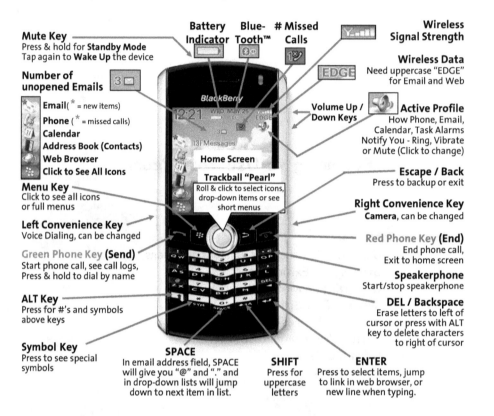

Mute Key
Press & hold for **Standby Mode**
Tap again to **Wake Up** the device

Number of unopened Emails

Email(* = new items)
Phone (* = missed calls)
Calendar
Address Book (Contacts)
Web Browser
Click to See All Icons

Menu Key
Click to see all icons or full menus

Left Convenience Key
Voice Dialing, can be changed

Green Phone Key (Send)
Start phone call, see call logs,
Press & hold to dial by name

ALT Key
Press for #'s and symbols above keys

Symbol Key
Press to see special symbols

Battery Indicator

Blue-Tooth™

 # Missed Calls

Wireless Signal Strength

Wireless Data
Need uppercase "EDGE" for Email and Web

Home Screen

Trackball "Pearl"
Roll & click to select icons, drop-down items or see short menus

Volume Up / Down Keys

Active Profile
How Phone, Email, Calendar, Task Alarms Notify You - Ring, Vibrate or Mute (Click to change)

Escape / Back
Press to backup or exit

Right Convenience Key
Camera, can be changed

Red Phone Key (End)
End phone call, Exit to home screen

Speakerphone
Start/stop speakerphone

DEL / Backspace
Erase letters to left of cursor or press with ALT key to delete characters to right of cursor

SPACE
In email address field, SPACE will give you "@" and "." and in drop-down lists will jump down to next item in list.

SHIFT
Press for uppercase letters

ENTER
Press to select items, jump to link in web browser, or new line when typing.

TIP: Multi-Use Buttons – Red Phone Key

Many buttons do more than one thing depending on where you are. **Try pressing the Red Phone key when you're not on a call.**

Icons: What do they all do?

Your Pearl gives you lots of information right on the Home Screen. The table below shows you what each icon does and where to get more information in this book.

NOTE: Your icons may look somewhat different from the ones shown below, however when you roll over them you will see the same name. Some BlackBerries may have icons to organize or group other icon together in sub-groups (sub-menus) like

"Applications" which may contain Tasks, MemoPad, Calculator, Voice Note, BlackBerry Messenger, Password Keeper,

Brick Breaker game, or "Settings" which may contain Alarm, Screen/Keyboard, Mobile Network, and Options. Finally, some BlackBerry providers may have additional services like "Push to Talk" (PTT – a Walkie-talkie type feature), or specialized icons to reach the Internet or their own web stores where ring-tones, games, and other applications are sold for your BlackBerry.

Icon / Name	What it does
Messages	Your email inbox, also for SMS text messages, MMS (Multi-Media Messages) and you can even configure your voice call logs (missed, placed, received) to show up here also so you have all communication in a single place. (See page 75 for email setup help and page 246 for turning on 'Call Logs' in Messages.)
Address Book / Contacts	Stores your names, addresses, email addresses, phone numbers and notes related to each entry. (See Chapter 4 for how to share your addresses between your computer and your BlackBerry and Chapter 5 for Address Book tips & tricks)
Calendar	See day, week, month and agenda views. (Chapter 4 for how to share your Calendar between your computer and your BlackBerry and Chapter 6 for the best way to use the Calendar.)
Browser, Internet Browser, BlackBerry	Your small wireless connection to the entire Internet. This works best when you learn how to use Bookmarks and which sites work best on your BlackBerry browser. (See Chapter 15 for all the best on the Browser.)

Browser	
Enterprise Activation	Use this icon to connect your BlackBerry to a BlackBerry Enterprise Server ("BES"). Your organization may have a BES, or you may purchase access to a BES from several third-party "Hosted-BES" providers. (Learn more about 'Hosted-BES' on page 514) Key benefits of the BES-connected BlackBerry include: enhanced email security, full 2-way wireless synchronization of your contacts, calendar, tasks and memo items.
Setup Wizard	Use this to do your initial setup including email, owner information, languages, fonts, date/time and even learn some good tips and shortcuts. See below: Setup Wizard Device Setup Language Date and Time Introduction to BlackBerry Import SIM Card Contacts Personalization Owner Information Font Email Setup Shortcuts Did You Know?
Phone & Call Logs	This is your phone and call logs screen. You can instantly see it by tapping the Green Phone Key. TIP: Press and hold the Green Phone key to dial by name from your Address Book.

	7:11AM SAT, AUG 18 edge GPRS Test Network 2 2 My Number: 1 519 888 7465 Jaydeep Barn... (W) 7:11a +13865551222 7:10a Cecily Barnes (W) 7:10a Martin Traut... (W) 7:09a
BlackBerry Messenger	This allows you to have instant messenger or "IM" conversations with other BlackBerry users. Learn about BlackBerry and other Instant Messenger programs in Chapter 13.
Media Player	This is where you can store and view or play your videos, ringtones, music and pictures. **TIP:** If you are viewing a picture, just tap the Menu key and select "Set As Home Screen Image" to use it as a background behind your icons. Media Music Video Ringtones Pictures
Camera	Take pictures with your BlackBerry Pearl. What's great is that you always have a camera with you and it is so easy to share pictures by sending them in email to anyone at anytime. **TIP:** Many times your right convenience key will be mapped to immediately start the camera. See Chapter 16 for all the details.

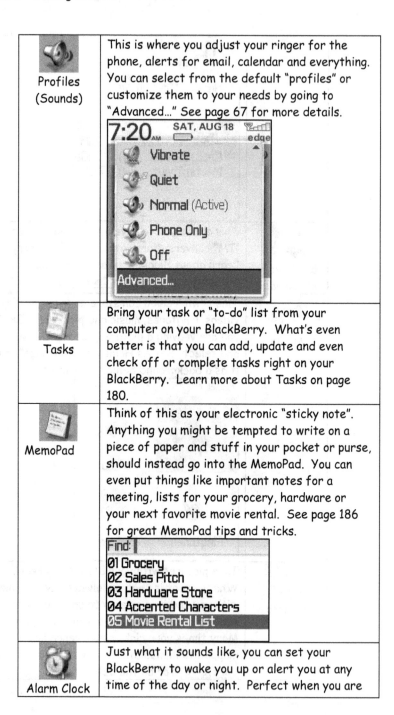 Profiles (Sounds)	This is where you adjust your ringer for the phone, alerts for email, calendar and everything. You can select from the default "profiles" or customize them to your needs by going to "Advanced..." See page 67 for more details.
Tasks	Bring your task or "to-do" list from your computer on your BlackBerry. What's even better is that you can add, update and even check off or complete tasks right on your BlackBerry. Learn more about Tasks on page 180.
MemoPad	Think of this as your electronic "sticky note". Anything you might be tempted to write on a piece of paper and stuff in your pocket or purse, should instead go into the MemoPad. You can even put things like important notes for a meeting, lists for your grocery, hardware or your next favorite movie rental. See page 186 for great MemoPad tips and tricks.
Alarm Clock	Just what it sounds like, you can set your BlackBerry to wake you up or alert you at any time of the day or night. Perfect when you are

	traveling and need an important (or backup) wakeup alarm. You can even set the alarm to be 'weekday only' by setting 'Active on Weekends' to "No". **12:11** PM SAT, AUG 18 edge GPRS Test Network Daily Alarm: On Time: 6:00 AM Snooze: Off Active on Weekends: No Alert Type: Tone Tune: Alarm_Antelope Volume: Medium Number of Beeps: 2
Voice Dialing or Voice Command	A great feature to increase your safety while you cannot look at your screen, for example driving. Check out Chapters 10 and 11 for more on Voice Dialing. Also, check out page 503 for our "mini" guide to Third party software and services. Several of these services even allow you to have your BlackBerry "read" all your emails and even "speak" email replies that are "typed" as text email. Some even allow you to add new calendar events by speaking!
Calculator	Calculate anything from basic tips to converting units from English (Lb., Miles, Inches, etc.) to Metric (Kg., Kilometers, Centimeters, etc.) 0. Help To Metric From Metric Switch Application Close in -> cm ft -> m yd -> m mi -> km lb -> kg F -> C US gal -> L UK gal -> L US mpg -> L/100km
Password	Pick one password to securely store all your important usernames and passwords / PIN numbers in one easy to access location.

Keeper	**New Password** Title: Amazon.com Username: myusername Password: password Website: http://www.amazon.com Notes:
Search	This is a fantastic tool to help you find almost anything in your BlackBerry using a "full text" search of Messages (Email), Calendar, Address Book, MemoPad and Tasks. **TIP**: Make sure to put a person's name in your calendar events (meetings, etc.) so you can later answer the question "When did I last meet with Sally Parker?" using the Search icon. See Chapter 7 for more. **Search** Text: Sally Parker Name: ☑ Messages ☑ Calendar ☑ Address Book ☑ MemoPad ☑ Tasks Search Deselect All Full Menu
Options (May be inside the "Settings" icon)	This is where you configure all the settings for your BlackBerry and can perform advanced troubleshooting. After you install new third party software, some of their settings will be located in this icon here also.

	Options About Advanced Options Auto On/Off AutoText Custom Wordlist Date/Time Localisation Network Owner Screen/Keyboard Security Options ▼ SMS Status Theme Voice Dialing And in "Advanced Options" you see: Options – Advanced Applications Browser Browser Push Cell Broadcast Enterprise Activation Host Routing Table Media Card Message Services Service Book SIM Card TCP	
Turn Wireless Off	Clicking this will turn off your BlackBerry radio receiver. You must do this when you are in an airplane. **TIP**: Turn off the radio if you are away from a wireless signal to prolong your battery life. See the best wireless troubleshooting tips in Chapter 19 on page 413 and our Battery Life tips on page 472.	
Manage Connections	**In newer versions of the BlackBerry software,** you may see an icon that will say "Manage Connections" and allow you to manage all your connections, whether to the Mobile "Cell" network, Bluetooth, or WiFi (newer models). This is a great area to help with troubleshooting	

	if email and/or web are not working. (See Chapter 19)
	
	 Turn All Connections Off
	 ☑ Mobile Network
	 ☐ Bluetooth
	 Services Status
	 Set Up Bluetooth
	 Mobile Network Options
	 Bluetooth Options
	
	 "Services Status" shows you this:
	
	 Services Status
	 Voice Services
	    Status available
	     Connection: Mobile Network
	 BlackBerry Internet Service
	     Connection: Mobile Network
	 BlackBerry Enterprise Server
	     Connection: not connected
	 Mobile Network ▽..ᴀᴤ
	    EDGE
	 Mobile Network Provider
	    AT&T
	 Bluetooth
	    Off

Keyboard Lock	Click this icon to lock your BlackBerry when you slip it into your pocket or purse. It prevents accidental key presses (which could result in an embarrassing surprise speed dial call!). TIP: You can also press and hold the MUTE key on the top of your Pearl to enter Standby Mode (See page 47)
Power Off	Note: This icon is not available on all Pearl models – it depends on your Phone Company / Carrier. Click this icon to power off your BlackBerry. You may also press and hold the power key (Red Phone Key) for 3 seconds to power off.
Screen/ Keyboard	Brings you directly to the Screen/Keyboard settings screen (Normally, you get to from the Options icon). Change font sizes & types (page 40), backlight brightness (page 474), trackball settings (page 65), and convenience key programming (page 48).

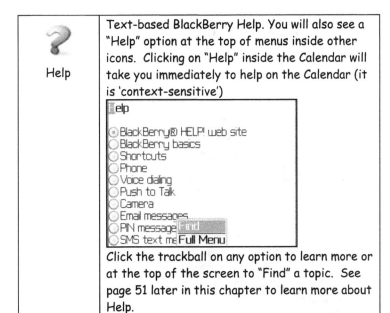Help	Text-based BlackBerry Help. You will also see a "Help" option at the top of menus inside other icons. Clicking on "Help" inside the Calendar will take you immediately to help on the Calendar (it is 'context-sensitive') Click the trackball on any option to learn more or at the top of the screen to "Find" a topic. See page 51 later in this chapter to learn more about Help.

Starting and Exiting Icons

Your "Home Screen" as it is called is just like your desktop on your computer is the source of your most vital information. You can jump back to this Home Screen from any program (by pressing the Red Phone key) and it is highly customizable. You can change the background image (called "Home Screen Image") from your Media player or camera. You can change the look and feel or "Theme" of your BlackBerry by going into the Options icon and selecting Theme (See page 41). You can also move around or hide the icons (page 35).

1.   **Starting & Exiting Icons**

Start Icons:
Roll and click (press in) the trackball "Pearl"

Exit Icons/Back Out:
Press the ESCAPE / Back Key

2.   See full menus and (in some Themes) see all your Icons.
     Press the Menu key

3.   Jump to the Home Screen, except on a Phone Call (while
     leaving what you are working on running in the
     background).

If you are on a phone call, pressing the Red Phone Key will
end your call. Pressing the Red Phone key any other time
will immediately bring you to your Home Screen from any
application.

TIP: Multi-Task with Red Phone Key

You can **"Multi-Task"** using the **Red Phone key. Just press
it (when not on a call)** and you jump right to the Home
Screen.
Say you are writing an email and needed to check the
calendar or wanted to schedule a new event.
1. Press the Red Phone key to jump to the Home Screen.
2. Start the calendar to check your schedule.
3. Press the Red Phone key again to return to the Home
Screen.
4. Click on the Messages icon to return exactly to where
you left off composing your email message.

Moving and Hiding Icons

You may not need to see every single icon on your Home
Screen, or you may have your most popular icons and want
to move them up to easy access on the top row.   Learn how
in this section. The way you move and hide varies a little
depending on which "Theme" you have on your BlackBerry.

Move / Hide Icons (When icons are <u>not</u> in one long list)

After pressing the Menu key, if your icons are arranged in
rows (as shown below), then use the method described
here. (If not, then skip to the next section).
1. Roll over it to highlight the icon you want to move using
the trackball.
2. Press the Menu key to bring up the "Move/Hide" menu.

In this case, we are going to move the "Enterprise Activation" icon, because it is highlighted with the yellow circle behind it.

3. Once you select "**Move Application**", then you see a black square around it. Start moving it wherever you want by rolling the trackball.

4. Finally, click the trackball to "set" the moved icon at the new location.
5. You can repeat the procedure for "Hiding" icons – select "Hide Icon" instead of moving.

How do you get back hidden icons?

1. How to do this depends on your particular Theme. If you see a "**Revert to Defaults**" menu item, then selecting that will bring back all your icons in their

'default' list.

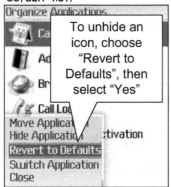

2. If you see a "**Show All**" menu item on the menu, select that and follow the directions below.

3. Then, select the icon to restore (may be shown grayed out, fainter than other icons, or with an "X" through it) and press the Menu key to bring up the menu and select "**Hide Application**" to restore it.

Move / Hide Icons (When icons are in a list)

After you press your Menu key (), if your icons are arranged in a vertical list as shown below, then you need to use a different method to move or hide icons.

1. After pressing the Menu key to see your icons in a long list, roll to the very bottom of the list and click on the **"Organize Applications"** button.

3. Once in the "**Organize Applications**" screen, press the Menu Key to select "**Move**" or "**Hide**" icons.

4. Now you can select "**Move**" to move an application icon, "**Hide**" to hide an application icon.
5. To see all your hidden icons, select "**Revert to Defaults**"

Seeing your Top 5 Icons on the Zen Theme

Just a note for those of you who like the "Zen Theme" (image below) which shows only five icons on the "Home Screen", you may want to know how to change those icons. (See the Themes section below for help on selecting the Zen Theme)

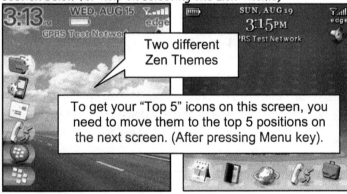

To have your top five icons shown on the Zen "Home Screen", follow the instructions to Move icons in on page 35 and make sure your top 5 icons are moved to be across the top row or in the top of the list.

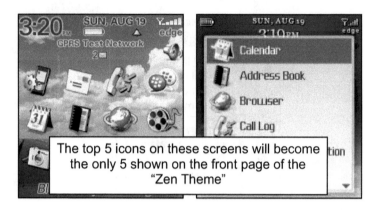

The top 5 icons on these screens will become the only 5 shown on the front page of the "Zen Theme"

Changing Your Font Size and Type

You can fine-tune the font size and type on your BlackBerry Pearl to fit your individual needs.

Do you need to see more on the screen and don't mind small fonts? Then go all the way down to a micro-size 7-point font.

Do you need to see bigger fonts for easy readability? Adjust the fonts to a large 14-point font and make it bold.

Here's how to adjust your font size and type:
1. Click on the Options icon. You may need to press the Menu key and roll up or down to find it.
2. Click on "Screen/Keyboard" to get to the screen to change your fonts.
3. Click the trackball to select a different font family, size, style or type as shown below. You can even see a preview of your currently selected style and size to make sure it

will fit your needs.

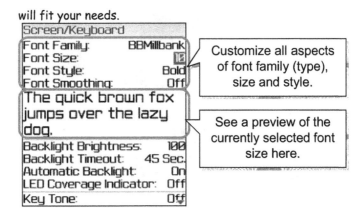

Customize all aspects of font family (type), size and style.

See a preview of the currently selected font size here.

Themes: The "Look & Feel" of Your BlackBerry

You can customize your Pearl and make it look truly unique. One way to do this is to change the "Theme" or look and feel of your BlackBerry. Changing Themes usually changes the layout and appearance of your icons and the font type and size you see inside each icon. There are at least four different Themes already included on your Pearl and literally hundreds more available for download at various web sites.

CARRIER-SPECIFIC THEMES: The Following Themes are included from various carriers around the world on their versions of the Pearl. Note: Unless you have a BlackBerry from the indicated carrier, you will not be able to see the Theme.

T-Mobile (US)
Zen
Theme

T-Mobile (Europe)
Zen Theme

MORE STANDARD/GENERIC BLACKBERRY THEMES:

Most of the 'Standard' Themes shown below are on every BlackBerry (or can be downloaded from mobile.blackberry.com). Unless your BlackBerry provider has specifically removed these Themes, they should be available on your BlackBerry in the Options > Themes or Settings > Options > Themes area. Learn more how to change and download Themes below.

BB Dimension Icon
Theme

BB Dimension
Zen Theme

BB
Dimension
Today
Theme

Your screen should look similar to one of the screens above with possible slight deviations. Much of this book uses screen shots from the "Today" Theme.

Downloading New Themes:
Note of caution: The authors have downloaded many Themes on their BlackBerry handhelds. Some Themes can cause problems with your BlackBerry. (lockups, not seeing everything on the screen, etc.) We recommend only downloading Themes from a web site you know and trust.

To download new Themes for your Pearl:

1. Start your web browser on your BlackBerry.
2. Click the Menu key and select "**Go To...**"
3. Type in "**mobile.blackberry.com**" - will read "http://mobile.blackberry.com" - Click "OK" to go to it.

4. Go to the "**Downloads**" link and click on it with the trackball.
5. On the next screen roll down to the "**Personalization**" section and click on 'Themes'
6. On the Terms & Conditions page, click "**I accept**" to continue if you accept these terms.
7. Try all the different Themes to see what you like best.

Selecting new Themes already on your Pearl

Experiment with these additional Themes to see which gives you the most appealing view of your information.

1. Move the Trackball to "Options" and click.
2. Scroll down to "Theme" and click.
    - You should now see a few possible Themes with a preview window below.

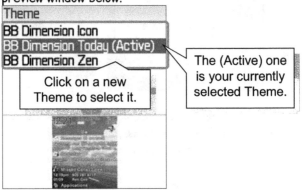

    - Scroll to each Theme to see it shown in the small preview window at the bottom of the screen
    - Choose the Theme you want and click the trackball
3. Your Home Screen now reflects the new Theme layout

Changing the Home Screen Picture

Now that you have the font size, type and Theme that you like – you may also want to change the background image or picture on your Home Screen. You may use any image that is stored on your Pearl – either in the BlackBerry's main memory or on the Expansion Card. And since the BlackBerry Pearl has a camera, you can even snap a photo and immediately use it for your Home Screen image. Grab a picture of your favorite person, a beautiful sunset or any landscape for your own personalized Pearl background.

To use a picture or image you already have on your BlackBerry:

1. Click on the "Media" icon.

2. Choose the "Pictures" icon and click.

- Using the trackball, navigate to the location of the picture you wish to use – either in the My Pictures, Device Pictures, Pre-loaded Media, Device Memory or Media Card folders

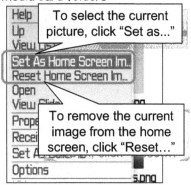

- Find the thumbnail of the picture you wish to set as your Home Screen.

- Move the trackball to highlight the thumbnail and press the Menu key and click
- Scroll up to "**Set As Home Screen Image**" and click

To use a picture or image directly from your camera:

1. Take the picture. (Learn all the details about the camera in Chapter 16 on page 332)
2. Click on the "Crop" icon as shown below and select "Set as Home Screen Image"

Standby Mode (Avoid Embarrassing Speed Dial!)

Have you ever needed to put your BlackBerry into your pocket, purse or bag and don't want keys to be accidentally pressed? If yes, then "**Standby Mode**" is the perfect answer .

Turn On Standby Mode:

Just press and hold the Mute Key on the top right of your BlackBerry until you see the "Entering Standby" message.

Turn Off Standby Mode: (Come back to life)

Tap the Mute key to bring your BlackBerry back "on".

TIP: You can also press and hold the SYM key (next to your SPACE key at the bottom) to lock your BlackBerry.

Changing Your Convenience Keys

The two keys on the middle of the sides of your BlackBerry Pearl are actually programmable keys called "convenience" keys. This is because each of the two keys can be set to 'conveniently' open any icon on your BlackBerry, even new Third Party icons that you add. (Check out our Guide to Third Party Software and Services starting on page 503)

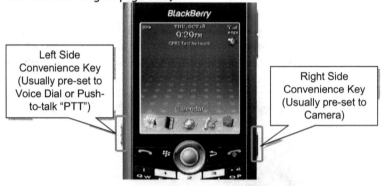

Left Side Convenience Key (Usually pre-set to Voice Dial or Push-to-talk "PTT")

Right Side Convenience Key (Usually pre-set to Camera)

In order to change your convenience keys you need to:
1. Click on the "Options" icon (press the Menu key if you don't see it listed.)
2. Scroll down and click on the "**Screen/Keyboard**" item.
3. Scroll down the screen until you see "Right Side Convenience Key Opens:" and "Left Side Convenience Key Opens:"
4. To change the icon / application these keys open, just click on the item to see the entire list. Then roll and click on the icon you want.

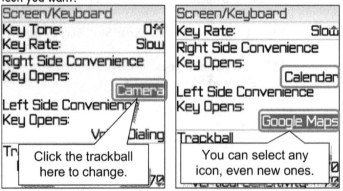

Click the trackball here to change.

You can select any icon, even new ones.

5. Then press the Menu key and select "Save" to save your changes.
6. Now give you newly set convenience keys a try – **they work from anywhere**, not just the Home Screen.

Using MicroSD Memory Cards "Media Card"

Your BlackBerry Pearl comes with about 64 MB of main memory, but that won't all be available to you. Operating system and installed software takes up some of that room and so will all your personal information. (The image of the SanDisk MicroSD card and the SanDisk logo are copyrights owned by SanDisk Corporation)

Since your Pearl is also a very capable Media device, you will want more room to store things like Music files, Videos, Ringtones and pictures.

That's where the "MicroSD" memory card comes in. We recommend a 1GB or 2GB micro SD memory card. Prices keep falling daily, but at the time of publishing this book, a 2GB MicroSD card was less than US $30.00. The larger 4GB cards were under $50.00.

Installing your Memory Card

Some of the newer Pearls (e.g. 8130) and newer actually have the MicroSD card on the outside of the device, so it is very easy to insert.
On the earlier models (e.g. 8100), the memory card actually goes underneath the battery, so follow the steps below and you can then load up your Pearl with hours of music and video.

1. Turn off your device by pressing and holding the Red Phone key (Power Key).
2. Remove the back cover of your Pearl. Pay special attention to where the connections are located. You will need to re-insert it the same way.

3.   Remove the battery.
4.   Close to the Camera end of the Pearl you will see a small, metal plate – this is the media card holder. Slide the metal plate up (follow the arrows.)
5.   Insert your memory card with the gold connectors lined up with the gold receivers. You need to stand the memory card up first and then lay it down.
6.   Slide the metal door downward to lock it in place.

Checking the Media Card Installation

Once installed, it is a good idea to double check that the card is installed correctly.

1.   Turn the phone on.
2.   Use the trackball to roll to the "Options" icon and click on it. You may need to press the Menu key to the left of the trackball to see this icon if it is not visible.
3.   Scroll up to the top and select "Advanced Options" and click. TIP: Pressing the first letter of an entry in the Options screen (or in menus) will jump to the first entry in the list starting with that letter. So pressing "A" will jump to the first entry starting with "A", pressing it a second time will jump to the next "A" entry.
4.   Scroll down to 'Media Card."

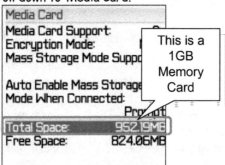

•   Look at the total space figure at the bottom of the screen. A 1GB card will read 952.19MB (1GB equals about 1,000 MB). If you see that, all is good.

- To see how to transfer Media files to the Media Card, go to see page 351 (for Windows™) and page 357 (for Mac™ computers).

Using BlackBerry Help

There might be times when you don't have this book or our video tutorials (www.blackberrymadesimple.com) handy and you need to find out how to do something right away on your Pearl.

Fortunately, almost every application on the Pearl has a built in contextual help menu that can answer some of your basic questions.

Using the "Help" Menus

The Help menu can be accessed from virtually any application. For our purposes, we will take a look at the Help menu built into the Calendar Program.

1. Locate the Calendar icon on the application screen and click the trackball.

2. Once in the Calendar or most any other program on your BlackBerry, press the Menu key and scroll all the way up to the top and you will see "Help." (This is true for most applications.)

Help
Today
Go to D
Prev D
Ne
Pr   Almost all of your
Ne   Icons will have a
Ne   "Help" item at the
            top of the menus.
Vie   (After you press the
Vie   Menu key)
Vie
Options

3. Click on "Help" and five options appear: Calendar Basics, Meetings, Calendar Settings, Calendar Shortcuts and Calendar Troubleshooting.

4. Move the cursor to "Calendar Basics" and click to see the screen below.

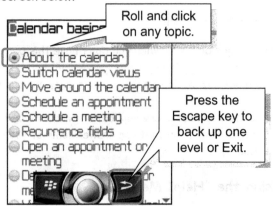

5. Then just roll and click the trackball on topics you would like to learn about. Press the ESCAPE key to back up one level in the help menus.

Help Menu Tips and Tricks

Like pretty much every other feature on the BlackBerry, there are some tips and tricks when using the "Help" menu.

1. Navigate to the "**Help**" menu as you did in step 3 above.

2. Do not move the cursor down to one of the options (keep it up at the top) and click in the trackball.

3. Now three options; "**Find**," "**Index**" and "**Full Menu**" are available.

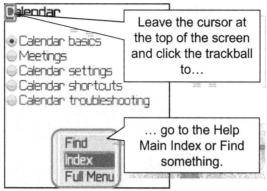

4. Click on "**Index**" and the full index of every help menu is now shown to you.

5. Navigate to the topic you desire, click the trackball and help topics for that subject will be displayed.

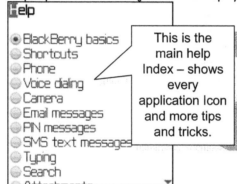

Typing and Sounds (Profiles) on Your Pearl

Chapter Contents:

- SureType™ and Multitap Typing Modes
- Typing Tips
- Editing Tips
- Using Symbols
- Save Time with AutoText
- The Custom Word List
- Multi-use SPACE bar
- The Trackball
- Setting Your Profiles (Ringtones, vibrate, mute, loud, custom)

SureType™ and Multitap Typing

There are two ways to type on your BlackBerry:
(1) SureType™ and (2) Multitap.

SureType is an innovative technology from BlackBerry that predicts what you are typing from the keys pressed, even though most keys have two letters on them. You only press a key once and the BlackBerry "guesses" which letter you wanted to type based on the context (what you have typed before it) and even what is in your Address Book. It even learns from you!

Multitap is the more standard cell phone typing technology, where you press the key once for the first letter on the key and twice for the second letter. For example, with the "ER" key, you would press it once for "E" and twice to get the "R" in Multitap mode. TIP: You will see the letters "ABC" in the upper right corner whenever you are in Multitap mode. You can switch back and forth by pressing the Menu key and selecting "**Enable SureType**" or "**Enable Multitap.**"

2
Typing, Sounds

NOTE: The BlackBerry always switches to **Multitap** mode when you are in a password field.

SureType:

When typing with **SureType** you will see the pop-up window below (or above) what you are typing. The highlighted word is the one currently being "guessed."

If you need to correct it, roll the trackball to highlight or select a different word or group of letters.

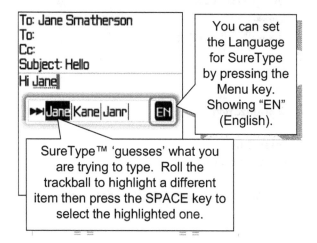

1. **Editing Text**

    Just roll the **trackball** back to the letter(s) that need to be corrected.

Subject: h

Press the **backspace** key to erase letters to the **left** of the cursor;

Subject: he

or, press **ALT + backspace** to **DELETE** characters under the cursor.

Subject: hel

Subject: hello

2. **Capitalization**

   Press & hold the
   letter to capitalize it.

3. **Use Multitap if SureType™ is not working**

TIP: SYM Key to Change Typing Mode

While typing, if you press and hold the **SYM key** (to the left of the SPACE key) you can switch between **SureType™** and **Multitap** typing modes. *NOTE: This trick seems to work only on certain versions of BlackBerry software.*

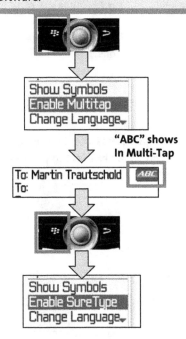

Show Symbols
Enable Multitap
Change Language

"ABC" shows In Multi-Tap

To: Martin Trautschold
To:

Show Symbols
Enable SureType
Change Language

Switching between typing modes:

– Switch between SureType and Multitap modes by **pressing and holding** the **SYM** key to the left of the SPACE key. *(NOTE: This SYM key trick seems to work only in certain versions of software on your BlackBerry)*

– You can also press Menu Key and select "**Enable Multitap**" or "**Enable SureType**"

- Long-term Solutions:

    If you use a particular word that is difficult to type, then add the word to your "**Custom Word List**" (See page 63 for details.)

    After adding the word to your Custom Word List, your BlackBerry should more easily recognize it when you type it.

    The other option is to use the **AutoText function** on your BlackBerry (See page 60 for details.)

Automatic Period & Cap at End of Sentence

At the end of a sentence, just press the **SPACE** key twice to see an automatic "." (period) and the next letter you type will be automatically capitalized.

Using Symbols

You can quickly add symbols to your text.

Press the "Symbol" key to the left of "Space"
This key brings up the Symbol menu

    Select the symbol by pressing the associated letter or rolling and clicking the trackball.

Editing Text

Making changes to your text is so easy with the Pearl

Scrolling Left and Right

Just roll the trackball back and edit using the DEL or ALT+DEL.

1. Roll the trackball left/right to scroll back/forth a character at a time.

2. Use DEL key to erase characters to the left of the cursor.

3. Press & Hold the ALT Key to delete characters UNDER the cursor.

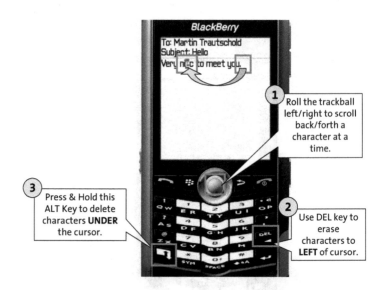

1. Roll the trackball left/right to scroll back/forth a character at a time.

3. Press & Hold this ALT Key to delete characters **UNDER** the cursor.

2. Use DEL key to erase characters to **LEFT** of cursor.

Saving Time with AutoText

Sometimes, typing on the SureType keyboard produces less than desirable results. Most of the time, it is fine – but strange word do appear from time to time. Fortunately, for the more common occurrences, you can create an "AutoText" entry to solve this problem. AutoText as shown below, is typically used to correct common typing mistakes, like leaving out an apostrophe in the word "aren't" (see below). Knowing AutoText is there helping you get things right will allow you to type on your Pearl much more quickly... most normal spelling mistakes and contractions are already pre loaded on your Pearl. You can even use AutoText for much more advanced things like automatically typing your entire customized email signature (See page 234), driving directions, a "canned" email, routine text describing your products or services, legal disclaimer text, anything!

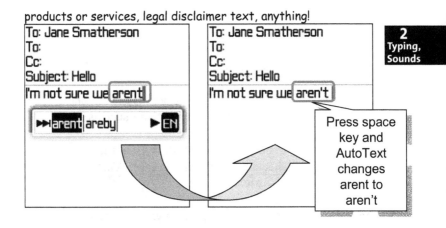

Press space key and AutoText changes arent to aren't

Creating an AutoText Entry

Pay attention to common text problems you are having. For example, when you type "I'm" and you forget the apostrophe, what happens? If the Pearl is putting "Im" instead of "I'm" – just do the following:

1. Select the "**Options**" icon from your Home Screen, Applications or Settings menus.
2. Select the "AutoText" item by clicking the trackball to see a list similar to the one shown below:

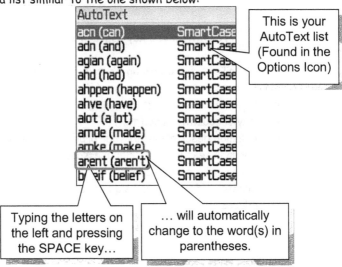

This is your AutoText list (Found in the Options Icon)

Typing the letters on the left and pressing the SPACE key...

... will automatically change to the word(s) in parentheses.

You will see a list of all the AutoText entries already on your BlackBerry.

3.   Press the Menu key and select "**New**"

Under the word "Replace" type the commonly miss-used word or letter combination – such as "Im"

Under the word "With" type in the new word that should be used – in this case, "I'm."

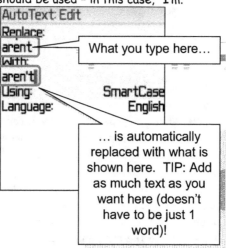

4.   Press the Menu key "Save" your new AutoText entry.

Use AutoText for anything that is repetitive:
✓   Directions to your home or office
✓   Legal disclaimer text
✓   Any frequently typed text
✓   Common descriptions of your products or services
✓   Common text used in email messages
✓   Your work or home address
✓   Create different email signatures (example: formal with full address and informal)

Using Custom Word Lists

Each of us has those words that are unique to our own vocabulary. It can be someone's last name that we email frequently or our favorite restaurant or something particular to our occupation. These words tend to not be included in the 'standard' dictionaries and word lists.

Fortunately, you can add your own Custom Word Lists to the Pearl making your unique words part of the Pearl vocabulary.

Adding a Custom Word

Let's say that you are a Stamp collector and you have the need to use the word "Philatelist" on many occasions. Here is what you would do to make this word part of the SureType vocabulary.

1. Move the Trackball to "Options" and click.
2. Scroll up to "**Custom Word List**" and click
3. Press the Menu key
    a. All the menu options will now be displayed for you
    b. Choose "**New**" and simply type in the new Custom Word

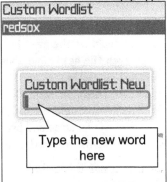

    c. Push escape and save your entry and now your word is a regular part of the vocabulary of your pearl

The Mighty SPACE Bar

Like many of the keys on the Pearl, the SPACE Bar can do some very handy things for you while you are typing.

Using the SPACE Bar while typing an email

On most handhelds, when you want to put in the "@" or the "." in your email, you need a complicated series of commands – usually a "**SHIFT**" or "**ALT**" or something.

On the Pearl, you don't need to take those extra steps. While you are typing the email, after the user name (for instance martin) just press the SPACE Bar once and the Pearl will automatically insert the "@" "martin@"
Type in the domain name and then press the Space Bar again and, presto - the Pearl automatically puts in the "."
"martin@blackberrymade." No additional keystrokes necessary. Just finish the email address with the "com"
"martin@blackberrymadesimple.com"

Using the SPACE bar to change drop down lists.

Another thing that the SPACE bar does is to move you down to the next item in a list. It could be the next hour, next 15 minutes, next month, or even the next time zone.

Give it a try. Open up a new calendar event, roll down to the month and press the SPACE key, then roll over to the hour and press SPACE, finally roll to the minutes and press SPACE. Notice that you moved: one month forward, one hour forward and 15 minutes forward. These are all great tricks to quickly re-schedule calendar events.

Using LETTER keys to change drop down lists or quickly select menu items or other lists

You can even use the letter keys on your keyboard to instantly jump down to the first item matching either letter on the key (if there are two letters), or jumping down to a matching menu item, or jumping down to a matching item in a list (like the long list in the "Options" icon).

The Trackball

The newest feature of the BlackBerry Pearl is the inclusion of the trackball as opposed to the familiar trackwheel or "Jog dial" along the right hand side. While this may take some getting used to for seasoned BlackBerry users, you will quickly see that the trackball gives you lots of freedom to scroll up and down and left to right using your thumb. It is incredibly intuitive to use.

The other thing that is great is that clicking in the Trackball will give you an innovative "short menu" that is context sensitive. Sometimes, it is so sensitive that it almost seems as if it reading your

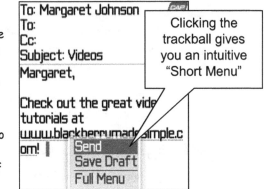

thoughts. Like showing "**Send**" after you finish typing an email and click the trackball.

There are also some neat features that are user adjusted with regards to the trackball.

Adjusting the Trackball sensitivity and Audible Roll

Each user is different in how quickly we like to navigate the Home Screen and how sensitive we like the trackball to be. To adjust the Trackball sensitivity just:

1. Move the trackball to "Options" and click
2. Scroll down to "Screen/Keyboard" and click
3. Scroll down and you will see "Trackball" and under it three user adjustable fields

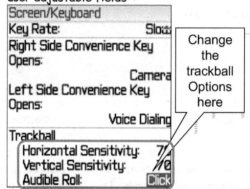

a. Click on either/both horizontal or vertical sensitivity number (70 is the default) and change it
   i. Higher is more sensitive, lower is less
b. At the end of the "Audible Roll" line either "Click" or "Mute" is highlighted ("Click" will produce an audible click when you move the trackball and "Mute" makes Trackball movement silent.)
   i. Click on whichever you see and you have the choice of changing to the other

Adjusting the Trackball lighting options

Normally, when a call comes in the Phone rings and information appears on the screen. You also have the option of having the Trackball light up and change colors when a call comes in. This is particularly useful if your phone is in Standby or Silent mode – and, it is very cool.

1. Press the green "Phone" key.
2. Press the Menu key and scroll to "Options" and click.
3. Scroll to "General Options" and click.
4. Scroll down to "Ringtone Lighting" and click where you see the word "off."
   a. When you click, you will see the option to choose "Trackball."

b. Choose "Trackball" and click, then Save your settings.

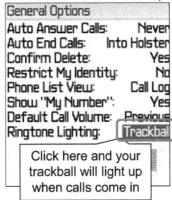

TIP: There is even an inexpensive Third Party software that will allow you to change the color of your Trackball to red, yellow, blue and even flash like disco lights. See page 509.

Understanding Profiles

Your BlackBerry Pearl is highly customizable – everything from Ringtones to vibrations to LED notifications can be adjusted. Traveling on an airplane but sill want to use your calendar or play a game without disturbing others? No problem. In a meeting and don't want the phone to ring – but you do want some sort of notification when an email comes in? No problem.

Virtually any scenario you can imagine can be dealt with preemptively by adjusting the profile settings.

Basic Profile Settings:

By default, the Pearl is set to a "Normal" profile – meaning that when a call comes in, the phone rings and when a message comes in, the phone plays a tune.

Changing your Profile:

To set or change the profile settings:

1. Depending you your selected Theme and BlackBerry carrier (Phone Company), how you get to your profiles icon will be slightly different.

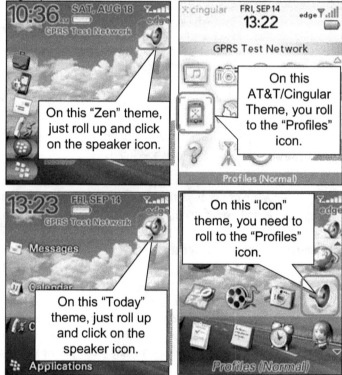

If you don't see this speaker icon on your screen, press the Menu key to see the entire list of icons, then scroll to the "**Profiles**" icon and click on it.

2. Six basic 'preset' settings are available from which you can choose: Loud, vibrate, Quiet, Normal, Phone only and Off.

Next to one of those options the word "Active" will be

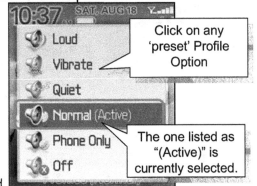

Click on any 'preset' Profile Option

The one listed as "(Active)" is currently selected.

displayed.

a. For most users, "**Normal**" will be the active profile which rings during phone calls and either vibrates or plays a tone when a message arrives.

b. "**Loud**" increases the volume for all notifications.

c. "**Vibrate**" enables a short vibration for meetings, movies or other places where cell phone rings are discouraged.

d. "**Quiet**" will display notifications on the display and via the LED.

e. "**Phone Only**" will turn off all email and SMS notifications.

f. "**Off**" will turn off all notifications.

Advanced Profile Options

There may be some situations where you want a combination of options that one profile alone cannot satisfy. The Pearl is highly customizable so that you can adjust your profile options for virtually any potential situation. The easiest way to accomplish this is to choose a profile that is closest to what you need and "Edit" it as shown below.

To enter the Advanced Profile Menu:

1. Click on "Profiles" icon as you did above.

2.   Scroll down to "Advanced" and click.

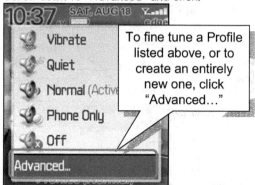

3.   Each of the profiles can be adjusted by scrolling to the profile you desire to edit, pushing the Menu Key and select "**Edit**."

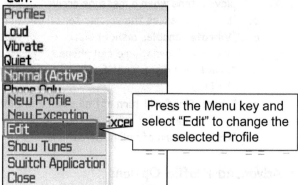

4.   Browser, Calendar, Level 1 Messages, Email, Messenger (Alert and New Message,) Phone, SMS and tasks can all be adjusted with regards to tone, vibration, volume, tune and

LED notification.

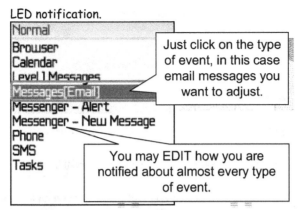

Just click on the type of event, in this case email messages you want to adjust.

You may EDIT how you are notified about almost every type of event.

5. For example, choose "**Email**" and notice that you can make adjustments for your Pearl both "Out of Holster" and "In Holster". (A "holster" may be supplied with your device or sold separately. This is essentially a carrying case that clips to your belt and uses a magnet to notify your BlackBerry it is "In Holster" and should turn off the screen immediately among other things.)

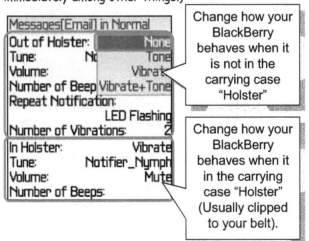

Change how your BlackBerry behaves when it is not in the carrying case "Holster"

Change how your BlackBerry behaves when it in the carrying case "Holster" (Usually clipped to your belt).

Understanding and Using the LED Notification

One of the features that BlackBerry users love is the little LED that blinks in the upper right hand corner. It is possible to have this light blink different colors:

"Red"   when you receive an incoming message (MMS, SMS or Email) or calendar alarm rings,

"Blue"   when connected to a Bluetooth Device,

"Green"   when you have wireless coverage, and,

"Amber"   if you need to charge your Pearl.

TIP: As we mentioned earlier, there is even an inexpensive Third Party software that will allow you to change the color of your Trackball to red, yellow, blue and even flash like disco lights. See page 509.

To make adjustments to the "Red" Message LED notification:
1.   Go into the **advanced options** as in steps 1-5 above.
2.   Notice that one of the options is "**Repeat Notification**" and that when clicked, you can choose to enable or disable the LED

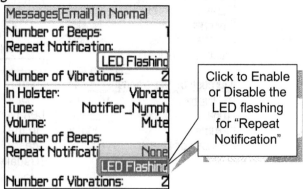

To turn on or off the Bluetooth LED notification:
1.   From the applications menu, click on "Options" and then scroll to "Bluetooth" and click.
2.   Press the Menu key, scroll down to "Options" and click
3.   You can then turn the LED Connection Indicator to "On" or "Off."

To Turn On or Off the "Green" coverage indication LED:

1. Navigate again to the "Options" icon in the applications menu and scroll to "Screen/Keyboard and click. Scroll down to LED Coverage Indicator and select either "On" or "Off"

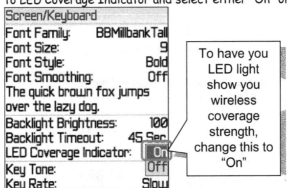

To have you LED light show you wireless coverage strength, change this to "On"

Hearing a different tone when someone special calls

You may decide that you want to customize a particular profile to meet your specific needs. You can make adjustments in any number of custom fields for a particular type of notification or you can create a totally new custom profile on the Pearl.

To set a Custom Notification Profile:

1. Get to the "**Advanced**" menu in the Profiles menu as shown above.
2. Press the Menu key and scroll to "**New Exception**" and click.
3. Type in any name for this new Profile in the field marked "**Exception**"
4. Then, roll down to "**From**" and press the Menu key
5. Click "**Add Name**" and select a contact for whom this new profile will apply
6. Press the **ESCAPE key** and save the new profile. In the example below, I want the Phone to ring loud specifically when my friend Martin calls so I don't miss the important call.

> Exception:
> From: Martin Trautschold
> Use Profile: Active Profile
> ✓ Custom Phon   Loud
>   Ringer   Vibrate
>   Quiet
>   Normal
>   hone Only
>   Off
>
> You can set it up so calls from a specific person are always "Loud"

Setting Up Your Email

Chapter Contents:

Creating your BlackBerry Email Account

Your BlackBerry Pearl is designed to retrieve your email from up to 10 different email accounts and, if you are connected to a BlackBerry Enterprise Server, one corporate email account. When your BlackBerry receives your email, all your messages will be displayed in your messages inbox.

Create new BlackBerry Email Address (Optional)

This is an optional step, and you do not need to create a new email address unless you want one. BlackBerry email will work fine without this new email address. If you do not currently have an email account, or would simply like to add a new one just for your Blackberry, then you can create one right from your BlackBerry. Your new account will be [new user name]@tmo.blackberry.net if you are on T-Mobile (US). If you are on another carrier, you will most likely have a similar format of [user name]@[carrier name].blackberry.net.

1. Press the Menu key and move trackball to **"Setup Internet Email"** or **"Setup Personal Email"**

2. Click the trackball.
3. NOTE: You may need to create your account on your BlackBerry, if you have not yet created one.
4. Using the trackball, navigate to **"Create a BlackBerry email address"** and click the trackball
5. Choose a user name and type it in.
6. Move the trackball to the "Next" link and click.
7. Move to "Ok" and click.

    o If your new BlackBerry email user name is accepted (does not conflict with a user name already setup by someone else), you will be told so on the next screen and your new email address is setup!
    o If your new user name is already 'in use' by someone else, then you will be told to select a different one.

Set Up Personal (Internet) Email from the BlackBerry

There are a couple of different ways to set up your Internet or Personal Email right on your BlackBerry Pearl. This is usually an email account that is 'hosted' by a company such as "gmail.com" "aol.com" "msn.com" or might be your own private domain name like "blackberrymadesimple.com"

3
Email
Setup

Option 1: Setup your email using the Setup Wizard
When you turn on your Pearl for the first time you are taken to the setup wizard. In the wizard, select the option **"I want to create or add an email address"**
1. Move the cursor to **"Next"** and click.
2. Agree to the terms and choose your language.
3. Enter your user name of your personal email account and your password and click **"Next"**.
4. You should receive confirmation on the next screen that your email was successfully set up.

Option 2: Setup you email from the Home Screen
1. Press the Menu key
2. Move the trackball to **"Setup Internet Email"** (it may say **"Setup Personal Email"**) and click the trackball
3. Click on "**E-Mail Accounts**" (or setup your login account, if not yet done.)
4. If asked, find the appropriate time zone and click **"Next"**
5. Decide if you want to agree to the terms and conditions (it is a good idea to read them).
6. Type in your complete email address (hint: if you press the space bar after the user name, the "@" sign will automatically be displayed. Press the

> **TIP!**
>
> Press the **SPACE** key to get the "@" and "." In your email address: sara@company.com. Type: sara **SPACE** company **SPACE** com

SPACE bar again after the domain name and the "." will be put in for you.

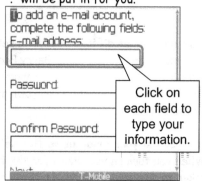

7. Type in your password and move the cursor to "**Next**" and click.

8. You should receive confirmation of the activation of your account – click "**OK**" and you are done.

Setting Up Your Corporate Email ("Enterprise Activation")

This process is also known as "**Enterprise Activation**". If your Help Desk or Information Technology department does not do this for you, all you need is your activation password and you can set this up on your own – right from the Pearl.

IMPORTANT: If you have not received your "**Activation Password**", then you need to ask your Help Desk or Technology Support department for that password before you may complete this process.

Option 1: Setup Using the Setup Wizard

1. Choose **"I want to use a work email account with a BlackBerry Enterprise Server"** from the setup menu.
2. Type in your email address.
3. Type in the activation password you received from your Help Desk or System Administrator.
4. Move the trackball and navigate to "Activate."
5. Then you should see a series of messages that talk about Security, Establishing Connection, Verifying Connection, Loading Contacts, Calendar, etc.
6. Once completed, and this could take 5 minutes or more, you should see a confirmation screen.
7. The best way to test is to try to send yourself or your colleague a test email message from your newly connected BlackBerry. Make sure it arrives and you can reply to a new message received.

Option 2: Setup your corporate account from the Home Screen

1. Press the Menu key.
2. Click on the **"Enterprise Activation"** icon.
3. Enter your corporate email address and the password given to you by your administrator.

4. Press the Menu key and click "Activate"
5. You should receive a confirmation screen and then a confirmation email letting you know that activation was successful

Benefits of Being Connected to a BlackBerry Server

What is a BlackBerry Enterprise Server "BES"?

A BlackBerry Enterprise Server (or "BES" for short) is a server that typically sits behind your corporate firewall and securely connects your BlackBerry to corporate email, as well as wirelessly synchronizes (shares) contacts, calendar, tasks and memo items between your corporate computer and your BlackBerry.

Can I get access to a BES if I'm an individual or small office BlackBerry User?

Yes! Just check out the list of "Hosted BES" providers on page 514

What are the benefits of being connected to a BES?

Connecting your BlackBerry to a BES (v4.0 and higher) will give you all of the following benefits:

Strong Encryption of Email Within Your Organization

All email sent from your BlackBerry to other users in your organization will be fully encrypted with "military-grade" Triple-DES encryption provided by the Server.

Full 2-Way Wireless Synchronization

Full 2-way wireless updates between your BlackBerry and corporate desktop account for:
- ✓ Address Book
- ✓ Calendar
- ✓ Task List
- ✓ MemoPad (Notes)

This means you will be able to add new information or make changes to anything in your address book, calendar, task list or MemoPad on your BlackBerry and in minutes it will appear on your Desktop Computer.

Global Address List (GAL) Lookup

Using a feature called the Global Address Book (GAL) lookup or just "Lookup" for short, you can immediately lookup anyone in your organization from your BlackBerry, even if there thousands of people at your organization.

Email Auto Signature From BlackBerry

Unlike non-Server connected BlackBerry handhelds, you may create or edit your Auto Signature right on your BlackBerry. Non-BES connected users, cannot truly adjust their Auto Signature except by logging into their wireless carrier's web site from their computer (not their BlackBerry). However, using the AutoText trick, anyone can have multiple signatures. See page 60 to learn how.

3
Email
Setup

NOTE: BlackBerry keeps upgrading the BlackBerry Internet Service, so non-Server connected BlackBerry handhelds may well be able to adjust their Auto Signatures from the BlackBerry in the future.

Out of Office Auto Reply

```
Email Settings
Send Email To Handheld:      Yes
Save Copy In Sent Folder:  Yes
Use Auto Signature:          Yes
  ▶ Martin Trautschold
BlackBerry Made Simple
www.blackberrymadesimple.c
om
Use Out Of Office Reply:   Yes
  ▶ I am out on vacation until
12/31/2007|
```

This is something you can turn on, off or change right from your BlackBerry if you are connected to a BlackBerry Server.

Meeting Invitations

Also, just like on your desktop computer, you may invite attendees to meetings you schedule right on your BlackBerry. And, just like on your desktop, you may accept, decline or tentatively accept meeting invitations you receive on your BlackBerry

IMPORTANT: On some carriers, such as AT&T (Cingular) in the USA, this "Invite Attendee" function is now available from a non-Server connected BlackBerry as well. We predict that most BlackBerry carriers will support this feature in the not too distant future.

Setting up Email Accounts and Signatures From Your Computer

Your personal email accounts can also be setup from your computer using your carrier's web site. You also might notice that when you send an email from the Pearl, the signature is something very basic like "Sent from BlackBerry Device via T-Mobile" or something similar depending on your carrier. You can easily change your signature from the Carrier Web Site as well.

Setting up email on the web

Find your way to your carrier's web site in Internet Explorer, Firefox or Opera. Once there, login to your personal account page.

NOTE: Below we use T-Mobile (USA) as an example. If your carrier is different, then the layout of the web site screens will be different, but some of the names like "Setup BlackBerry Email" and other key links or steps should be very similar.

On T-Mobile, the login is the "My T-Mobile" page. NOTE: You will need to initially set this up – usually by inputting your Mobile number and choosing a password. Some wireless carriers (phone companies) will send you a temporary password via SMS text message to your BlackBerry – then you login using that password and select a new one.

1.   Choose the tab that says something like "Phone & Accessories", "Device", "Handheld" or "Support" from your home page.

2.   Then click on "Setup BlackBerry Internet E-mail" or "Setup BlackBerry E-mail"

3. You should now see a screen similar to the one below.

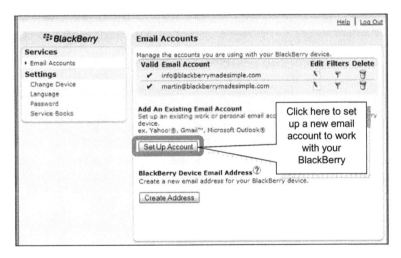

4. After clicking the "Setup Account" button, you will need to input your email address and password on the screen below.

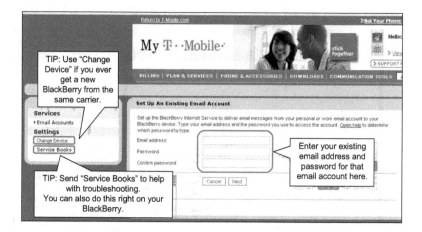

After the email account is successfully set up, you will then receive confirmation email on your BlackBerry usually titled "Activation."

- Shortly thereafter, your first email will come in on the Pearl
- Repeat this process for each of your email accounts
- Once you have all your email accounts configured you will see them listed as shown below. You can then customize ("EDIT"), filter email ("FILTER") or remove them ("DELETE") by selecting the icons on the right side.

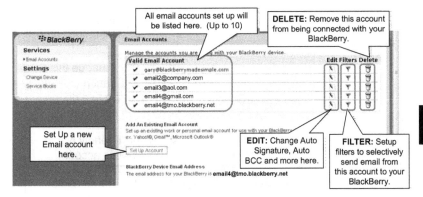

Setting up your Email Auto Signature

On your email accounts page you should see an icon for editing each of your accounts that you have set up. You can then add a unique signature – for every email account that you have set up.

1. Select the "Edit" icon next to the email account you wish to work with
2. Make any changes in the fields provided to you
3. In the signature box, simply type in the new signature you wish to appear at the bottom of that particular email account

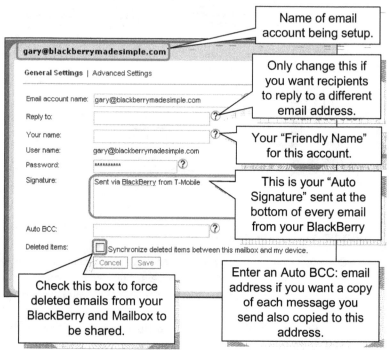

Name of email account being setup.

Only change this if you want recipients to reply to a different email address.

Your "Friendly Name" for this account.

This is your "Auto Signature" sent at the bottom of every email from your BlackBerry

Check this box to force deleted emails from your BlackBerry and Mailbox to be shared.

Enter an Auto BCC: email address if you want a copy of each message you send also copied to this address.

4. Click the save button. Test your new settings by sending an email from your Blackberry to yourself or another email account and verify that the new signature is included.

5. You can also add a signatures that can be selected "on the fly" from your BlackBerry while typing emails using the "AutoText" feature See page 60.

6. **Advanced Settings Screen:** Clicking on the "Advanced Settings" link at the top of the email EDIT screen will show you a screen similar to the one below. This will allow you to configure settings like your specific email server, the port number, and whether or not SSL (Secure Socket Layer) encrypted connection is required.

info@blackberrymadesimple.com

General Settings | **Advanced Settings**

Email server: mail.blackberrymadesimple.com

Email server type: POP3

Port: 995

Timeout: 120 seconds

SSL: ☑

[Cancel]   [Save]

3
Email
Setup

What to Do if the Email Program On the BlackBerry Can't Automatically Setup Your Email

While the Pearl is amazingly easy for setting up email and more often than not configures it automatically, there may be times when some email addresses cannot be configured this way. Don't worry, you will still be able to use your BlackBerry – you will just need to go through a few extra steps. Basically you will see a similar version of the "Advanced Settings" screen above on your BlackBerry.

Manually Setting up Mail

1. Click on the "Setup Internet Mail" icon from the applications menu and then click on "E-Mail Accounts."
2. Click on "Add and Email Address" and put in the address and password.
3. You will receive an error message telling you that the account could not be configure automatically and that you have to manually enter your settings. (Hint: if you are not sure of your email settings, open up Outlook or Outlook express on your PC and go to your "Accounts" menu and highlight the account you are trying to set up on the Pearl. Go to settings and copy down the email settings from your PC.

4. Just fill in each field exactly as it is on your PC – pay careful attention to note whether you have SSL connection checked or not.

5. If you are still having trouble with email setup, then please contact your email service provider and possibly your BlackBerry wireless carrier (phone company) technical support.

Moving On

Now that you know the basics of your BlackBerry and your email is setup, you are ready to move on to putting your names, addresses, calendar and more on your BlackBerry. We will show you how to get all that done in the next sections.

Section 2: Managing your Life with Your Pearl

Sharing or Synchronizing Information

Chapter Contents:
- Loading Addresses, Calendar, Tasks and Memo Items
- Microsoft™ Windows™ users: Desktop Manager Software
- Apple Mac™ users: PocketMac for BlackBerry™ or Missing Sync for BlackBerry
- Loading Information from a BlackBerry Enterprise Server

Loading Your Addresses, Calendar, Tasks & Memos

Like the Calendar, Task list and MemoPad, your Address Book can be shared with the same applications on your computer. How this works depends on whether or not your BlackBerry is connected to a BlackBerry Enterprise Server or "BES" for short. (Most medium to large organizations have these "BES" servers installed to increase security as well as provide full two-way wireless sharing of your personal information between your computer and BlackBerry.) If you are not at an organization with a BES server, but still want to enjoy the benefits of connecting to a BES, you can subscribe to a service from a Hosted BES Company (What's this? See page 514).

If your BlackBerry is connected to a BlackBerry Enterprise Server, and your Address Book is not yet loaded on your

BlackBerry, please consult the "Enterprise Activation" section on page 140 or call the Help Desk for support.

If you are an individual or small office user of BlackBerry, you will need to use either a USB cable or Bluetooth wireless to connect your BlackBerry to your computer to load up your Address Book. We provide help for getting this setup for both Windows™ computers (see page 95) and Apple Mac™ computers (see page 127).

What's an electronic organizer without all your important names, numbers, addresses and your calendar?

4
Sync
Setup

How your personal information (names, addresses, calendar, tasks and notes/memos) is first loaded and kept up-to-date between your BlackBerry and computer depends on a few factors. Like whether or not your BlackBerry is connected to a BlackBerry Enterprise Server (BES) and whether or not that Server provides wireless updates. For most users, without access to a server, you will need to install software on your personal computer to transfer all your information between your BlackBerry and your computer.

Loading Media (pictures, videos, music)
To transfer **media** (pictures, videos, music) you may either email them to yourself as attachments and "save" them on your BlackBerry or, the better option (much faster), is to use the desktop software (Desktop Manager for Windows – see page 351 - or PocketMac for Apple Mac computers) and a USB or Bluetooth connection to transfer them directly. (See page 348 for other media transfer details.) Learn more about the 'Mass Storage Mode' to transfer Media on page 357.

(1) If your BlackBerry is connected to a **BlackBerry Enterprise Server** ("BES"), your information is likely updated wirelessly and automatically. See page 140 for details on **Enterprise Activation**, the process which connects your BlackBerry wirelessly and securely to the Server. If you are allowed by your organization, you

may also install the Desktop Software (or PocketMac) to transfer media between your computer and your BlackBerry.

(2) With some Enterprise Server-connected BlackBerries, you may still be required to share your personal information using Desktop Manager (or PocketMac if you have an Apple Mac). This would be the case if the wireless synchronization service is not working or turned off at the BlackBerry Server.

(3) If you are an individual or small office BlackBerry user, then it is likely that your BlackBerry is not connected to a BlackBerry Enterprise Server. The only exception is when you decide to pay extra for access to a hosted BlackBerry Server. (See page 514). Without a wireless sync from the Server, you will need to connect your BlackBerry to your personal computer via USB or Bluetooth to transfer information. The software you need use on your computer depends on the operating system:

> **TIP**
>
> Even if you don't work at an organization with a BlackBerry Enterprise Server ("BES"), you can still gain access to one by subscribing to monthly service from one of a number of "BES Hosting" companies. See Page 385.

For Microsoft Windows™: **BlackBerry Desktop Software**
See page 93
For Apple Macintosh™: **PocketMAC™ or Other Software**
See page 127

How to connect to **BlackBerry Enterprise Server** – See page 140

For Microsoft Windows™ Users - Desktop Manager

What computer applications are supported by BlackBerry Desktop Software (v4.2) Source: www.blackberry.com August, 2007.

4
Sync
Setup

- Microsoft Outlook® 2000, Outlook 2002, Outlook XP, Outlook 2003 or Outlook 2007
- Lotus Notes® 5.0.6 or later, 6.0, 6.5, 7.0
- ACT!® 4.0.2, 5.0 (2000), 6.0
- Lotus Organizer® 6.1
- Microsoft Outlook Express 5.0, 6.0
- Novell® GroupWise® 6.0.1, 6.5.4 or higher and 7.0
- ASCII Importer/Exporter
- Yahoo! PIM

What follows are the steps you need to complete to first load your names, addresses, calendar, tasks and notes (and media – pictures, music and videos) and media (videos, music, pictures) from your personal computer onto your BlackBerry and keep them up-to-date or "synchronized".

Step 1: Locate the Install CD or Download the Software

Step 2: Install Desktop Manager Software (Page 99)

Step 3: Setup the Synchronization (Page 106)

Step 4: Perform the Synchronization (Page 120)

Ongoing: Sync often to keep everything up-to-date (Page 123)

Step 1: Locate the Install CD or Download the Software

If you recently purchased your BlackBerry, you will probably find a CD in the box. This CD should contain the most recent version of Desktop Manager Software and some other helpful information. **Can't find the CD?** Skip to page 95.

If you have this CD, then insert it in your computer drive and navigate to the link or image that says "**Install BlackBerry Desktop Software**" or "**BlackBerry Desktop Software**". (Your screen may look different from the one below.)

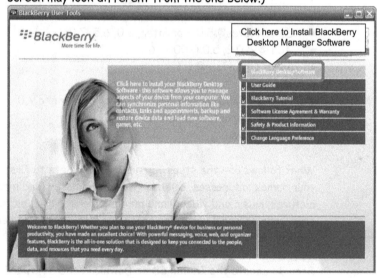

After clicking the first link, then you should see a screen similar to the one below.

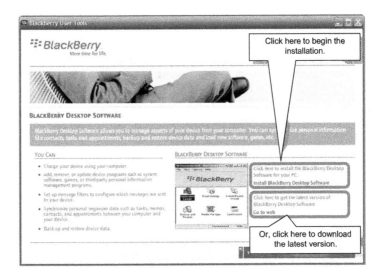

Notice that you are given the option of going to the web to download the latest version. This provides you another way to get to the BlackBerry.com download site, which we describe later in this chapter.

At this point, click the "**Install BlackBerry Desktop Software**" link to start the installation.

Now, skip to "Step 2" on page 99.

You don't have the CD...Find and download Desktop Manager from the Web

If you don't have a CD, then best way to get the latest version is to download the installation file directly from blackberry.com.

NOTE: Web site layouts and software versions and screens change frequently, so it is likely that something on the web or in the software will not look exactly like it does in this book. If not, please look for the correct link or correct words in order to continue working through the steps. If you find a mistake and have the time, please email us a correction for our next revision at info@blackberrymadesimple.com, we would greatly appreciate it!

1. To find the download link for Desktop Manager, type the search phrase "**blackberry desktop manager**" into your favorite web search engine.

2. The search results should show you a link from www.blackberry.com/downloads in one of the top positions. Click on that link. Then you will go to the BlackBerry.com site and see a page similar to the one below. On this BlackBerry software download page, you need to select the highest number version for your computer's operating system. Since you are using Microsoft Windows™, you will select "**BlackBerry Desktop Software**"

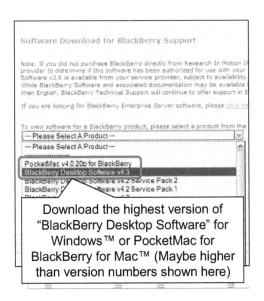

Download the highest version of "BlackBerry Desktop Software" for Windows™ or PocketMac for BlackBerry for Mac™ (Maybe higher than version numbers shown here)

3. Then click the Next button to see the page with the download button(s).

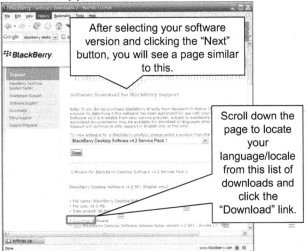

After selecting your software version and clicking the "Next" button, you will see a page similar to this.

Scroll down the page to locate your language/locale from this list of downloads and click the "Download" link.

4. Now you will need to enter your personal information in order to download the software.

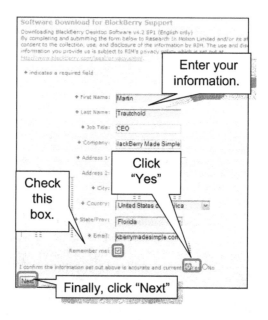

5. Now you will see a legal agreement similar to the one shown, you will need to click "**Agree**" and "**Next**" to continue to the download page.

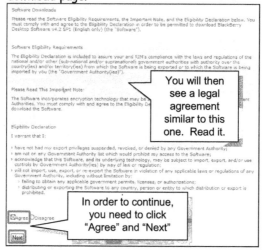

6. Now, verify you have selected the correct software and click the "Download" button to see the Download popup window below.

4
Sync
Setup

NOTE: A high-speed Internet connection is recommended because these download files can be 40 or more megabytes ("MB") and would take an hour or more to download on a slow or dial-up Internet connection, but just a few minutes on a high-speed connection.

7. When the download is complete, you now have the latest desktop manager installation file on your computer. Locate it and double-click on it (should look similar to the image to the right – probably with different or higher numbers) to get started with the installation. Then follow the steps below.

Step 2: Install Desktop Manager Software

After clicking the "Install Desktop Manager Software" link from the CD or double-clicking on the downloaded installation file, you should now see a screen very similar to the one below.

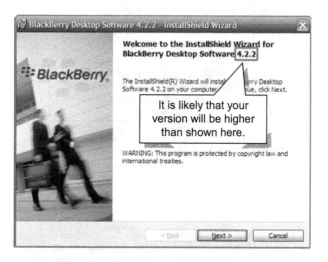

1. Click "**Next**" to begin the installation.
2. Then, select your country or region and click "Next"

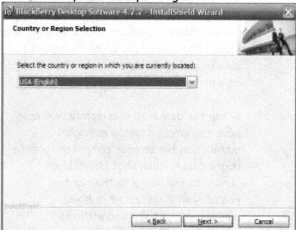

3. Review and determine if you "**Accept**" the user terms, click "**Next**"

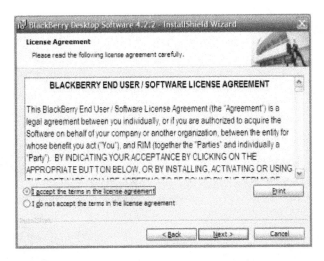

4. Now enter your **name** and **organization**, select if you want this software to only be available to your user login, or everyone who uses the computer. Click "**Next**"

5. Now, unless you need to change where the software is being installed, go ahead and click "**Next**" on the screen below. Otherwise click the "Change" button and alter the installation location.

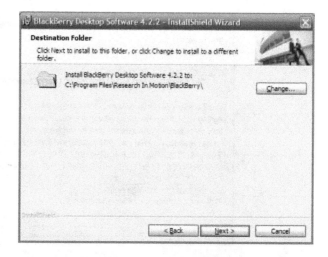

6. We recommend selecting "Typical" unless you have a special need for "Custom" on this screen.

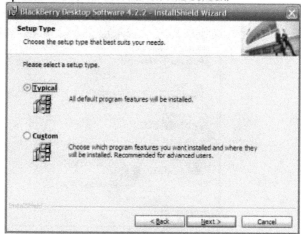

7. **Integration Options Screen:** Now you need to make a decision on this next screen based on whether or not your BlackBerry is connected to a **BlackBerry Enterprise Server** (or you want to use **Desktop Redirector** – the Redirector forces you to leave your computer on and connected to the internet 24 x 7 x 365 to 'redirect' all your email to/from your BlackBerry)

If your BlackBerry is connected to a server, then you will select the top option, **even if you want to use the BlackBerry Internet Service option for your personal email account integration.** **(See note at bottom of screen)**

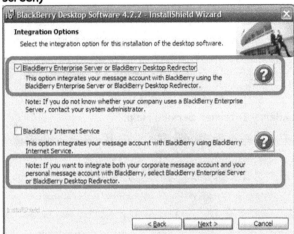

If you are an individual user, and your BlackBerry is not connected to a BlackBerry Server, then choose the bottom or "BlackBerry Internet Service" option.

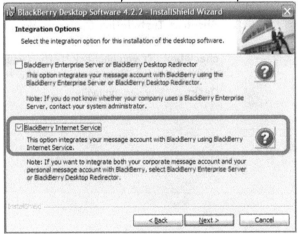

If you need more help on making your decision, click the help icons to the right of each choice. They will show you screens similar to the following.

BlackBerry Enterprise Server/Redirector Option Help:

BlackBerry Internet Service Help:

If you work at an organization that supplied your BlackBerry to you and are still unsure of which option to select, then please contact your Help Desk for support.

8. **Shortcut Installation Options.** You may want to uncheck the "**Start desktop manager automatically**" check box. If you uncheck it, then your computer will start up faster, however you need to then start Desktop Manager manually.

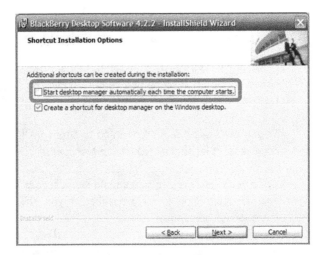

9. Now you will see the final screen before the installation starts, click **"Install"**

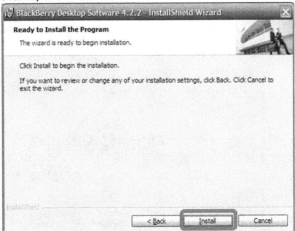

10. Then you will see a series of screens while the installation is working. Finally, when successfully completed you will see a "InstallShield Wizard Completed" screen.

You then may be asked to **re-start your computer** – you must do a re-start before the new installation can work correctly.

Step 3: Setup the Synchronization

Now that you've finished installing the software, go ahead and start it up by double clicking on the Desktop Manager icon.

Desktop Manager

If you don't see the icon, then go to Start > All Programs > BlackBerry > Desktop Manager.

Once you've started it, you should see a screen similar to this one. Depending on how you installed it, you may see fewer or more icons than shown here.

What does each Desktop Manager icon do?

Once you've started it, you should see a screen similar to the ones below (either version 4.2 or version 4.3). Depending on how you installed it, you may see fewer or more icons than shown here.

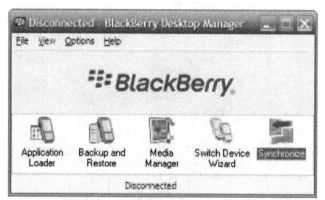

Desktop Manager v4.2 main screen

If you have installed version 4.3 or later, then you will see a screen similar to the one below.

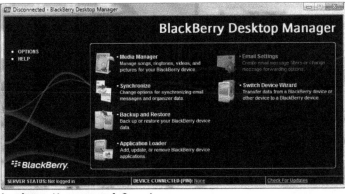

Desktop Manager v4.3 main screen

4
Sync
Setup

(Initially we received advance Desktop Manager v4.3 Images courtesy of Jibi at the "Boy Genius Report" - http://www.boygeniusreport.com, however by publishing time, v4.3 has been officially released.)

Differences between 4.2 and 4.3: You will notice that all the icons of the Desktop Manager are the same between 4.2 and 4.3. The grayed out Email Settings shown in the v4.3 image only appears "active" when you are using the Desktop Redirector or are in using your BlackBerry with a BlackBerry Enterprise Server. This is the same for v4.2.

Icon / Name (v4.3)	Description (v4.2 and v4.3)
	Load or remove software – including Third Party software. Upgrade your BlackBerry operating system "Device Software" see page 491.
	Backup and restore data from your device. Selectively backup, delete or restore just your address book, calendar, tasks and more. Automate the backup procedure.
	Transfer media (songs, ringtones, video and pictures / images) to and from your BlackBerry.

	Transfer all your personal data (addresses, calendar, tasks, memos) from a Palm OS, Windows Mobile/Pocket PC, or other RIM BlackBerry device to your new BlackBerry.
	Synchronize or share your personal organizer information between your computer and your BlackBerry (addresses, calendar, tasks and memo pad note items).

1. After you have installed and opened your BlackBerry Desktop Manager, connect your BlackBerry to your computer using the USB cable and ensure it shows your PIN number on the bottom left corner of the Desktop Manager window as shown below. (If it shows "None," you are not connected.)

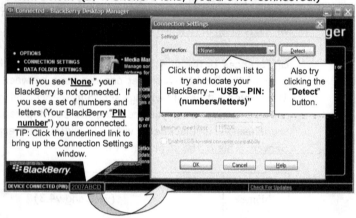

TIP: If you are having trouble seeing "Connected" for your USB Cable Connection:

First, try unplugging the USB cable and re-plugging it in.

Second, try a plugging it into a different USB port on your computer.

Third, if you have **password security** enabled on your BlackBerry, make sure you have entered your password on both your computer in the pop-up window after you connected your BlackBerry and on the BlackBerry itself. This also happens when you have "**Mass Storage Mode**" turned on.

Fourth, click the "**Options**" item in the left column and click on "**Connection Settings**" to see the screen. Try the "**Detect**" button and look at the pull-down menu to see if you see your device. Alternatively, you can try Bluetooth support if your computer has a Bluetooth receiver.

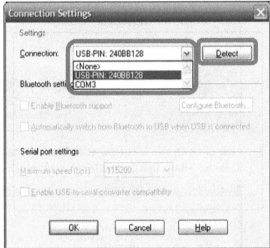

Fifth, try re-booting your computer.

Sixth, try re-booting your BlackBerry by powering it off, then removing the battery, waiting about 30 seconds, then replacing the battery.

2. Now that you have successfully connected your BlackBerry to your computer, double click on the Synchronize icon to see the screen below.

3. Now click on the "Configuration" tab at the top to see this screen. Then click on the "Configure synch..." button.

4. Now, click the check box next to the "Address Book" to start setting up the sync.

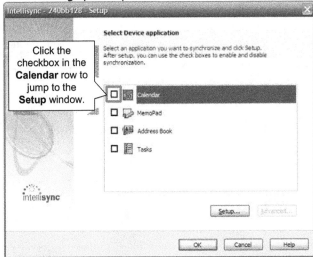

5. Click the computer software you use to manage your contacts, calendar, tasks and notes on your computer. In this example, we have clicked on "**Microsoft Outlook**" then click "**Next**"

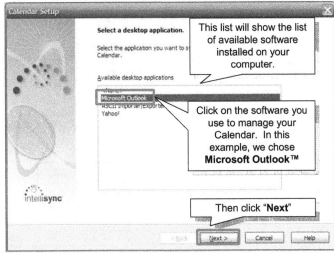

6. Now you will see options for Two way or one way sync. A **"Two way sync"** means any changes you make on your computer or BlackBerry will be synchronized to the other device. This is what you usually will want. Under special circumstances, you might require or want a One Way sync.

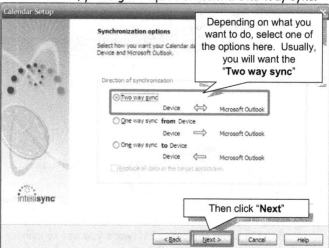

7. Now you are on the options screen for the Calendar. Select your profile if different. We recommend check is the "Remove alarm for past events" – this prevents a lot of annoying old alarms from ringing in your Outlook reminders box.

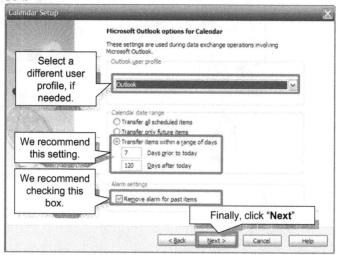

We also recommend selecting the radio button "**Transfer items within a range of Days**" and enter **7 days prior** and **120 days after.**

Why? The default is "Transfer only future items" – with this setting you might lose valuable calendar information entered or updated on your BlackBerry, especially if you forget to sync for a day or two. By setting it to 7 days prior to today, you have 7 days "grace period" before that calendar event data gets "lost forever" on your BlackBerry, never to make it to your computer.

4
Sync
Setup

After clicking "**Next**" you will see this screen. Click "**Finish**"

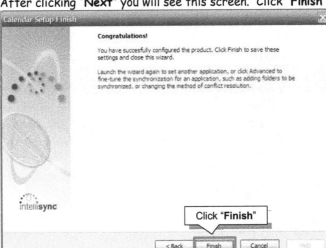

8. Notice that there is a 2-way arrow between the Calendar and Microsoft Outlook (or your selected application).

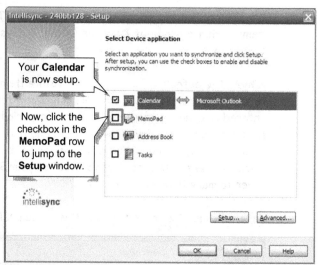

Now, click the "MemoPad" check box to configure that sync.

9. Now, select your desktop application. In this case, we selected Microsoft Outlook. Click "Next" and select Two-way or One-Way Sync. Click "Next" and select your Profile (or other option depending on your selected application). This will complete the setup of your **MemoPad**.

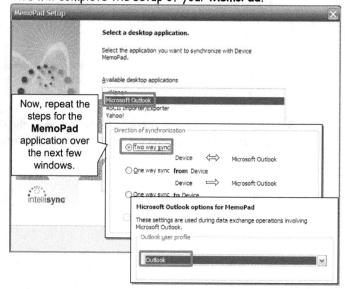

10. After clicking on the checkbox next to "**Address Book**" in the main Sync window, you will then repeat similar steps to configure it as shown.

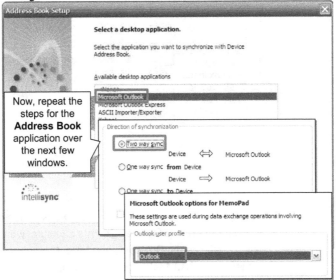

Now, repeat the steps for the **Address Book** application over the next few windows.

4
Sync
Setup

11. Once you finish the Address Book setup, then you will be back at the main Sync setup window shown below. Click the checkbox next to "**Tasks**" to configure that sync.

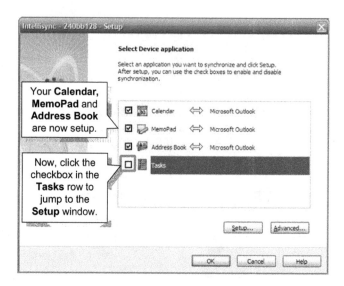

12. Check the checkbox next to Tasks and repeat the selection of your desktop software. In this example, we continued to select "Microsoft Outlook", you have the option of transferring "All tasks" or "only pending" tasks, depending on your preference.

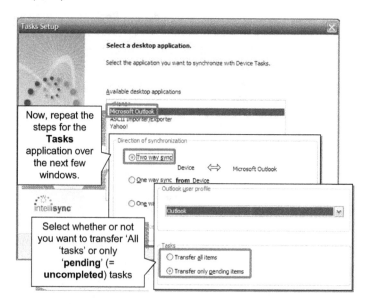

13. Finally, when all four applications are setup for sync, then you should see a screen similar to the image below. If you want to adjust advanced settings, then click on the "Advanced" button at the bottom.

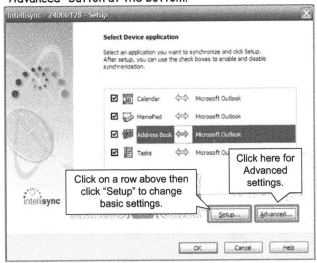

Advanced Sync Configuration Screens

The Advanced Sync setup screens will look like the one below. Click on the tabs at the top to see settings for each of the different applications.

Map Folder – Allows you to select one or several folders to map to sync your BlackBerry.

Conflict Resolution – Allows you to determine if you want to review each sync change and determine whether in conflicts the Handheld or your Computer will "win" (or you should be asked each time). Being asked each time is the default and recommended setting.

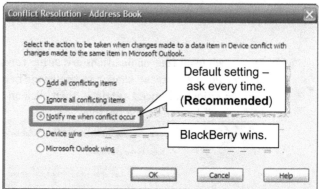

Filters - These allow you to filter data that is synchronized. This can be extremely useful if you have specific data that you do or do not want to be synchronized to your BlackBerry from your computer. With filters and creative use of information typed in your desktop application you can do just about anything you want.

Filter Example: You are traveling on a business trip to France, Germany and the United Kingdom; you want to put only people who have business addresses in these countries on your BlackBerry so you can easily find them.

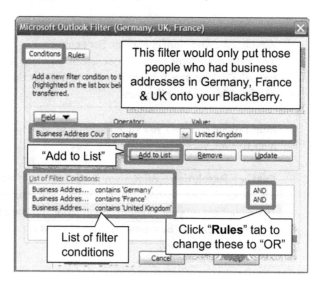

Click the "**Rules**" tab at the top to see the screen below.

Then you need to click the option "**One or more conditions must be met**" in order to change the conditions from "AND" to "OR". This way when only one of the conditions are true, then the contact is synchronized to your BlackBerry. For example, one person's business address will only be France, Germany or UK, not all three.

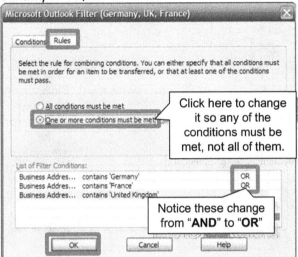

4
Sync
Setup

Field Mapping – This allows you to map individual fields from your computer application into your BlackBerry. This can be useful if you need to fine-tune the information that is put onto your BlackBerry.

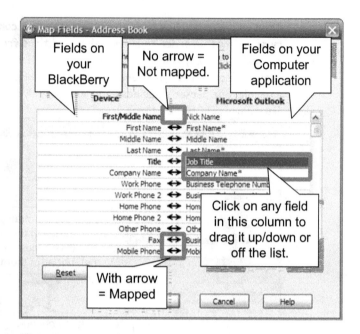

Click "OK" to get back to the "Synchronize" tabbed screen and click on the "Synchronize".

Congratulations, your synchronization setup is now complete. You are ready to try your first sync.

Step 4: Perform the Synchronization

1. Assuming you now have your BlackBerry connected to your computer and are on the screen shown above, go make sure the checkbox is checked next to "Synchronize organizer data" as shown in (#1) and then click the "Synchronize now" (#2) button as shown.

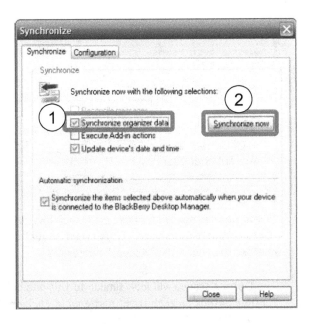

4
Sync
Setup

2. You will then see the sync status window pop up that looks something like this:

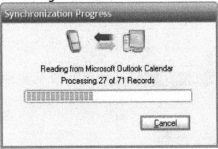

3. Then you will likely see a number of these screens that ask you to "**Confirm Calendar Edits**" or "Confirm Address Book Edits" and so on.

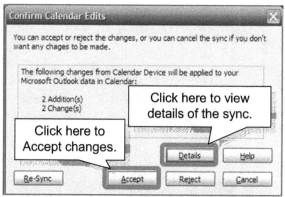

If you want to see what these edits look like, then click the "**Details**" button as shown. If you want to just approve the change, then click the "**Accept**" button.

The Details screen will look similar to this one below. To see further details on each item, just double-click on it to see the "Additional Details" window.

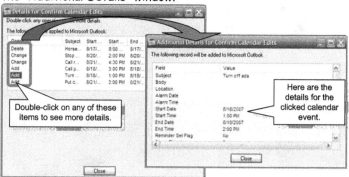

If everything looks OK then click the "**Accept**" button.

4. Then, if there are other notifications of "Edits" you can review and "**Accept**" or view "**Details**" or even "**Re-Sync**" if you think that the sync did not work correctly.

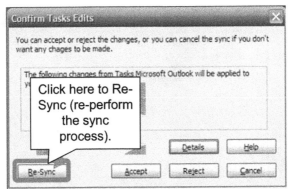

Once all four applications have finished synchronizing, then the pop-up windows will disappear and the sync will be completed.

4
Sync
Setup

How do I know when the Sync is completed?

Unfortunately, you will not see any window saying "Sync Completed." If you have your speakers turned up on your computer, you will hear a little "ding" sound, but other than that there is no notification of the completed sync.

To check that the sync worked, you need to disconnect your Blackberry and verify that changes from your computer made it to your BlackBerry and vice versa.

Automating Daily Synchronization

By default, the BlackBerry Desktop Manager should "auto-sync" every time you connect your BlackBerry to your computer. However, if for some reason it is not working for you, you need to check the "auto-sync" checkbox.

1. Double-click on the Synchronize icon from the Desktop Manager.
2. In this screen, make sure the check box for "Automatic Synchronization" is checked as shown.

Next time you connect your BlackBerry to your computer, it should start the synchronization process automatically.

Conflict Resolution during Synchronization

Conflicts seem to be handled well by the Desktop Manager software (at least for the Microsoft Outlook software we tested.)

Scenario 1: Changed Business (work) number on BlackBerry and added a Mobile number in Outlook on the computer.
Result: Both changes made it successfully to both the BlackBerry and Outlook.

Notice that the changes are highlighted with a red exclamation point in the "Additional Details" windows below.

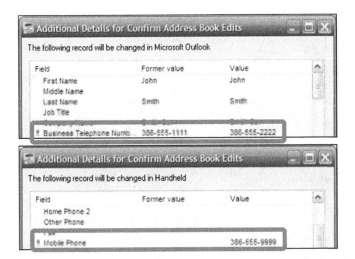

4
Sync
Setup

Scenario 2: Changed the Mobile number on both the BlackBerry and in Outlook to two different numbers before the sync.

Result: A conflict resolution window popped up showing the conflicting data, and I was allowed to make a choice as to which data to select by clicking on the correct item and selecting "OK"

Click the "View" button to see the entire field, useful for notes.

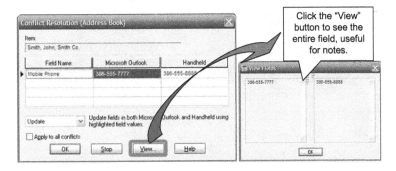

You have three choices: UPDATE, ADD or IGNORE

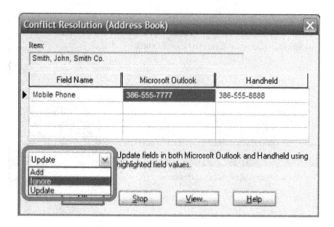

Go ahead and click on the correct data field (#1) (center column from the computer - in this case "Microsoft Outlook") or the right column, for the Handheld (BlackBerry).

Then select whether or not you want this applied to all future conflicts found during this sync by checking the box (#2)

WARNING: One of the authors has gotten into trouble by checking this "Apply to all" box. Please use with extreme care!

And finally, click "OK" to move on to the next conflict.

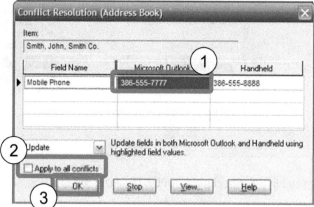

<u>SKIP TO CHAPTER 5</u>

If you are not an Apple Mac user, and/or your BlackBerry is not connected to a BlackBerry Enterprise Server, then please skip to Chapter 5 on page 144.

4
Sync
Setup

For Apple Macintosh Users – PocketMac for BlackBerry™ or Missing Sync for BlackBerry

Have a <u>Microsoft Windows</u>™ computer? Please go to page 93

IMPORTANT: BlackBerry themselves (Research In Motion or "RIM") have decided to license the PocketMac for BlackBerry™ software and make it available for all BlackBerry users for free. The authors, who do not use Mac computers, have noticed that there have been comments from vocal Mac users about some trouble they have experienced syncing some Mac software using "PocketMac for BlackBerry" software. While we have no means of verifying this, we have seen enough posts on forum web sites to believe that it does happen.

If you try PocketMac (free software) as described below, but are having significant trouble getting your information to sync, then we recommend trying another Mac-BlackBerry sync software called "**The Missing Sync for BlackBerry**" from the Mark/Space software company. You can learn more about this software by visiting the Mark/Space web site at <u>www.markspace.com</u>.

All that said, below we describe details about the free software available directly from BlackBerry for your Mac.

TIP: Get online up-to-date technical support and download the latest version by going to this link on your computer's web browser:

http://www.discoverblackberry.com/discover/mac_solutions.jsp

The screen may look different than the image below, but look for the links that say **"Download the latest version"** and **"Get technical support"**

Home > Discover BlackBerry > BlackBerry Solutions for the Mac World

BlackBerry Solutions for the Mac World

Together. At last.

If you're a Mac® user, it's easier than ever for you to take full advantage of a BlackBerry® device. PocketMac for BlackBerry requires MacOS 10.3.9 or 10.4 and above (including Intel Duo Technology). It lets you load new applications onto your BlackBerry as well as synchronize your email, contacts, calendar, tasks and notes with popular Mac applications, including:

- Mail.app Email
- Entourage® Email, Contacts, Calendar, Tasks and Notes
- Address Book Contacts
- iCal® Calendar and Tasks
- Now Contact®/Now Up-To-Date® Contacts, Calendars & Tasks
- Meeting Maker Contacts, Calendar, and Tasks
- Lotus Notes Contacts, Calendar, and Tasks
- Safari Bookmarks (One-Way sync)

PocketMac for BlackBerry is now available to BlackBerry customers as a free download. So you can stay on top of it all, wherever you go.

Download a copy of PocketMac for BlackBerry
Get technical support

PocketMac® for BlackBerry® features:
(courtesy www.pocketmac.com and www.discoverblackberry.com/discover/mac_solutions.jsp as of August 2007)

- ✓ Sync the following applications: Entourage Email, Contacts, Calendar, Tasks and Notes; Daylite; Address Book Contacts; iCal Calendar and Tasks; Lotus Notes Contacts, Calendar and Tasks; Mail.app Email; Meeting Maker Contacts Calendar and Tasks; Now Contact/Now Up-to-Date Contacts, Calendars & Tasks; Stickies Notes
- ✓ Install 3rd Party Applications from Mac to BlackBerry
- ✓ USB/Serial compatibility
- ✓ Password Support
- ✓ USB Charge while connected

✓ Requirements: Mac OS 10.4 or higher, 1 USB Port
✓ Only specific BlackBerry models are supported – please check their web site to see details
✓ *Check out www.pocketmac.com for the latest features and requirements.*

What follows are the steps you need to complete to first load your names, addresses, calendar, tasks and notes (and media – pictures, music and videos) and media (videos, music, pictures) from your personal computer onto your BlackBerry and keep them up-to-date or "synchronized".

4
Sync
Setup

Step 1: Download the PocketMac for BlackBerry™ Software

Step 2: Install the Software (Page 133)

Step 3: Setup the Synchronization (Page 134)

Step 4: Perform the Synchronization (Page 137)

Ongoing: How to Automate the Sync (Page 139)

Step 1: Download the PocketMac for BlackBerry Software

1. On your computer's web browser, go to http://www.discoverblackberry.com/discover/mac_solutions.jsp
2. Click the link at the bottom to download a copy of PocketMac for BlackBerry.
   NOTE: Web site layouts and software versions and screens change frequently, so it is likely that something on the web or in the software will not look exactly like it does in this book. If not, please look for the correct link or correct words in order to continue working through the steps. If you find a mistake and have the time, please email us a correction for our next revision at info@blackberrymadesimple.com, we would greatly appreciate it!

3. **Download the PocketMac© for BlackBerry©**
   Documentation: After clicking the "Download a copy.." link above, you be on the BlackBerry.com site and see a page similar to the one below. Select the highest version of "PocketMac for BlackBerry" available and click the "Next" button. (it is likely that the latest version will be higher than the one shown in the screen shot below) After clicking "Next", you will see new information appear below the "Next" button as shown.

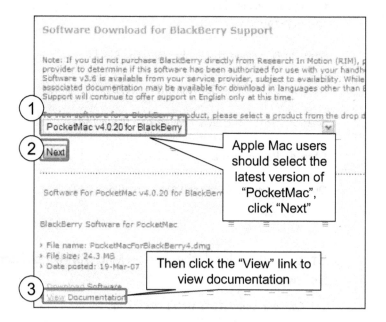

IMPORTANT: While you might be tempted to click the "Download" link, please click on the "View" documentation link first. This will give you the latest user guide (was 50 pages in August 2007) from the software vendor. With our book, we cannot re-create the excellent documentation supplied by PocketMac for BlackBerry® themselves. We strongly recommend you download and review their PDF manual in addition to ours.

4. After clicking "View Documentation" you will be on this page which gives you access to download the PocketMac for BlackBerry manual:

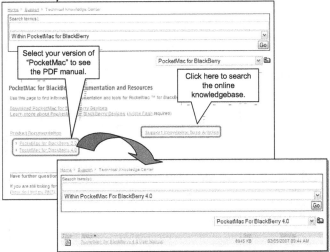

4
Sync
Setup

5. After you have the user guide, then click the "**BACK**" button a few times until you see the "**Download**" link at the bottom as shown below and now click on it.

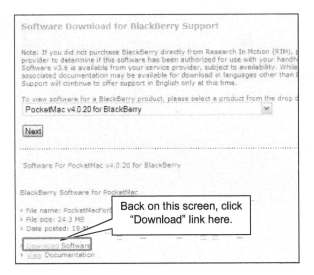

6. Now you will need to enter your personal information in order to download the software.

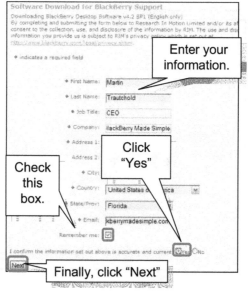

7. Now you will see a legal agreement similar to the one shown, you will need to click "Agree" and "Next" to continue to the download page.

8. Now, verify you have selected the correct software and click the "Download" button to see the Download popup window below.

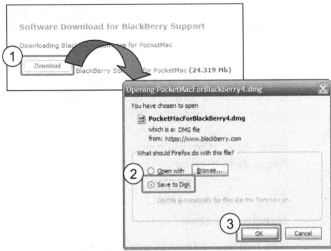

4
Sync
Setup

NOTE: A high-speed Internet connection is recommended because these download files can be 20 or more megabytes ("MB") and would a long time on a slow or dial-up Internet connection, but just a few minutes on a high-speed connection.

9. When the download is complete, you now have the latest PocketMac for BlackBerry installation file on your computer. Locate it and double-click on it to get started with the installation. Then follow the steps below.

Step 2: Install PocketMac for BlackBerry® Software

After double-clicking on the downloaded installation file, you will follow the onscreen installation instructions.

NOTE: Please use the **PocketMac for BlackBerry™ manual** to help guide you through the detailed installation steps. (How do I get this free guide? See page 130)

You have the option of installing support for Lotus Notes, if that is installed on your Mac.

TIP: Make sure your date/time and time zone on your BlackBerry match those on your Mac. Otherwise strange things could happen with scheduled calendar event start/end times.

You may sync either with a USB cable if you Mac has a USB port or a USB-Serial adapter. The manual describes details on how to user either connector.

After installation, you may be asked to **re-start your computer**. Please do so if asked.

Step 3: Setup the Synchronization

Now that you've finished installing the software, go ahead and start it up by double clicking on the PocketMac for BlackBerry™ desktop alias and a dock alias.

<u>NOTE</u>: Please use the **PocketMac for BlackBerry™ manual** to help guide you through the detailed installation steps. (How do I get this free guide? See page 130)

SCREEN SHOTS: Courtesy of PocketMac for BlackBerry™ v4.0 Manual from Information Appliance Associates.

1.   Setup the synchronization by clicking the "BlackBerry" icon inside the PocketMac for BlackBerry Sync Manager to see the nine tabs below the top gray bar like so:

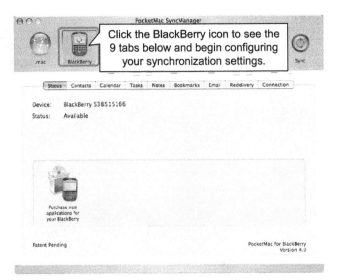

2. Now, you will need to select the Contacts, Calendar, Tasks, and Notes applications to synchronize to your BlackBerry by clicking the tabs near the top of the screen. (#1) Then select the checkbox (#2) if you want to share this application data with your BlackBerry. Select the particular Mac application (#3) that you want to configure. Finally, if you need to configure "Advanced Preferences"- click that button (#4).   Advanced preferences allows you to select only certain categories to sync to your BlackBerry or make it one-way synchronization (where your Mac data overwrites the BlackBerry or vice versa).

Shown below is the "Contacts" tab.

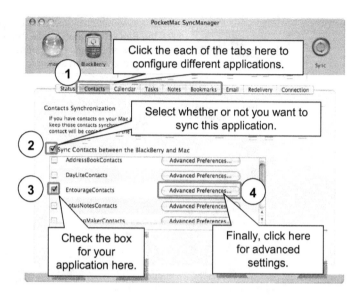

3. Repeat the above procedure for all the types of information: Calendar, Tasks, Notes, Bookmarks, etc.

4. You may choose to also setup Redelivery – this allows all email sent to your Mac (OS X Mail or Entourage v10.1.6 or v11) to be redirected to your BlackBerry. When you reply to this mail then it looks like you are replying from your Mac.

   CAUTION: Realize that using the Redelivery option will stop all email delivery as soon as you (1) turn off your Mac or (2) disconnect your Mac from the Internet.

   EMAIL SETUP: An alternative option to Redelivery is to use the BlackBerry Internet Service, which is available directly from the phone company that sold you your BlackBerry. Learn about how to setup Email integration right on your BlackBerry on page 77)

5. Connect your BlackBerry to your Mac. Make sure you see a status of "Connected and Ready" as shown below.

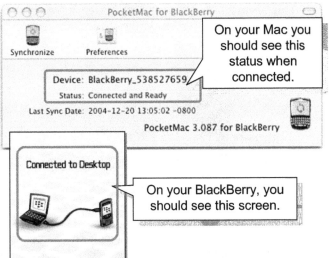

6. If you don't see "**Connected and Ready**", then click on the Preferences and make sure the connection settings are correct.

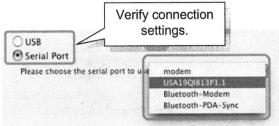

Step 4: Perform the Synchronization

1. Verify the following before you start your sync:

   ✓ The BlackBerry successfully connected to your Mac
   ✓ You have configured the Sync as shown in Step 3 above and followed detailed instructions from the PocketMac for BlackBerry™ User Guide.

2. Now, click the green sync button in the right side of the
   PocketMac for BlackBerry Sync Manager window as shown:

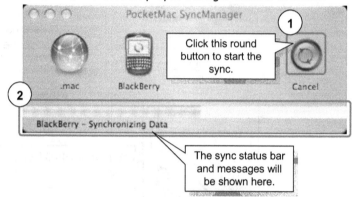

3. Depending on your preferences and
   whether or not this is your first sync, you will see various
   pop-up windows with important decisions to make.

   Sample popup windows:
   - Detected Deletion on Device
   - Detected Deletion on Mac
   - Sync Alert Message (may ask you to delete all calendars).

   WARNING: How you respond to these windows will be
   critical to protect your data. Please see the detailed
   instructions about each type of pop-up window in the
   PocketMac for BlackBerry™ User Guide.

How do I know when the Sync is completed?

Unfortunately, you will not see any window saying "Sync
Completed." If you have your speakers turned up on your
computer, you will hear a little "ding" sound, but other than that
there is no notification of the completed sync.

To check that the sync worked, you need to disconnect your
Blackberry and verify that changes from your Mac made it to
your BlackBerry and vice versa.

Automating Daily Synchronization

In the PocketMac for BlackBerry Scheduling preferences you may set the sync to happen when you first "Login" to your Mac, or run it automatically every so many (you set this) minutes. Please consult **PocketMac for BlackBerry™ User Guide** for details.

Conflict Resolution during Synchronization

Conflicts will be handled by PocketMac and shown to you during the synchronization. We strongly recommend consulting the **PocketMac for BlackBerry™ User Guide** for details.

4
Sync
Setup

SKIP TO CHAPTER 5

If your BlackBerry is not connected to a BlackBerry Enterprise Server, then please skip to Chapter 5 on page 144.

Loading Your Information for BlackBerry Server-Connected Handhelds

Most likely, if your BlackBerry was issued to your by your organization, it is now (or will be) connected to a BlackBerry Enterprise Server or "BES". If you received your BlackBerry from your organization, please contact your Technology Support group or the company that is providing access to your BlackBerry Server (for Hosted BES customers – learn more on page 514) These groups will help you getting your personal information loaded and email up and running. They will have to issue you what's called an "Activation Password" for you to complete the Enterprise Activation process.

My BlackBerry should be connected to a BlackBerry Server, how can I verify that my

BlackBerry is setup and "Activated" on the BlackBerry Server?

A simple rule of thumb is: If you can send and receive email and you have names in your BlackBerry address book, it has been successfully setup (the Enterprise Activation is complete.)
To verify if your BlackBerry successfully configured with your Server:

1. Start your BlackBerry Address Book.
2. Click the Menu key to the left of the trackball.
3. Roll the trackball up / down to find a specific menu item called "Lookup"
4. If you see "Lookup," then you are connected. (Note: This "Lookup" command allows you to do a "Global Address List" or "GAL" lookup from your BlackBerry Enterprise Server to find anyone in your organization - and then add them to your personal address book on your BlackBerry.)

Connecting to a BlackBerry Enterprise Server

If you have determined that your BlackBerry should be connected to your organization's server, then you should do the following:

1. Contact your Technology Support group and ask them for a BlackBerry Enterprise Activation Password.
2. Once you have your password, then you will need to start Enterprise Activation application on your BlackBerry.
3. You may have an icon specifically for "Enterprise Activation" - if you see that roll to it and click on it with the trackball. If you don't see an Enterprise Activation icon, locate and

click on the Setup Wizard icon on your BlackBerry.

4. If you go with the Setup Wizard option, either you will step through a number of screens to get to the "Email Setup" screen or simply be able to select "Email Setup" from the menu. It will look like this screen. Select the "Enterprise Server" option then roll down and click on 'Next >' with your trackball.

4
Sync
Setup

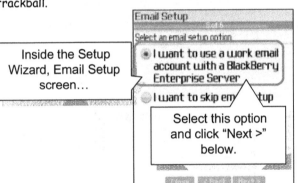

5. On the next screen, you will see the Enterprise Activation screen where you need to enter your work email address and activation password. After you enter it, click the trackball and select "Activate"

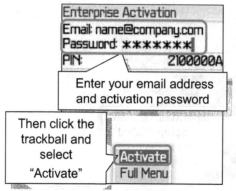

Enter your email address and activation password

Then click the trackball and select "Activate"

6. After selecting "Activate" you will then see many messages including the first one shown below. Then many more showing "Secure Connection", "Loading Address Book", "Email", "Calendar". The entire process may take 15 minutes or more depending on how much data is being sent as well as the strength of your wireless connection.

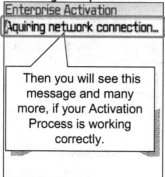

Then you will see this message and many more, if your Activation Process is working correctly.

7. If you see this error message, then verify your Wireless Radio is turned on and you are in a strong coverage area. If you still have problems, then please contact your Technology

Support group.

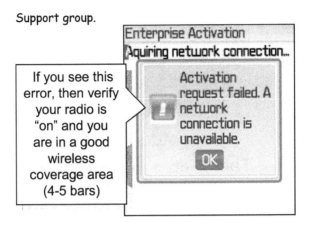

If you see this error, then verify your radio is "on" and you are in a good wireless coverage area (4-5 bars)

Enterprise Activation
Aquiring network connection...

Activation request failed. A network connection is unavailable.

OK

4
Sync
Setup

8. Once you have seen all the Enterprise Activation messages go by, and you see a completion message, then try email and check your address book and calendar to see if it looks like everything was loaded correctly. If not, then contact your Help Desk for support.

Your Address Book:
The "Heart" of Your Pearl

Chapter Contents:

The "Heart" of Your Pearl

Your Address Book is really the "heart" of your BlackBerry Pearl. Once you have your names and addresses in it, you can instantly call, email, send text ("SMS") messages or even pictures or Multi-Media Messages ("MMS") to anyone, Since your Pearl has a camera, you may even add pictures to anyone in your address book so when they call, their picture shows up as "Picture Caller ID." (See image)

How do I get my Addresses to my BlackBerry?

We describe exactly how to get this done on page 90.

How do I keep my Address Book in Sync with My Computer?

This works whether you are in a corporate environment, small office or are on your own. If you are a corporate user or subscribe to a hosted BlackBerry Enterprise Server (See page 514), the synchronization is wireless and automatic. Otherwise, you will use either a USB cable or Bluetooth wireless to connect your BlackBerry to your computer to keep it up to date. We show you how to set this up and keep it running for both Windows™ computers (see page 95) or an Apple Mac™ computer (see page 127).

When is Your Address Book Most Useful?

Your Address Book is most useful when two things are true:

1. You have **many names** and addresses in it.
2. You can **easily find** what you are looking for.

Our Recommendations:

We recommend keeping two "Rules" in mind to help make your Address Book most useful.

1. **Add anything and everything to your address book.**
    You never know when you might need that obscure restaurant name/number, or that plumber's number, etc.

2. **As you add entries, make sure you think about ways to easily find them in the future.**
    We have many tips and tricks in this chapter to help you enter names so that they can be instantly located when you need them.

How to <u>Easily</u> Add New Addresses

On your BlackBerry Pearl, since your Address Book is closely tied to all the other icons (Messages/Email, Phone and Web Browser) you have many methods to easily add new addresses:

Choice 1: Add a new address inside the Address Book.
Choice 2: Add an address from an email message in Messages.
Choice 3: Add an address from a phone call log in the Phone.
Choice 4: Add a new address from an underlined email address or phone number anywhere (Web Browser, Email, Tasks, MemoPad, etc.)

Choice 1: Add a new address in the Address Book.

This might be the most common way for you to get your Address Book up and running - just input the data directly into the Pearl.

1. Use the trackball and navigate and click on your Address Book.

2. Press the Menu key and select "New Address".

5
Address
Book

3. Type in the appropriate information in each field and then press the Menu key and "Save" the contact information.

TIP: Press the SPACE bar to get the "@" and "." in the email address.

Need to put in several email addresses for a person?
Just press the Menu key and select "Add Email Address"

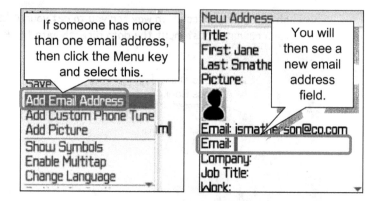

Need to enter a phone number that has letters?

Some business phone numbers have letters, like "1800-CALLABC". These are easier than you might think to add to your BlackBerry address book (or type while on the phone). The trick is to hold down your ALT key (lower left key with up/down

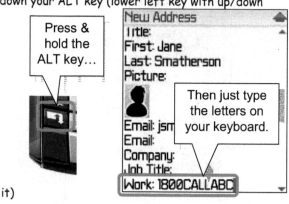

arrows on it)

Choice 2: Add an address from an email message in Messages.

Another easy way to update your address book is to simply add the contact information from emails that are sent to you.

1. Navigate to your message list and scroll to an email message in your inbox.

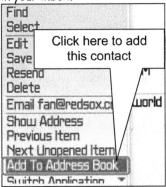

2. Click on the email message and press the Menu key.
3. Scroll to "**Add to Address Book**" and click.
4. Add the information in the appropriate fields, Push the ESCAPE key and "Save."

Choice 3: Add an address from a phone call log in the Phone

Sometimes you will remember that someone called you a while back, and you want to add their information into your address book.

1. Press the Green Phone button to bring up your call logs.
2. Scroll to the number you want to add to your address book.
3. Press the Menu key and select "**Add to Address Book**"
4. Add the address information, press the Menu key and select "Save".

Choice 4: Add a new address from an <u>underlined email address</u> or <u>phone number</u> anywhere (Web Browser, Email, Tasks, MemoPad, etc.)

One of the very powerful features of the Pearl is that you can really add your contacts from just about anywhere. While the next steps show on the MemoPad, they can be applied to Tasks, Emails (email addresses in the To:, From:, and CC: fields and in the body of the email), and Web pages. Let's say you wrote down

a contact's name and phone number in a memo, but never added it
to your address book;

1. Navigate to your
    MemoPad and click.
2. Scroll to the memo in
    which the contact
    information is stored and
    click.
3. Click on the memo and
    move the trackball to the
    phone number. The
    number will immediately
    become highlighted.
4. Press the Menu key and
    scroll to "Add Contact to Address Book" and follow the
    steps above.

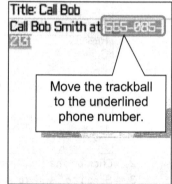

Title: Call Bob

Call Bob Smith at 555-085-213

Move the trackball
to the underlined
phone number.

How to Easily "Find:" Names & Addresses

Option 1: Locating the Address Book icon

The address book has a great "Find:" feature at the top that will
search for entries that match the letters you type in one of
three fields:

✓ First Name, Last Name or Company Name

Inside the Address Book, just type a few letters of a person's
first name, last name and/or company name (separated by
spaces) to instantly find that person.

See the entire address book:

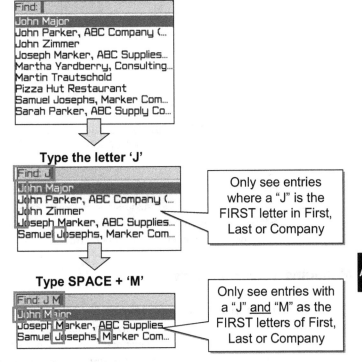

Type the letter 'J'

Only see entries where a "J" is the FIRST letter in First, Last or Company

Type SPACE + 'M'

Only see entries with a "J" <u>and</u> "M" as the FIRST letters of First, Last or Company

5
Address
Book

Option 2: Just start pushing buttons from your Home Screen

TIP: Press & Hold Green Phone Key

If you press & hold the **Green Phone key**, you will instantly be able to "**Dial by Name**" using your Address Book.

Sometimes, you just want to make a phone call to someone. If you just start dialing numbers or pressing letters from your Home Screen, the BlackBerry assumes you want to make a call. Then the phone is opened and the BlackBerry immediately starts searching for matching entries from your Address Book. If none can be found, you just see the digits being dialed.

1. Simply start typing in the name of your contact or phone

number.

2. Press the Green Phone key to immediately call this contact.
3. Or, you may press the Menu key and select Email, Call or SMS. You will only see these menu options if there is an email and phone number for this contact.

Managing your Contacts

Sometimes, your contact information can get a little unwieldy. Multiple entries for the same individual, business contacts mixed in with personal ones, etc. There are some very powerful tools within the Address book that can easily help you get organized.

Basic Contact Menu Commands

One of the first things to do is to make sure that all the correct information is included in your contacts. To do this, you will follow the steps to select and edit your contact information.

1. Select the Address Book icon and click on it.
2. Type in a few letters of the first, last or company name to "Find:" the contact or just scroll through the list.

3. Highlight the contact you want to manage with the trackball.

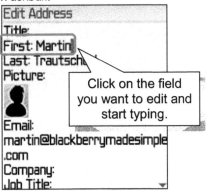

4. Press the Menu key and choose "Edit" to access the detailed contact screen and add any information missing in the fields.

Adding a Picture to the Contact for Caller ID

Sometimes it is nice to attach a face with the name. If you have loaded pictures onto your Media Card or have them stored in memory, you can add them to the appropriate contact in the Address Book. Since the Pearl has a camera, you can simply take the picture of the person and add it as "Picture Caller ID" right from the camera.

1. Select the contact to edit with the trackball as you did above.

2. Scroll down to the "picture" and click the trackball.

3. Choose "Add Picture" from the short menu.

4. You have the choice of finding a picture already stored on your BlackBerry or taking a new one with the camera.

| Click here or roll down to select a picture stored on your BlackBerry. | Click here to take a new picture with your camera. |

5. If you want to use a stored picture, then navigate to the folder in which your pictures are stored by rolling the trackball and clicking on the correct folder. Once you have located the correct picture, click the trackball on it and you will be prompted to "crop" the picture and save it.

6. If you want to use the camera instead to take a picture right now, then click on the camera and take the picture. Move the box to center the face, click the trackball and select "**Crop and Save**"

    Take the picture, then move this crop frame to center the image.

    Finally, click the trackball, select "Crop & Save"

7. The picture will now appear in that contact whenever you speak to them on the phone.

Changing the way Contacts are Sorted

You can sort your contacts by First Name, Last Name or Company Name.

1. Click on your Address Book – but don't click on any particular contact.
2. Press the Menu key and scroll down to "Options" and click.
3. In the "Sort By" field click on the trackball and choose the way you wish for your contacts

TIP
On any menu, you can jump down to an entry by pressing the key with the first letter. E.g. to jump down to "Options" press the "OP" key.

5
Address Book

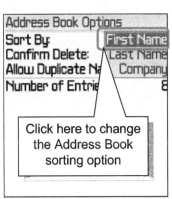

Click here to change the Address Book sorting option

TIP
On any drop down list like "First Name, Last Name, Company" in "Sort By", pressing the first letter of the entry will jump there. Ex. Pressing the letter "L" will jump to the entry starting with "L-Last".

to be sorted. You may also select whether to allow duplicate names and whether to confirm the deleting of contacts from this menu.

Using Categories

Sometimes, organizing similar contacts into "Categories" can be a very useful way of helping to quickly find people. What is even better is that the Categories you add, change or edit on your BlackBerry are kept fully in sync with those on your computer software.

1. Find the Contact you want to assign to a Category, click the trackball to view the contact, then click it again and select "Edit" from the short menu.

2. Click the Menu key and select "Categories."

3. Now you will see the available categories. (The default are Business and Personal.)

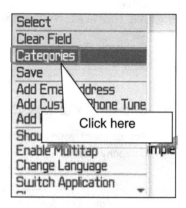

- If you need an additional category, just press the Menu key and choose "New."

- Type in the name of the new category and it will now be available for all your contacts.

TIP: Unlimited Categories

You can assign a contact to as many categories as you want!

- Scroll to the category in which you wish to add this contact and click.

Filtering your Contacts by Category

Now that your have your contacts assigned to categories, you can filter the names on the screen by their Categories. So, let's say that you wanted to quickly find everyone who you have assigned to the "business" category.

1. Click on your Address Book.
2. Press the Menu key, scroll up and select "Filter"
3. The available categories are listed. Just click the trackball (or press the SPACE key) on the category you wish to use as your filter. Once you do, only the contacts in that category are available to scroll through.

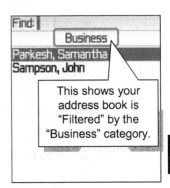

This shows your address book is "Filtered" by the "Business" category.

5
Address Book

Un-Filtering your Contacts by Category

Unlike the "Find" feature, you cannot just press the ESCAPE key to un-filter your categories. You need to reverse the "Filter" procedure.

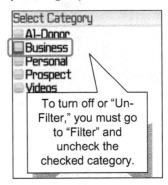

To turn off or "Un-Filter," you must go to "Filter" and uncheck the checked category.

1. Inside your Address Book, press the Menu key.

2. Select "Filter" and roll down to the checked category and uncheck it by clicking on it or pressing the SPACE bar when it is highlighted.

Use Groups as Mailing Lists

Sometimes, you need even more "Organizing Power" from your BlackBerry. Depending on your needs, grouping contacts into mailing lists might be useful so that you can send "Mass Mailings" from your Pearl.

Examples:
- ✓ Put all your team in a group to instantly notify them of project updates.
- ✓ You're about to have a baby – put everyone in the "notify" list into a "New Baby" group – then you can snap a picture with your BlackBerry and instantly send it from the hospital!

Creating and Using a Group Mailing List

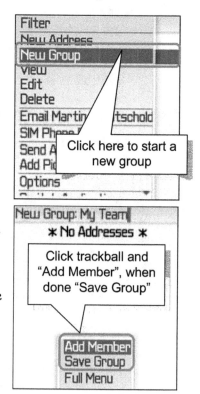

1. Scroll to the Address Book and click the trackball.
2. Press the Menu key and Scroll to "New Group" and click.
3. Type in a name for your new group.
4. Press the Menu key again and scroll up to "Add Member" and click.
5. TIP: Make sure each member has a **valid email address**, otherwise you will not be able to send them email from the group.
6. Scroll to the contact you want to add to that group and click. Their name is now under the name of the Group.

7. Continue to add contacts to that group or make lots of groups and fill them using the steps above.

Sending an Email to the Group

Just use the Group Name as you would any other name in your address book. If your group name was "My Team" then you would compose an email and address it to "My Team." Notice, that after the email is sent, there is a separate "To:" for each person you have added to the group.

Using the SIM Card to Store Contacts

Your SIM card is the small plastic card that you inserted when you activated your phone. SIM stands for Subscriber Identity Module and is stores your phone number and other personal information. You can remove your SIM card and put it into another GSM phone in the future, so it can be valuable to have your contacts on your card.

You can put approximately 250 contacts on your SIM card by following the steps below. **Note:** The SIM Address Book only stores name and telephone number, nothing else.

Copying A Contact from your BlackBerry Address Book to the SIM Phone Book

1. Click on the Address Book and navigate to the contact you want to add to your SIM card.
2. Click on the Contact and then press the Menu key.
3. Scroll up to "Copy to SIM Phone Book" and Click.

Adding all SIM Contacts to the BlackBerry Address Book

Sometimes you want to do the reverse and put your SIM contacts into your Device.

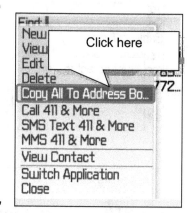

1. Click on the Address Book.
2. Press the Menu key and scroll to SIM Phone book and click.
3. Press the Menu key and scroll to "Copy All to Address Book."

Editing or Deleting SIM Card Contacts

1. Click on the Address Book and scroll to your SIM Phone Book and click.
2. Scroll to the contact you wish to Edit or Delete and press the Menu key.
3. Choose the desired action from the menu.

Storing SMS messages on the SIM Card

Sometimes you want to make sure you save a message. Because SMS messages are at times purged after a certain period of time or deleted accidentally, storing them on your SIM card keeps them preserved.

1. From your Home Screen, locate and click on the "Options" icon.
2. Press the "S" key a few times or roll the trackball down to the **SMS** line and click.
3. You second option is to leave your SMS messages on the SIM card. The default is "No," but if you click you can change this to "Yes."

SIM Card Security Options

Sadly, we live in a world that requires us to be constantly worried about security. With a GSM phone, like your BlackBerry, if your phone was every lost or stolen, your SIM card could be removed and used to activate another phone. Also, if you have put your contacts on your SIM card, that is information that you may want to protect. Fortunately, setting security on your SIM card is very easy to do.

1. Click on "Options" and scroll up to "Advanced Options" and click.

2. Scroll down to SIM card and click.

3. The menu will allow you to:

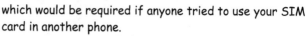

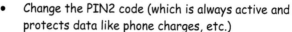

- Enable Security – by assigning a new PIN Code which would be required if anyone tried to use your SIM card in another phone.
- Change the PIN2 code (which is always active and protects data like phone charges, etc.)

Organize with Calendar, Tasks and MemoPad

Chapter Contents:

Calendar Icon:
- Switching Views in the Calendar
- The Quickest Way to Schedule Appointments
- Working with Meeting Invitations
- Customizing Your Calendar Options
- Calendar Hot Keys / Shortcuts
- Copy and Paste Information Into the Calendar
- Recurring Appointments
- Snoozing Alarms and Rescheduling Appointments

Tasks Icon:
- Adding Tasks
- Using Categories
- Finding Tasks
- Completing Tasks
- Sorting Tasks

MemoPad Icon:
- 1,001 Uses
- Adding New Memos
- Quickly Finding Memos
- Ordering Frequently Used Memos
- Organizing with Categories

Multi-Tasking with ALT+ESCAPE

Organizing You Life with Your Calendar

For many of us, our calendar is our life line. Where do I need to be? With whom am I meeting? When do the kids need to be picked up? When is Martin's birthday? The calendar can tell you all these things and more.

The Calendar on the Pearl is really simple to use, but it also contains some very sophisticated options for the power user.

How do I get my Calendar from my Computer to my BlackBerry?

We describe exactly how to get this done starting on page 90.

How do I keep my Calendar in Sync with My Computer?

This is also described on page starting on page 90.

Switching Views and Days in the Calendar

The calendar is where you look to see how your life will unfold over the next few hours, day or week. It is quite easy to change the view if you need to see more or less time in the Calendar screen.

Option #1: Using the Trackball (Fastest way)
1. Navigate to your Calendar icon and click. The default view is the "Day" view which lists all appointments for the current calendar day.
2. Move the Trackball left or right to a previous day or an upcoming day.
3. Notice the date changes in the upper left hand corner.

Option #2: Using the Menu key
1. Click on your Calendar icon as you did above.
2. Press the Menu key and scroll up to either "Next Day," "Prev. Day" or "Go to Date" and click. If you clicked "Go to Date" just input the date you wish to view.

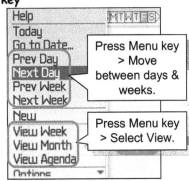

Changing View to Week View, Month View or Agenda View
1. Click the Calendar icon as above.
2. Press the Menu key and scroll to "View Week", "View Month" or "View Agenda"
3. Use the trackball to navigate left and right to view past or future weeks or months.
4. Roll the trackball up and down to move an hour at a time (Week View), a week at a time (Month View), or up/down through your scheduled appointments or free time (Agenda View).

Scheduling Appointments

Putting your busy life into your BlackBerry Pearl is quite easy. Once you start to schedule your appointments or meetings, you will begin to expect reminder alarms to tell you where to go and when. You will wonder how you lived without your BlackBerry for so long!

Quick Scheduling (Use for simple meetings)

It is amazingly simple to add basic appointments (or reminders) to your calendar. In Day view, roll the trackball to the correct day and time, press the ENTER key and start

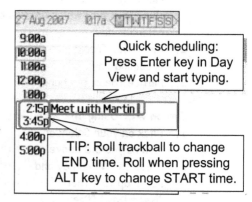

typing your appointment right in day view. If you need to change the start time, press the ALT key (up/down arrow in lower left corner) while rolling the trackball up/down.

TIP

Quick Scheduling is so fast you can even use your calendar for reminders like:
"Pick up the dry cleaning"
"Pick up Chinese food"
"Pick up dog food"

To change the ending time, just roll the trackball by itself. When you're done, click the trackball or press the ENTER key.

Detailed Scheduling (Use when you need advanced options)

1. Click on the Calendar icon. You should be brought to today's date with appointment times shown hourly.

2. Scroll with the trackball to the designated hour of the appointment you wish to schedule and click.

3. Input the appropriate information in the Subject line as well as the location of the appointment.

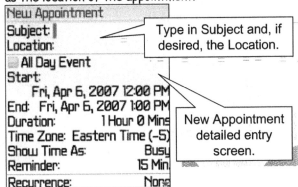

4. If this is an all day event, check the radio box next to "All Day Event."

6
Calendar
Task, Memo

5. Scroll down to where it reads "Start" and use the trackball to highlight the date, year or time.

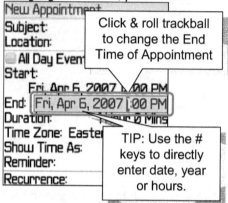

Click & roll trackball to change the End Time of Appointment

TIP: Use the # keys to directly enter date, year or hours.

Click on the field you need to change (if any) and put in the correct information.

6. You can skip changing the end time of the appointment, and instead just change the length of the appointment by scrolling to "Duration" and putting in the correct amount of time.

7. You can show the time as "Busy" (default) or "Free," "Tentative" or "Out of Office" by clicking on that field and scrolling to the appropriate label.

TIP

Use your **number keys (1, 2, 3...)** to enter specific dates, years and times. Example type in "45" to change the minutes to "45".

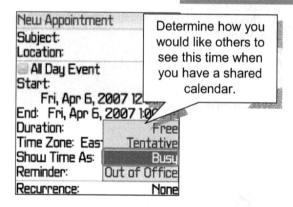

Determine how you would like others to see this time when you have a shared calendar.

8. Set a reminder alarm by clicking on "Reminder" and setting the reminder time for the alarm from five minutes prior to nine hours prior. TIP: The default reminder time is usually 15 minutes, but you can change this by going into your Calendar Options screen. (See page 172)

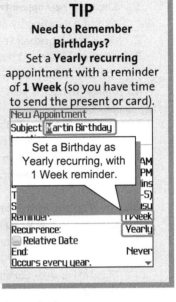

TIP

Need to Remember Birthdays?

Set a **Yearly recurring** appointment with a reminder of **1 Week** (so you have time to send the present or card).

Set a Birthday as Yearly recurring, with 1 Week reminder.

9. If this is a recurring appointment, click on Recurrence and select "Daily," "Weekly," "Monthly" or "Yearly".

10. Mark your appointment as "Private" by clicking on the radio box.

11. If you would like to include notes with the appointment, simply input them at the bottom of the screen.

12. Press the Menu key and select "Save."

6
Calendar
Task, Memo

Inviting Attendees and Working with Meeting Invitations

If your BlackBerry Pearl is connected to a BlackBerry Enterprise Server ("BES") in your office (or from a Hosted BES provider – See page 514), you can invite people to appointments, respond to invitations and really use the Pearl to manage your life at the office.

NOTE: Some BlackBerry phone companies may soon give this same meeting invitation capability to BlackBerry users who are not connected to a BlackBerry Enterprise Server. (What is a BlackBerry Enterprise Server? See page 80)

To Invite Someone to Attend this Meeting

1. Create a new appointment in your calendar or "Open" an existing meeting by clicking on it with your trackball.
2. Click the trackball to see the Short Menu.
3. Click on "Invite Attendee" and follow the prompts to find a contact and click on that contact to invite them.
4. Follow the same procedure to invite more people to your meeting.
5. Click on the Trackball and select "Save."

To respond to a meeting invitation

1. You will see the meeting invitation in your Messages (Email Inbox).
2. Open up the invitation by clicking on it with the trackball, then press the Menu key.
3. Several options are now available to you. Click either: "Accept" or "Accept with Comments," or "Tentative or "Tentative with Comments" or "Decline or "Decline with Comments."

To Change List of Participants for Meeting

1. Click on the meeting in your calendar application.
2. Navigate to the "Accepted" or "Declined" field and click the Contact you wish to change.
3. The options "Invite Attendee," "Change Attendee" or "Remove Attendee" are available. Just click on the correct option.

To Contact your Meeting Participants

1. Open up the meeting or your meeting invitation or even one of the responses from the participants.
2. Simply highlight the contact and press the Menu key
3. Scroll through the various ways you can contact that contact – email, PIN message, SMS, etc. or Call the contact directly

To Send an Email to everyone who is Attending the Meeting

1. Navigate to the meeting in your calendar and click on the trackball.
2. Click on "Email all Attendees" and compose your email.

3. Click on the Trackball and select "Send."

Customizing Your Calendar with Options

You can change a number of things to make your Calendar work even better.

NOTE: Some of the screen shots in this section are different colors than the rest of the book – this is because we took these images from an AT&T / Cingular Themed BlackBerry

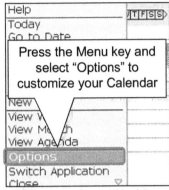

Press the Menu key and select "Options" to customize your Calendar

Pearl to give you a flavor that the "Theme" of your BlackBerry can change everything from colors, font sizes and types. Learn more about Themes on page 41.

Before you can make any of the changes below, get into your Calendar Options screen. To get there, first open the calendar, press the Menu key and select "Options" from the menu.

6
Calendar
Task, Memo

Change your Initial View (Day, Week, Month, Agenda or Last)

If you prefer the Agenda view, week view or month views instead of the default Day view when you open your Calendar, you can set that in the options screen. Click the drop down list next to "Initial View" to set these.

Select your default view when you first open the calendar.

Change your Start and End of Day Hours
If you are someone that has early morning or evening appointments, the 9a – 5p calendar will not work well. You will need to adjust the 'Start of Day' and 'End of Day' hours in the options screen.

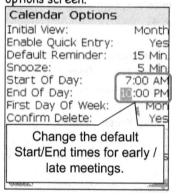

Change the default Start/End times for early / late meetings.

TIP: Use the number keys on your keypad to type in the correct hours (e.g. type 7 for 7am and 10 for 10pm). This is faster than clicking the trackball and rolling to an hour.

Changing the Default Reminder (Alarm) and Snooze Times
If you need a little more advanced warning than the default 15 minutes, or a little more snooze time than the default 5 minutes, you can change those also in the options screen.

Calendar Navigation Hot Keys or Shortcuts

Some of us like using the trackball, scrolling and clicking to set our appointments. Others of us would like to use keyboard short cuts - or "**Hot Keys**" to navigate through the scheduling tasks. The Pearl can accommodate whichever method you prefer.

If you want to **turn on** calendar navigation hot keys, then you will need to set "**Enable Quick Entry**" to "**No**" in the **Calendar Options** screen.

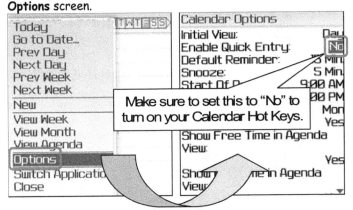

Make sure to set this to "No" to turn on your Calendar Hot Keys.

Once you have turned off Quick Entry, then the following Hot Keys will work from the keyboard:

6
Calendar
Task, Memo

CALENDAR HOT KEYS:

Press this key	In order to...
!	Go to Today
2	Previous Hour (Day View)
8	Next Hour (Day View)
4	Previous Day (Day View)
6	Next Day (Day View)
5	Open Appointment / Schedule New
.	New Appointment
SPACE	Next Day
DEL	Delete Selected
SHIFT + roll trackball	Select several hours (Day View)

Copying and Pasting Information into Your Calendar

The beauty of the Blackberry Pearl is how simple it is to use. Let's say that you wanted to copy part of a text in your email and paste it into your calendar. A few good examples are:
- Conference Call information via email
- Driving directions via email
- Travel details (flights, rental cars, hotel) via email

1. First, roll the trackball to select the email from which you want to copy and open it.
2. Then, highlight the text by moving the cursor to the beginning or end of the section you want to highlight.

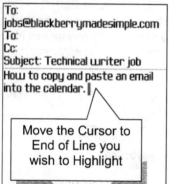

3. Next, press the **SHIFT** key (also the "#" key). Then all you do is roll the trackball to move the cursor to the end (or beginning) of the section you want to highlight. The text that you just highlighted will turn gray.

4. Just press the Menu key and select "Copy."

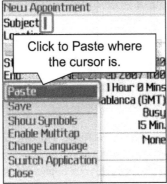

Press Menu key, select "Copy"

5. Click the trackball and your text is now in the clipboard.
6. Press the **Red Phone key** to "jump" back to your Home Screen and leave this email open in the background.
7. Roll to and click on the "**Calendar**" icon to open it.
8. Start a new appointment by clicking the trackball in day view or selecting "**New**" from the Calendar menu. Move the cursor to the field you want to insert the text that is in the clipboard. Then click the trackball or press the Menu key and select "**Paste**"

Click to Paste where the cursor is.

9. Click the **trackball** once and your copied text will appear in your calendar.
10. Press the **ESCAPE key** (to the right of the trackball) and select "**Save**" when prompted. Now your text is in your calendar. Now it's available exactly when you need it. Gone are the days of hunting for the conference call numbers, driving directions or asking yourself "What rental car company did I book?"

Alarms and Recurring Appointments

Some appointments are ones that occur every week, month or year. Others are easy to forget, so setting an alarm is helpful to remind us where to be or where to go.

To Schedule an Alarm:
1. Navigate to the Calendar icon and click.
2. Begin the process of scheduling an appointment as detailed above.
3. In the New Appointment screen, scroll down to "**Reminder.**"
4. The default reminder is 15 minutes – click on the highlighted field and change the reminder to any of the options listed.

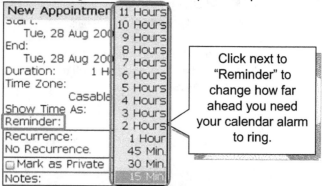

Click next to "Reminder" to change how far ahead you need your calendar alarm to ring.

5. Press the **ESCAPE** key or the Menu key and select "**Save**".

To Change the Calendar Alarm to Ring, Vibrate or Mute:
1. Scroll to the upper right hand corner and click on the "**Profile**" icon or scroll through your applications and select "**Profiles**" and click.
2. If you only see a listing of "Loud", "Vibrate", "Quiet", etc. as shown below, then you need to roll down and click on

"Advanced"

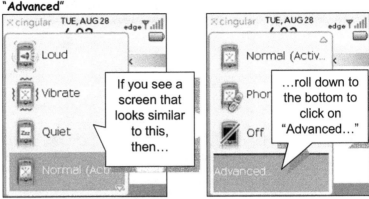

3. Now you should see a screen similar to the one below with **"Profiles"** at the top.

4. In the Profiles screen, press the Menu key and select "Edit" (make sure that your **"Active"** or **"Enabled"** profile is highlighted when you do this.)

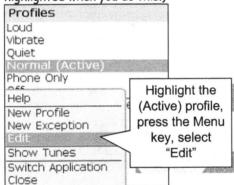

6
Calendar
Task, Memo

5. Scroll down to "Calendar" and click on it.

6. Scroll to "**Tune**" and click on the highlighted field. Navigate trough the possible tunes on your Pearl, either in the Device memory or on your Micro SD card and select the tune you wish to use for reminders.

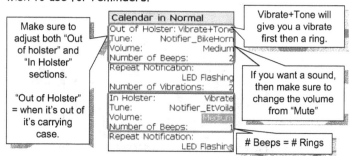

7. Press the **ESCAPE** key or the Menu key and select "**Save**".

To Set a Recurring Appointment

1. Click on your Calendar icon.
2. Click on an empty slot to bring up the scheduling screen.
3. Scroll down to "**Recurrence**" and click in the highlighted field.
4. Select either "**None**," "**Daily**," "**Weekly**," "**Monthly**" or "**Yearly**."

5. Press the **ESCAPE** key or the Menu key and select "**Save**".

To Snooze a Ringing Calendar or Task Alarm

When a calendar or task alarm rings, you can "Open" it, "Dismiss" it or "Snooze" it.

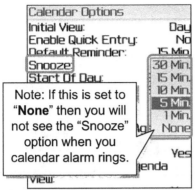

Note: If this is set to "**None**" then you will not see the "Snooze" option when you calendar alarm rings.

If you don't see a "**Snooze**" option, then you need to change your setting in your Calendar or Task options screen from "None" to some other value. Clicking on the "**Snooze**" option does just that – it will snooze 5 minutes, 10 minutes, or whatever you have set in the Calendar or Task options screen.

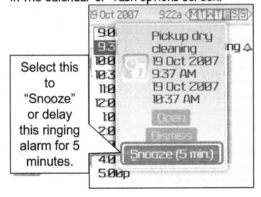

Select this to "Snooze" or delay this ringing alarm for 5 minutes.

But what if your 'pre-set' snooze time is not going to work for you?
In this case you should select "**Open**" and scroll down to the scheduled time and change that. Use the **number keys** on your BlackBerry to **change the date or time**. For example, typing

"30" in the minutes field would change the time to ":30."

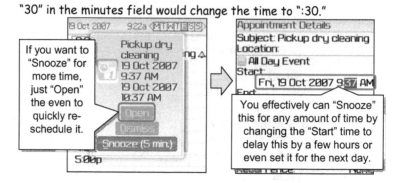

If you want to "Snooze" for more time, just "Open" the even to quickly re-schedule it.

You effectively can "Snooze" this for any amount of time by changing the "Start" time to delay this by a few hours or even set it for the next day.

The Task Icon

Like your Address Book, Calendar and Memo Pad, your Task list becomes more powerful when you share or synchronize it with your computer. Since the BlackBerry Pearl is so easy to carry around, you can update, check-off, and even create new tasks anytime, anywhere they come to mind. Gone are the days of writing down a task on a sticky note and hoping to find it later when you need it.

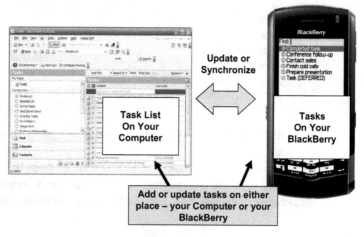

Update or Synchronize

Task List On Your Computer

Tasks On Your BlackBerry

Add or update tasks on either place – your Computer or your BlackBerry

How do I Sync my Task List to my BlackBerry?

We describe exactly how to get this done starting on page 90.

Viewing Tasks On Your BlackBerry

To view your tasks, locate and click on the "**Tasks**" icon. It will

look something like this: 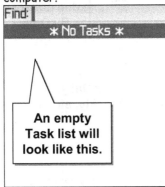 and say "**Tasks**" when you roll over it. You may need to press the Menu key to the left of the trackball to see all your icons.

The first time you start tasks on your BlackBerry, you may see an empty task list if you have not yet synchronized with your computer.

Find:

✳ No Tasks ✳

An empty Task list will look like this.

6
Calendar
Task, Memo

Adding A New Task

Press the Menu key and select "**New**." Then you can enter information for your new task. TIP: Keep in mind the way the "**Find**" feature works as you name your task. For example, all tasks for a particular "Project Red" should have "Red" in the name for easy retrieval.

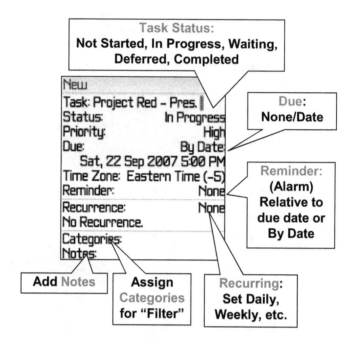

Categorizing Your Tasks

Like Address Book entries, you can group your tasks into Categories. And you can also share or synchronize these categories with your computer.

To assign a task to a category:
1. Highlight the task, click the trackball and "**Open**" it.
2. Press the Menu key and select "**Categories**"
3. Select as many categories as you would like by checking them with the trackball or pressing the **SPACE key**.
4. You may even add new categories by pressing the **Menu key** and selecting "**New**"
5. Once you're done, press the **Menu key** and select "**Save**" to save your Category settings.
6. Press the **Menu key** and select "**Save**" again to save your Task.

To filter your tasks by category:

This works the same as in your Address Book, so what you learn here you can apply in the Address Book as well. To filter by a particular Category:

1. Open the task list by clicking on the Tasks icon.
2. Press the **Menu key** and select "**Filter**"
3. Roll to a Category and **press the trackball** to select that category. Note: You may only filter by one category at a time.

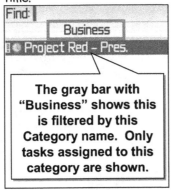

To turn off the "Filter" by Category:

1. Press the Menu key and select "**Filter**"
2. Roll the trackball and **click** on the checked category to uncheck it.

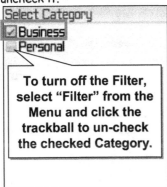

6
Calendar
Task, Memo

Finding Tasks

Once you have a few tasks in your task list, you will want to know how to quickly locate them. One of the fastest ways is with the

"**Find**" feature. The same "**Find**" feature from the Address Book works in Tasks. Just start typing a few letters to view only those that contain those letters.

In the example below, if we wanted to quickly find all tasks with "John" in the name, then we type the letter "jo" to quickly see them.

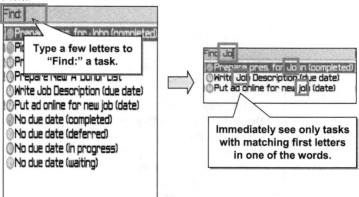

"Checking-Off" or Completing Tasks

Roll the trackball down to a task to highlight it and press the **SPACE key**. (Press **SPACE key** again to "un-check" it).

Note, you can change a task to "**Waiting**" or "**Deferred**" by first "**Opening**" by clicking the trackball and changing the status.

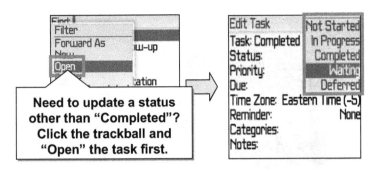

Sorting Your Tasks & Task Options

You may sort your tasks by the following methods in your Task Options screen: **Subject (default), Priority, Due Date** or **Status.**

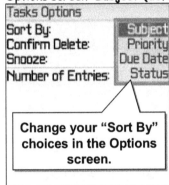

You may also change "**Confirm Delete**" to "**No**" (default is "**Yes**"). You may also change the default Snooze from "**None**" to "**30 Min.**"

6
Calendar
Task, Memo

The MemoPad

One of the simplest and most useful programs on your BlackBerry is the included MemoPad. Its uses are truly limitless. There is nothing flashy about this program – just type your memo or your notes and keep them with you at all times.

How do I Sync my MemoPad to my BlackBerry?

We describe exactly how to get this done starting on page 90.

1,001 Uses for the MemoPad (Notes) Feature

OK, maybe we won't list 1,001 uses here, but we could. Anything that occupies space on a sticky note on your desk, in your calendar or on your refrigerator could be written neatly and organized simply using the MemoPad feature.

Common Uses for the MemoPad:
1. Grocery list
2. Meeting Agenda
3. Packing list
4. Daily agenda
5. BlackBerry Made Simple Videos you want to watch
6. Movies you want to rent next time at the video store.
7. Your parking space at the airport, mall or theme park.

Using the Memo Features

Using the MemoPad is very easy and very intuitive. The following steps guide you through the basic process of inputting a memo and saving it on your BlackBerry Pearl. There are two basic ways of setting up Memos on the Pearl, either compose the note on your computer organizer application and then synchronize (or transfer) that note to the Pearl or compose the Memo on the Pearl itself.

Synching Memos from your computer

1. Compose your Memo (Note) in your computer's Personal Information Manager such as Microsoft Outlook or another supported organizer Program (For a full list of compatible organizer programs for Windows™ computers see page 93, For an Apple Mac™ see page 128)
2. For complete instructions on how to setup desktop synchronization between your computer and your BlackBerry Pearl, please see Chapter 4.
3. After the synchronization is complete, the notes (memo items) you created on your computer should appear in the MemoPad program on your BlackBerry.
4. The sync works both ways, which extends the power of your desktop computer to your BlackBerry – add or edit notes anywhere and anytime on your BlackBerry – and rest assured they will be back on your computer (and backed up) after the next sync.

6
Calendar
Task, Memo

Composing New Memos on the Pearl

1. Navigate to the **MemoPad** icon and click on it. Your icon may look different from the one shown below. You know you're on the MemoPad when you see the word "**MemoPad**" at the bottom (or top) of the screen when you roll over the icon.

2. If you have no memos in the list, then to add a new memo, simply press in the trackball and start typing.

3. If you have memos in the list, and want to add a new one, you must press the **Menu key** and select "**New**."

4. To open an existing memo, just roll to it and click on it. Depending on the version of software on your BlackBerry, you may already be in "**Edit**" mode. If you cannot type in the memo, then click one more time with the trackball and select "**Edit**"

5. When typing a new memo, you will want to enter a title that will be easy to "**Find**" later.

6. Using the trackball, scroll down and begin composing the Memo in the main screen.

7. Press the **ENTER key** to go down to the next line.

8. When the memo is complete, press the **Menu key** and select "Save."

Quickly Locating or 'Finding' Memos

The memo pad has a **"Find"** feature to help you locate memos quickly by typing the first few letters of words that match the title of your Memos. Example, typing **"gro"** would immediately show you only memos matching those three letters in the first part of any word like **"grocery."**

Use the 'Find' feature. Type a few letters to find matching Memo items.

Ordering Frequently Used Memos

For frequently used memos, type numbers (01, 02, 03, etc.) at the beginning of the title to force those memos to be listed in order at the very top of the list. (The reason we started with zero is to keep memos in order after the #10):

TIP: Using numbers at the beginning of your memo titles will force them to stay at the top of the list – easy access!

6
Calendar
Task, Memo

Viewing Your Memos

Roll the trackball down to a memo or type a few letters to '**Find**'

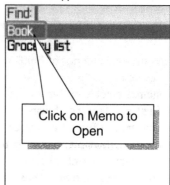

Click on Memo to Open

the memo you want to view.

Click the trackball to instantly view the memo.

TIP

Typing "**ld**" (stands for 'Long Date') and pressing the SPACE key will insert the date "Tue, 28 Aug 2007" and "**lt**" ('Long Time') will enter the time: "8:51:40 PM" (will be in the local date/time format you have set on your BlackBerry)

Organizing your Memos with Categories

TIP

Categories are shared between your Address Book, Task List and MemoPad. They are even synchronized or shared with your desktop computer.

Similar to your Address Book and Task list, the MemoPad application allows you to organize and filter memos using Categories.

First, you must assign your memos to categories before they can be "**Filtered**"

One way to be extra organized with your MemoPad application is to utilize Categories so all your Memos are "filed" neatly away. The two default categories are "Personal" and "Business" but you can easily change or add to these.

To file a memo in a New or Existing Category:
1. Start the **MemoPad** icon by clicking on it.
2. Locate the memo you want to file to one or more categories by rolling and clicking on it or by typing a few letters and using the "Find" feature at the top.
3. Press the Menu key and select "Edit"
4. Press the Menu key again and select "Categories". Now you will see a screen similar to the one below. Roll the trackball to a category and click to check/uncheck it. You can add a new category by pressing the Menu key and selecting "New"

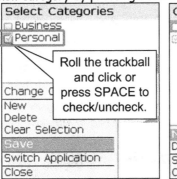

5. Then "Save" your category settings, and "Save" the memo.

To Filter memos using Categories / To only see memos in a specific Category
1. Start the MemoPad by clicking on it.
2. Press the Menu key and select "Filter"

3. Now roll to and click (or press SPACE) on the Category you would like to use to filter the list of memos.

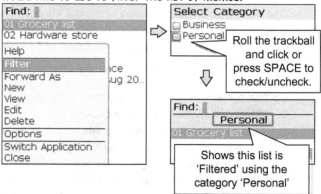

To 'Un-Filter' (Turn Off the Filter) on Your MemoPad:
You probably noticed that pressing the ESCAPE key (which clears out the 'Find:' characters typed) will do nothing for the Filter - it just exits the MemoPad. When you re-enter, you still see the filtered list. To 'un-filter' or turn off the filter, you need to:
1. Press the **Menu key**.
2. Select "**Filter**"
3. Roll to and uncheck the checked category by **clicking the trackball** on it or pressing the **SPACE key**.

Switch Application / Multi-Tasking

Selecting the "**Switch Application**" menu item allows you to "**Multi-task**" and leave whatever you are working on in the MemoPad (or any icon) open and jump to any other icon on your BlackBerry. This is especially useful when you want to copy and paste information between icons.

Here's how you jump or "switch" applications:
1. Press the **Menu key** and select "**Switch Application**"
2. You will now see the "**Switch Applications**" pop-up window which shows you every icon that is currently running.
3. **If you see the icon you want** to switch to, just roll and click on it.

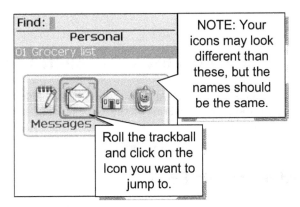

4. **If you don't see the icon you want**, then click on the "**Home Screen**" icon. Then you can locate and click on the right icon.

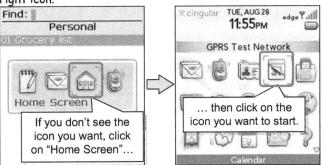

6
Calendar
Task, Memo

5. You can then jump back to the MemoPad or application you just left by selecting the "**Switch Application**" menu item from the icon you jumped to.

TIP: ALT+ ESCAPE to Multi-Task

Pressing & holding the **ALT key** and then tapping the **ESCAPE key** is the shortcut to bring up the "Switch Application" pop-up window.

Forward Memos via Email

You might want to send a memo item via email, BlackBerry PIN message or SMS text message to others. If so, you can use the "**Forward As**" command from the menu.

1. Highlight the memo you want to send and press the **Menu key**.
2. Select "**Forward As**", then select if you want **Email**, **PIN** or **SMS**.
3. Finally finish composing your message, click the trackball and select "**Send**"

You can forward any memo item as an Email, PIN message or SMS text message.

Other Memo Menu Commands

There may be a few other things you want to do with your memos, these can be found in the more advanced menu commands.

1. Start the **MemoPad** icon.

2. Some of these advanced menu items can only be seen when you are either writing a "**New**" memo or "**Editing**" an existing one.

3. So you either select "**New**" and begin working on a new Memo or select "**Edit**" and edit an existing Memo.

4. From the Editing screen, press the Menu key and the following options become available to you:

TIP: Shortcuts for Select & Copy

Select - Press the **SHIFT key** (to right of the SPACE key) to start "Select" mode.

Copy - To copy selected text, **hold the ALT key** (lower leftmost key – up/down arrow) and **click the trackball**.

a. **Paste** – Suppose you have copied text from another program and want to paste it into a Memo. Select and copy the text (from the calendar, address book or another application) and select "Paste" from this menu. The text is now in your Memo.

b. **Select** – Allows you to do just the reverse – click here and select text from the Memo, then press the Menu key again and select "Copy." Now, use the "Switch Applications" menu item to navigate to another application and press the Menu key and select "Paste" to put the text in that application.

c. **Clear field** – Clears all contents of the entire memo item – USE WITH CAUTION!

d. **Save** – Saves the changes in the Memo.

e. **Categories** – Allows you to file this Memo into either the "Business" or "Personal" categories. After selecting "Categories" you can press the Menu key again and select "New" to create yet another category for this Memo. (Learn more on page 190)

f. **Delete** – Deletes the current Memo.

g. **Show Symbols** – for quickly adding a Symbol. (TIP: You can also just press the **SYM key** to see the symbol list.)

h. **Enable Multitap** – to change from SureType to Multitap typing mode. Multitap is a slower but more exacting way

6
Calendar
Task, Memo

to type text forcing you to press each key once to type the first letter on it and twice to get the second. For example, pressing the "OP" key once would type an "O" and twice would type a "P".

TIP: Remember the shortcut for switching between Multitap and SureType is **pressing and holding the SYM key**.

i. **Change Language** - to compose the Memo in another language - this allows the SureType™ system to guess words in the new language selected.

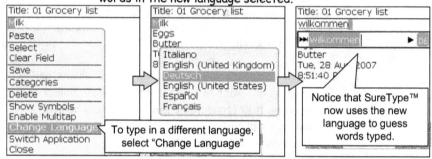

To type in a different language, select "Change Language"

Notice that SureType™ now uses the new language to guess words typed.

j. **Switch Application** - this is explained on page 192.
k. **Close** - similar to pressing the ESCAPE key.

Memo Tips and Tricks

There are a couple of tricks you can use to make your filing and locating of memos even easier.

1. Add separate items for each store in which you need to shop - This can help eliminate the forgetting of one particular item you were supposed to get at the hardware or grocery store (and save you time and gas money!).
2. Put numbers at the beginning of your Memo names. - This will then order them numerically on your BlackBerry. This is a great way to prioritize your memos and keep the most important ones always at the top of the list.

6
Calendar
Task, Memo

Search Icon -
Find Just About Anything

Chapter Contents:
- Understanding "Search"
- Choosing which Fields to Search
- Searching for Names or Text
- Search Tips and Tricks

TIP: Finding Calendar Events

With the **Search** icon, you can even answer the questions like:
When is my next meeting with Sarah?
When did I last meet with her?
(For this to work, you need to type people's names in your calendar events like "Meet with Sarah" or "Lunch with Tom Wallis")

Understanding How Search Works

Once you get used to your BlackBerry, you will begin to rely on it more and more. The more you use it, the more information you will store within it. It is truly amazing how much information you can place in this little device.

At some point, you will want to retrieve something – a name or a word or phrase – but you may not be exactly sure of where you placed that particular piece of information. This is where the "Search" icon can be invaluable.

Finding the Search Icon

In your applications menu there is a **Search** Icon.

1. From your Home Screen of icons, use the trackball to find the Search Icon. It may be located within the "Applications" icon as shown below.

You may have to first click on "Applications"

Then, you will see the "Search" icon

Or, you may just have to press the Menu key to see a list of all your icons, if you are in the "Zen" Theme that only shows five icons on your Home Screen.

Search: A full text search of your information.

7
Search

Expanding Your Search to Several Icons:

It is possible that the desired text or name could be in one or several different places on your BlackBerry. The Search tool is quite powerful and flexible. It allows you to narrow down or expand the icons you want to search. If you are sure your information is in the calendar, then just check that box, if not, you can easily check all the boxes using the "Check All" from the menu.

1.   Click on the **Search** Icon and the main search screen is visible.

2.   By default, only the "**Messages**" field is checked

3.   To search all the Icons for your Name or Text, press the **Menu key** and scroll to "**Select All**" and click.

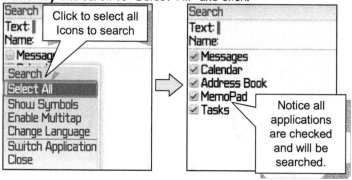

Searching for Names or Text

1. In the "Name" field, you can search for a name or email address. The "Text" field allows you to search for any other text that might be found in the body of an email, inside a calendar event, in an address book entry, in a memo or task.

2. If you decide to search for a name, then you can either type a few letters of a name, like "Sara" or press the Menu key and "**Select Name**"

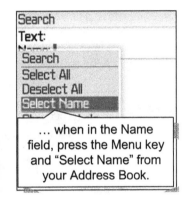

3. If you are looking for a specific text, like a word, phrase or even phone number that is not in an email address field, then you would type it into the "**Text:**" field.

7
Search

4. When you are ready to start the search, click the trackball and select "**Search**"

5. The results of the search are displayed with the number of found entries. The image below shows that there were two total matches found, one in the Messages (Email) and one in the Calendar. Then you click on any application to expand it.

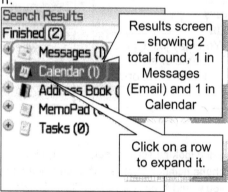

6. After clicking on the Calendar row, you will see all matching calendar entries from the search. You can even click on the listed event and open it up to look at details. You may have typed a few notes from your last meeting with Martin and want to refresh your memory before you step in the door

for your next meeting.

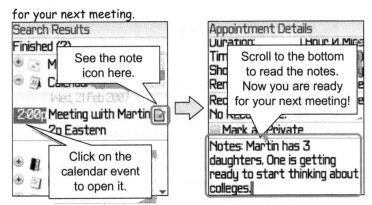

7. In a few seconds, you have located your most recent meeting with martin on Wednesday, February 21st 2007 and have good notes about some things of interest to Martin. Now you can surprise Martin by asking about his three daughters and if the oldest has figured out which college to consider.

TIP: Add Notes to Calendar Events

Remember to add notes to your calendar events and the 'notes' field at the bottom of your contacts. You can do this right on your BlackBerry or on your computer and sync them. Use the Search icon to find key notes later on your BlackBerry right when you need them.

7
Search

Search Tips and Tricks

You can see that the more information you enter on your BlackBerry (or enter on your desktop computer and sync to your BlackBerry), the more useful it becomes. When you combine a great deal of useful information with this Search tool, you truly have a very powerful handheld computer.

As your BlackBerry fills up, the possible places where your information is stored increases. Also, the search might not turn up the exact information you are looking for due to inconsistencies in the way you store the information.

Here are a few Search Tips:

1. Try to be consistent in the way you input someone's name – for example, always use "Martin" instead of "Marty" or "M" or any other variation. This way the Search will always find what you need.

2. Occasionally check your address book for "Doubles" of contact information. It is easy to wind up with two or three entries for one contact if you add an email one time, a phone number another and an address another – try to keep one entry per contact. It is usually easier to do this clean up work on your computer, then sync the changes back to your BlackBerry.

3. If you are not sure whether you are looking for "Mark" or "Martin," just type in "Mar" and then search. This way, you will find both names.

4. Remember, if you want to find an exact name, then roll to the "Name" field, press the Menu key and choose "Select Name" to select a name from your address book.

5. Do your best to put consistent information into calendar events. Example: if you wanted to find when the next

Dentist appointment for Gary was, you could search for "Gary Dentist" in your calendar and find it. But only if you made sure to put the full words "Gary" and "dentist" in your calendar entry. It would be better to just search for "dentist."

6. If you wanted to find a phone number and just remembered the area code, then you would type that area code into the "Text" field and search the Address Book.

7. If you wanted to find when the name "Gary" was in the body of an email, not an email address field (To:, Cc:, From:, Bcc:) then you would enter the name in the "Text" field, not the "Name" field on the Search screen.

7
Search

Section 3: Communicating With Your Pearl

Getting Started with Email

Chapter Contents:
- Composing email
- Adding contacts to email
- Basic email menu commands
- Advanced email menu commands
- Replying to messages
- Using email folders
- How to use email message filters

Getting Started with Email

The BlackBerry Pearl, even though 'small and stylish,' is a BlackBerry to the core – a powerful email tool. This chapter will get your up and running with your email. In minutes, you will be an emailing pro!

Composing Email

The BlackBerry Pearl, like all BlackBerries, gives you the freedom to email on the go. With the cellular network, you are no longer tied to a Wi-Fi hotspot or your desktop or notebook; email is available to you at all times almost anywhere in the world.

Option #1: Emailing from the "Messages" icon

This first option is perhaps easiest for learning how to initially send an email.

1. Move the trackball to your "Messages" icon 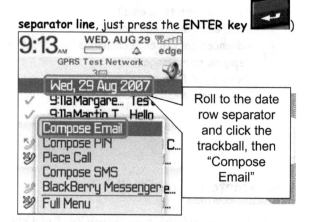 on the Home Screen and click.
2. A fast way to start writing a new email is to click on a date row separator and click the trackball to select "Compose Email" (Shortcut: From the same **Date Row**

   separator line, just press the **ENTER key**)

Roll to the date row separator and click the trackball, then "Compose Email"

You may also press the **Menu key** and scroll down to "**Compose Email**" and click.

Press Menu key and click here

But the fastest way to compose a new email is to use the **shortcut key "L"** on your keyboard.

The fastest way to compose a new email is to simply press the "L" key.

3. Type in the recipient's email address in the "To" field, if your BlackBerry finds a match between what you are typing and any Address Book entries, those are shown in a selectable drop-down list (see below). Then you may just select the correct name by clicking on it.

When you start typing, you will see matching Address Book entries, select one by clicking on it.

TIP

Press the SPACE bar for the "@" and "." in the email address. EXAMPLE: To type susan@bbms.com, you would type "susan" **SPACE** "bbms" **SPACE** "com"

4. Repeat this to add additional "To:" and "Cc:" addressees.
5. If you need to add a Blind Carbon Copy ("Bcc:"), then press the Menu key and select "Add Bcc:"

8
Email
Basics

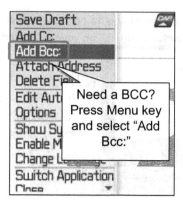

6.   Then type the Subject and Body of your email message, when you are done, just press the trackball and click "send." That's all there is to it.

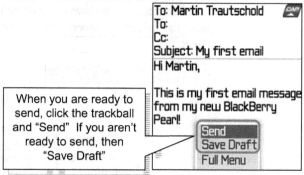

If you have several email addresses integrated with your BlackBerry, you can select which one to send your email from the "**Sent From**" or "**Send Using**" address. To learn exactly how to do this, please see page 228.

Sending Email from your Address Book

After you have entered or synced your names and addresses to your Pearl (See Chapter 4 for help on synchronization.), you may send emails directly from your Address Book.

1.   Navigate to your **Address Book** icon and click the trackball.

2. Begin to type a few letters from your person's first and last name to "**Find**:" them.

3. Once you see the name you want, then press the **Menu key** and select "Email (name)". The only time you will not see the option to "Email" someone is if you do not have an email address stored for that contact.

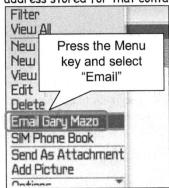

4. Alternatively, if you are already looking at the person's detailed address screen, then you can roll to the "**Email**:" field and **click the trackball** to see the short menu and select "Email"

8
Email
Basics

5. Click on that option with the **trackball** and their name now appears in the "To" field. Complete and send the email as outlined above.

Tip To See a Person's Email Address

When you receive email on your BlackBerry, many times you will see the person's real name: "Margaret Johnson" and not their email address in the "From" field. Sometimes you want to quickly see their true email address, many times it can tell you exactly where they work. The trick to do this is to roll up and highlight their email address and press the "Q" key on your keyboard. Their name will switch to the email address and if you press "Q" again, it switches back.

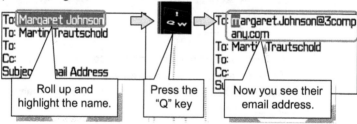

Replying To Messages

Once you get the hang of emailing on the Pearl, you will quickly find yourself checking your email and wanting to respond quickly to your emails. Replying to messages is very easy on the Pearl.

TIP: "!" = Reply

The shortcut hot key to reply to a message is the exclamation point key "!" – pressing this key either when reading a message or just viewing a received message in the message list (inbox) will open up a "Reply" email.

1. Open your email inbox by clicking on the **Messages** icon (which will have a red asterisk or might be flashing to indicate you have received new mail)
2. Scroll to the email you wish to open and click the trackball to open it and read it.
3. Press the Menu key or click the trackball and scroll to "**Reply**" and click.
4. The recipient is now indicated in the "**To**" field.
5. Type in your message, and click the trackball when done. Choose "**Send**" and your email is sent.

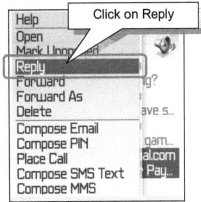

Attaching an Address Book Entry to Email

At times, you might need to send someone an address that is contained in your BlackBerry Address Book.

TIP: "," (comma) = Compose Message

The shortcut hot key to compose a new message is the comma key "," – pressing this key in the message list (inbox) will open up a "Compose Email" screen and allow you to start addressing and typing your new email.

1. Start composing an email by pressing the "," (comma) key or selecting "Compose Email" from the Menu in Messages Icon.
2. Press the **Menu key** and scroll to "**Attach Address.**"
3. Either type in the name of the contact or use the trackball to scroll to the contact desired and click.
4. You will now see a little address book icon in the main field of the email.

Attaching a File to Email

NOTE: Depending on the version of your Pearl software, this "Attach File" menu option may not be available for you.

NOTE: At publishing time, the only files that could be attached to an email message were media files (pictures, songs, videos). However, this may expand to include all file types in future releases of the "system software" that runs your BlackBerry.

The Pearl is a powerful business tool. As such, there are times that you might need to attach a file (much like you would do on your PC) to the email you send from the Pearl.

1. Start composing an email message and press the Menu key.

2. Select "**Attach file**" from the menu.

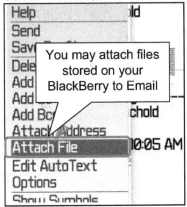

3. Next, you need to locate the directory in which the file is stored. Your two initial options are "**Device Memory**" or "**Media Card**."

4. Use the trackball to navigate to the folder where the file is stored. Once you find the file, simply click on it and it will appear in the body of the email.

8
Email
Basics

Setting the "Importance" of the Email:

Sometimes, you want your email to be noticed and responded to immediately. The Pearl lets you set that importance so that your recipient can better respond.

1. Begin composing a new email message then press the **Menu key**.
2. Select the "**Options**" menu item. (Shortcut tip: Pressing the letter key that matches the first letter of the menu item -- the "O" key a couple of times will jump you down to that item.)
3. In the Options screen, you will see a line that says "Importance" and the default "Normal" at the end of the line. Click on the word "**Normal**" and you see the options "**High**" or "**Low**".

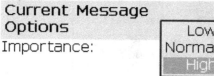

4. Just click on the appropriate option. Press the Menu key and "**Save**" your choice to return to the email message. Then press the trackball and "**Send**" the message.
5. Finally, you will see high importance and low importance messages marked with special icons in your messages list (Inbox).

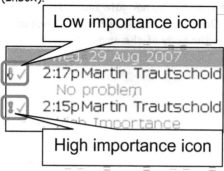

Opening Email Attachments & Supported Formats

One of the things that makes your BlackBerry Pearl more than just "another pretty smartphone" is its serious business capabilities. Often, emails arrive with attachments of important documents; Microsoft Word™ files, Excel™ Spreadsheets or PowerPoint™ Presentations. Fortunately, the Pearl lets you open and view these attachments and other common formats wherever you might be.

Supported Email Attachment Formats:

- Microsoft® Word (DOC)
- Microsoft Excel® (XLS)
- Microsoft PowerPoint® (PPT)
- Corel® WordPerfect® (WPD)
- Adobe® Acrobat® PDF (PDF)
- ASCII text (TXT)
- Rich Text Format files (RTF)
- HTML
- Zip archive (ZIP)
- (Password protected ZIP files are not supprted)
- MP3 – Voice Mail Playback (up to 500Kb file size)
- Image Files of the following types: JPG, BMP, GIF, PNG, TIFF
- (Multi-page TIFF files are not supported)

Features available in attachment viewing:
Images: Pan, Zoom or Rotate.
Save images to view later on your BlackBerry.
Show or hide tracked changes (e.g. in Microsoft Word)
Jump to another part of the file instead of paging through it
Show images as thumbnails at the bottom of the email message.

Source: BlackBerry Technical Solution Center Knowledgebase Article number: KB03265 on www.blackberry.com.

Do you need to **edit** your Microsoft Office™ documents?

Check out the Third Party software in our Software Guide on page 515.

How do you know if you have an email attachment?
You will see an envelope with a paperclip as shown below.

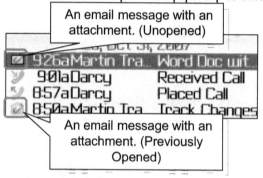

An email message with an attachment. (Unopened)

An email message with an attachment. (Previously Opened)

To Open an attached file:
1. Navigate to your unread messages and scroll to the message with the attachment and click on it.
2. At the very top of the email, in parenthesis, you will see **[1 Attachment.]** or [2 Attachments], depending on number of attachments.
3. Click the trackball and select "**Open Attachment**"

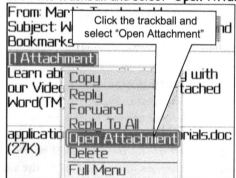

Click the trackball and select "Open Attachment"

4. Some files (e.g. wordprocessing) will offer you the option of opening either a table of contents or the full document.
5. Click on the option you desire and the document will be retrieved into the Pearl.
6. If you get an error message such as "**Document Conversion Failed**" you it is very likely that the attachment is not a

format that is viewable by the BlackBerry Attachment Viewer. Check out the list of supported attachment types on page 217.

To view or hide "Tracked Changes"

1. Open an attachment which has '**Tracked Changes**' turned on. (Usually a Microsoft™ Word™ document. **TIP:** In Word™ 2003, you can turn on 'Track Changes' by going to the 'Tools' menu and selecting 'Track Changes'.)

2. You first see the document in it's "Final" format with all changes hidden. To show the changes, click the trackball and select "**Show Changes**."

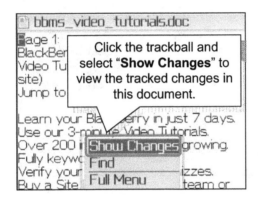

3. Now you will see all changes highlighted with underlines and strike-through text. When you highlight a specific change, you can see the person's name who made the change at the top of the screen as shown.

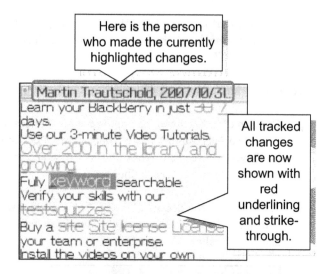

4. To turn off viewing changes and see the 'Final' document again, click the trackball and select "**Hide Changes**."

To 'Find' text in an Email Attachment (Shortcut "F")

1. Open up the attachment as described above.

2. Press the **trackball** select "**Find**" or use the shortcut key "**F**"

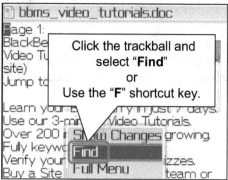

3. Enter your search text (letters or numbers), then select whether or not you want the search to be '**Case Sensitive**' (match your search text exactly - upper / lower case), you

need to check the checkbox using your **SPACE key** or clicking the **trackball** on it.

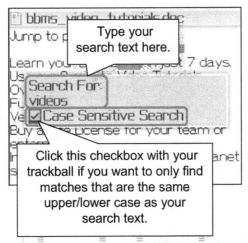

4. **TIP:** To quickly 'Find' the same text again later in the document, press the "F" key again. To search for different text, click the trackball and select "Find."

To change the way the attachment looks on the BlackBerry
1. Open up the attachment as described above.
2. Press the **Menu key** and select **"Options."**
3. Choose a new Font from the Font Family to change the display font of the document.

To open a Presentation file or Spreadsheet
1. Follow the same steps you did earlier when you opened the wordprocessing document.
2. Click on **"Open Attachment"** and select Table of Contents
    *   In a Spreadsheet, you will see the available worksheets.

8
Email
Basics

- In a Presentation file you will see the available slides.

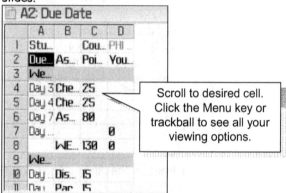

Scroll to desired cell. Click the Menu key or trackball to see all your viewing options.

3. Click on the individual slide or sheet or the "full document" option to open the file.

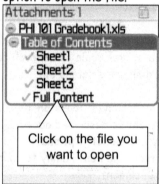

Click on the file you want to open

4. When done reading, press the **Menu key** and click on "**Close**".
5. Press the **ESCAPE key** twice to return to the message screen.

To Open a Picture

1. Click on the [1 **Attachment**] or [2 **Attachments**], etc. at the top of email message. Click on the image file names to open them.
2. Once you have opened the pictures, then the next time you view that email, you will see the thumbnails of all the pictures attached to that email at the bottom of the message. You can then just roll down to them and click on them to open them.

3. To save the picture, press the Menu key or click the trackball and click on "**Save Image**." The picture will be saved where you specify, either on your 'Media Card' or the main 'Device Memory'.

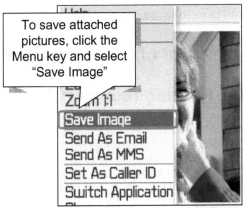

To save attached pictures, click the Menu key and select "Save Image"

4. Other menu options include "**Zoom**" **(to expand the image)** or "**Rotate,**" (which will rotate the image) or "**Send as Email**" (Email as an attachment) or "**Send as MMS**" (Multi-Media Message = imbed image as part of email message).

5. To save it as a "Caller ID" picture in contacts, select "**Set as Caller ID**" from the Menu and then begin to type in the contact name.

   • Navigate to the correct contact and save as prompted.

Email Attachment Tips and Tricks

Like all features of the Pearl, there are some shortcuts and tricks that might prove helpful when working with attachments:

1. To search for specific text inside an attachment, press "Q."
2. To switch between the table of contents and the full content of the attached file, press "O".
3. If you want to change the size of a column in a spreadsheet, press "Z."
4. If you want to move to a specific cell inside a spreadsheet, press "A" and then scroll to that cell.

8
Email
Basics

5. If you wish to view the content of a cell in a spreadsheet, press the "Space" key or simply click on the trackball.
6. To view a slide show presentation, press "**A**."
7. If you want to stop the slide show presentation, hold the **ESCAPE** key.
8. To switch views in the presentation, press "**Z**."

Filtering Your Messages for SMS, Calls and More

TIP: Filtering Your Messages Inbox

The shortcut to filter your Messages Inbox are:
"**ALT + S**" = Show only SMS Messages
"**ALT + I**" = Show only Incoming messages and phone calls.
"**ALT + P**" = Show only Phone Calls
"**ALT + V**" = Show only Voicemail Messages

Just like on your computer, using email folders can help you be more organized and productive. Also, if you have saved many messages and are not sure which are email inbox messages and which are SMS inbox messages, using the folder commands can help.

1. Go to your "**Messages**" icon and click. The press the Menu key.

2. Scroll down to "**View Folder**" and click. You will now see a listing of all the message folders on your device.

3. Choose, let's say "**SMS inbox**" and you will now see only the SMS messages in your inbox and none of the other

messages.

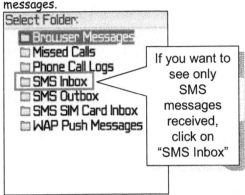

4. You can also use these folders to see your missed calls, MMS messages, WAP Push messages and your Browser Messages.

Filing a Message

Make sure that in the screen (in the Email Reconciliation lesson above,) that Wireless Synchronization was, in fact, turned on. This is necessary in order to file messages.

1. Click on the **Messages** icon from your Home Screen.
2. Highlight the message you wish to file
3. Press the **Menu key** select "**File**"
4. Then choose the folder in you wish to use to store the message.

Changing Folder Names or Adding Folders

In order to do this, you must be using your BlackBerry together with a BlackBerry Enterprise Server with wireless synchronization. If you are unsure whether you are using Wireless Sync, most likely you are not using it.

1. On your desktop (or notebook) computer that you use to Sync your BlackBerry, simply change or add a folder to the email client you use to sync the BlackBerry.
   - Changes you make on the desktop or notebook will be reflected in the folders available on the BlackBerry.

8
Email
Basics

Creating and Using Email Message Filters (Only for BlackBerry devices connected to a BlackBerry Enterprise Server.)

While receiving your email on your BlackBerry is a wonderful thing, there might be some email messages that, for whatever reason, you don't want sent to your BlackBerry. Fortunately, you can use an Email Filter to tell your BlackBerry just which messages you want sent to the Pearl and which ones stay on the server.

1. Click on your **Messages** icon.
2. Press the **Menu key.**
3. Scroll down to "**Options**" and click.
4. Click on "**Email Filters**" and then press the Menu key and click on "**New.**"

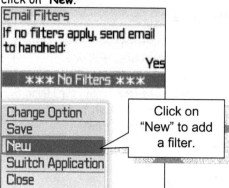

Click on "New" to add a filter.

5. You can now type a name for the new filter and set the options.
6. Press the **Menu key** and choose "**Save.**"

To Use the Email Filter:
1. Click on your **Messages** icon.
2. Press the **Menu key** and select "**Email Filters**"
3. Just use the trackball and click the radio button next to the filter you wish you use.

Advanced Email Topics

Chapter Contents:

Introduction

Given the Email power of the Pearl, there might be some things that you would want to do right from your handheld that were usually done from your desktop. You can write emails in other languages, select any one of your integrated email accounts to "send from," and easily create and select various email signatures and auto-signatures.

Writing Email in Other Languages

Let's say you have a client in Latin America and you wish to compose your email in Spanish. Because of the SureType™ and special characters and accents, you will want to change your language selection to the one in which you are composing the email.

1. Compose a new email message and then press the **Menu key**.
2. Scroll to "**Change Language**" and a list of the available languages are made available to you.

To:
Cc:
Subject:

English (United States)
Deutsch
English (United Kingdom)
Español
Français
Italiano

Click on a new
language

3. Scroll down to "**Español**" and click.
4. When you begin typing, you will now have the Spanish language dictionary loaded and you can type your email in the new language. You will see the "**ES**" (**Español**) next to the SureType™ selection list while typing instead of the "EN" for English

Messages "Inbox" Housecleaning ("Delete Prior")

It is possible for your Messages mailbox to get a little unwieldy, just follow these suggestions to manage and clean your mailbox.

To clean out old messages:

1. Start your Messages Icon and press the Menu key.
2. Highlight the date row separator (e.g. "Mon, Sep 4, 2007") under the most recent message you desire to keep, press the Menu key and select "**Delete Prior**."
   • All "older" messages will then be deleted
3. To delete an individual message, just click on the message, press the Menu key and choose "Delete."

   IMPORTANT: If you have turned on Call Logs in your Messages Inbox, then "Delete Prior" will ALSO delete all your Call Logs.

Sending From a Different Email Account ("Send Using")

Like many of us, you might have a separate email account for business and for personal matters, or several just for work. You can easily change which email account you use to send the email on your BlackBerry.

1. Get to the main email screen and scroll to the top where it says "**Send Using.**"

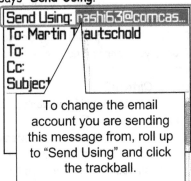

To change the email account you are sending this message from, roll up to "Send Using" and click the trackball.

2. The "**Default**" is chosen, but you can highlight the word "**Default**" and click and all your available email accounts will show up in the window.

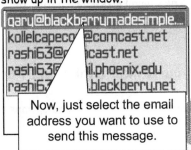

Now, just select the email address you want to use to send this message.

9
Email
Advanced

3. Just click the email account you wish to use to send this particular email.

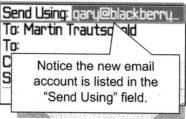

Send Using: gary@blackberry...
To: Martin Trautsc old
To:

Notice the new email account is listed in the "Send Using" field.

Setting your Default "Sent From" Email Address

You can change your default "**Sent From**" email address on your BlackBerry. To get this done, you need to:

1. Go into your **Options** icon. "Options" may be located within the **Settings** icon if you cannot find it from your Home Screen of icons.
2. Click on "**Advanced Options**"
3. Click on "**Message Services**" (or if you don't see this item, then click on "**Default Services**")
4. Then you will see a screen that shows you "**Messaging (CMIME) Web Client**" or something similar. Click on the item to see a list of all your integrated email accounts.
5. Select your new default email account for sending new messages you compose on your BlackBerry.
6. Press the Menu key and select "**Save**"
7. Now compose a new email message – notice that your new default email account is used at the top in the "Send Using" field.

Changing the Way your Email Looks and Functions

You can change many of the more advanced options for email by doing the following:

1. Navigate to your "**Messages**" icon and click.
2. Press the **Menu key** and scroll down to "Options" and click.

3. Click on "**General Options.**"

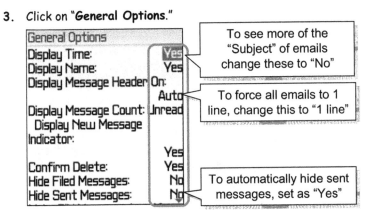

General Options

Display Time: Yes
Display Name: Yes
Display Message Header On: Auto
Display Message Count: Unread
Display New Message Indicator: Yes
Confirm Delete: Yes
Hide Filed Messages: No
Hide Sent Messages: No

To see more of the "Subject" of emails change these to "No"

To force all emails to 1 line, change this to "1 line"

To automatically hide sent messages, set as "Yes"

- You can choose whether to display the time, name, message header, new message indicator, confirm the deletion of messages, hide file and sent messages and change the level of PIN Messages. (Learn more about PIN Messages on page 285.)

4. Click on the desired change. When done, press the Menu key to "**Save**" your changes and they will now be reflected in your email screen.

Email Reconciliation

Depending on the type of email accounts you have set up and your messaging services, there are options that may be available to the advanced user.

1. Open your **Messages** icon, press the **Menu key**, select "**Options**". Then select "**Email Reconciliation.**"
   - If one of your integrated email accounts is an IMAP4 account, that email address will be listed next to "**Messaging Services.**"

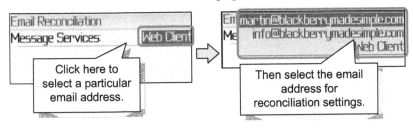

Email Reconciliation

Message Services: Web Client

Click here to select a particular email address.

Email

martin@blackberrymadesimple.com
info@blackberrymadesimple.com
Web Client

Then select the email address for reconciliation settings.

9
Email
Advanced

- You can click on that email address and your other available email addresses that have been integrated to your BlackBerry will be shown.
- Select the account you want to work with.

2. You have the options to change the way deletion of messages is handled.
   - Click on the word "Prompt" which is the default setting, and choose either "Handheld" or "Mailbox and Handheld." NOTE: "Mailbox" means your email inbox on your email server and "Handheld" means your BlackBerry handheld.

When you delete a message on your BlackBerry:
"Handheld" = Delete on BlackBerry only
"Mailbox & Handheld" = Delete message on BlackBerry and your main Mailbox
"Prompt" = Ask you every time.

   - **IMPORTANT:** If you choose "**Mailbox and Handheld**" then (unless you download all your email to your computer very regularly from the server) the next time you look at your email on the server or on your computer – that message you deleted on your BlackBerry will also be deleted from your regular email inbox. Choosing this option will delete your message from your mailbox on the email server itself.

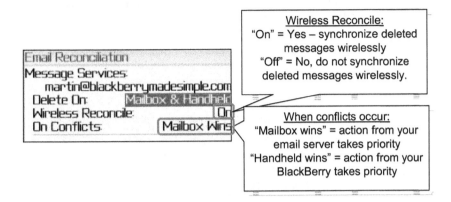

3. You can also turn on or off Wireless Reconciliation by clicking **"On"** or **"Off"** after the words **"Wireless Reconcile."**

4. Lastly, you can choose whether your server or your handheld wins if there is a reconciliation conflict. The default setting is **"Mailbox Wins"** which means that your main email box changes win over changes from your BlackBerry.

Easily Adding Signatures to Your Emails

There are various ways to setup email signatures. You may setup what are called "Auto Signatures" which are attached automatically to every email message you send, or use something called "AutoText" to select a specific signature whenever you need it.

Option #1: Setting up Signatures from your BlackBerry Carrier's Web site

This option is described in detail in Chapter 3 starting on page 85. Using this feature, you have the ability to add a unique "Auto Signature" to each of your integrated email accounts.

Option #2: Setting up Email Signatures for those Using BlackBerry Internet Service Email

If you use BlackBerry Internet Email (POP3 and IMAP 4 Accounts) we will need to set up your signatures a little differently.

1. Since there is no "**Auto Signature**" option when using BlackBerry Internet email, we will need to set up the signature using the **AutoText** feature.
2. Locate and click on the **Options** icon. It may be inside the **Applications** or **Settings** icons on your BlackBerry. It

    usually looks like a wrench 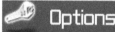 or gears

    .
3. Select "**AutoText**" near the top of the

Options
About
Advanced Options
Auto On/Off
AutoText

    list.
4. Press the Menu key and select "**New.**"
5. In the "Replace" field type any combination of letters – we would recommend putting your initials. If you plan to have several different signatures, possibly one for work and one for personal use, then you might want to use a number or extra letter after your initials like "(initials)w" (for work) and "(initials)p" for personal.
6. In the "**With**" field, type in your full email signature exactly as you would like it to appear in your emails.
7. Choose "SmartCase" if you want the BlackBerry to capitalize the letters according to the correct context in the sentence when they are replaced. Select "Specify Case" to replace these letters with the capitalization exactly as you have entered them in the AutoText entry. For example, if you entered "DeSoto" with "Specified Case"

then it would always replace the words as "DeSoto" never "Desoto".

8. Then, in language, select "**All Locales**" for this AutoText entry (signature) to work in every language or specify only one language for this to work. This setting would be useful if you had different signatures for different languages.

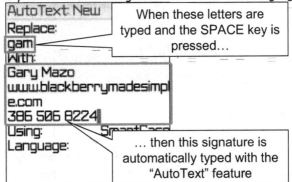

9. Press the Menu when you are done and select "Save."
10. Now, each time you type in your initials and press the space key, your complete signature will appear "Automatically."
11. To setup an Auto Signature from the Carrier Web Site – see page 85.

Option #3: Setting up Email Signatures for BlackBerry devices connected to a BlackBerry Enterprise Server

1. If your BlackBerry is using the BlackBerry Enterprise Software, navigate to the messages list and press the Menu key.
2. Click on "**Options**" and scroll to "**Email Settings**"

3. One of the options in the Email Setting screen is the "**Use Auto Signature**" field – just set the default to "**Yes.**"

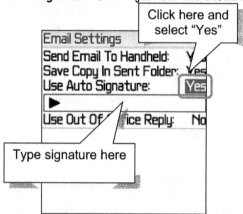

4. You will then be prompted to add in your signature.
5. Press the Menu key and save the changes.

Your Phone and Voice Dialing

Chapter Contents:

Your Pearl Phone and Voice Dialing

We have already covered many of the exciting and powerful features of your BlackBerry Pearl in this book. First, and foremost, however, your Pearl is your phone – your lifeline for communication. It is a very good and full-featured phone and includes the latest voice dialing capabilities.

What's My Phone Number?

You have your phone, and you want to give your number to all your friends – you just need to know where you can get your hands on that important information. There are a couple of ways of doing this:

Press the Green Phone Key and read "My Number"

1. Press the **Green Phone key**.

2. Above your call log is should say
   "My Number: nnn-nnn-nnnn"

Press the Green
Phone key to see this
screen. Your Number
is shown here.

Changing Your Ringtone

To select any song on your BlackBerry as a new ringtone, please check out the steps in our Media section on page 367.

Calling Voice Mail

The easiest way to call voice mail is to press and hold the number "1" key. This is the default key for voicemail.

If it is not working correctly, then please call your phone company technical support for help in correcting it.

To setup voice mail, just call it and follow the prompts to enter your name, greeting, password and other information.

Placing a Call

The BlackBerry Pearl truly excels as a phone – making phone calls is easy and there are many ways to place a call.

Making a Call – Not from Contact

1. Just start dialing numbers from your Home Screen.
2. As soon as you type your first number or letter key, the Pearl automatically knows you are trying to make a call and the Call screen is displayed.

   First, the Pearl will try to match the letters you are typing to Address Book entries. If it cannot find any, then it will just show you the digits you have typed as shown below.

Dial the phone number and press Green Phone Key to start the Call

3. You will notice that a small image of the **Green Phone key** is immediately after the cursor. Once all the numbers are punched in, just press the **Green Phone key** and the call will be placed.

Answering a Call

Answering a call couldn't be easier. When you call comes in, the number will be displayed on the screen. If you have that particular number already in your **Address Book** the name and/or picture will also be on the screen (if you have entered that information into that particular contact.)

When a call comes in:

1. Push either the **Green Phone key** or click the **trackball** to answer the call.

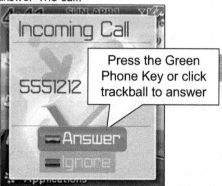

Press the Green Phone Key or click trackball to answer

2. If you are using a Bluetooth Headset, you can usually click a button on the headset to answer the call, see Chapter 14 on page 299.

Why do I see Names and Numbers in my Call Logs?

You will see both phone numbers and names in your phone call logs. When you see a name instead of a phone number, you know that the person is already entered in your BlackBerry Address Book.

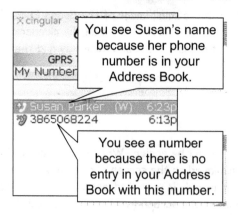

You see Susan's name because her phone number is in your Address Book.

You see a number because there is no entry in your Address Book with this number.

It is easy to add entries to your Address Book right from this phone call log screen. Below we show you how.

Add New Addresses from Your Phone Call Logs

If you see just a phone number in your call log screen, then there is a good chance you will want to add that phone number as a new Address Book entry.

Note: Call log entries are generated whenever you receive, miss, ignore or place a call from your BlackBerry.

1. Get into the call log screen by tapping the Green Phone key once. (**TIP**: If you press and hold the Green Phone key, the BlackBerry will think you want to "Dial from Address Book" and show you your address book instead.)
2. Highlight the phone number you want to add to your Address Book.

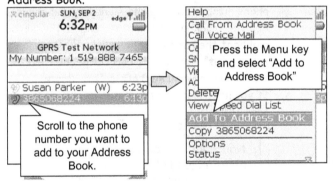

3. Notice that the phone number is automatically placed in the "Work" phone field.

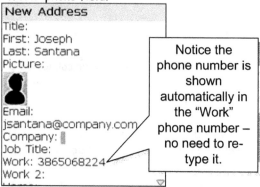

4. Enter the address book entry information for this person, press the Menu key and select "Save."

5. **TIP:** If this phone number is not the person's "WORK" phone, then you can select, cut and paste it into the correct phone number. To select, roll to the beginning or end of the phone number and tap the Menu key and choose "**Select**". Roll the trackball to the other end of the number to highlight the number. Then click the Menu key again and select "**Cut**". Roll to the correct phone field, click the trackball (or Menu key) and select "**Paste**"

6. If you need more tips on entering new addresses, please see page 146.

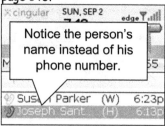

Ignoring and Muting Phone Calls

Sometimes, you can't take a call and you need to make a decision to ignore or perhaps mute the ringing of an incoming call. Both of these options can be achieved quite easily with your Pearl.

Ignoring a Call to Immediately Stop the Ringing.

1. When the phone call comes in, instead of answering by pushing the Green Phone Key, simply press the Red Phone Key to ignore.

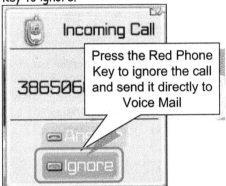

Press the Red Phone Key to ignore the call and send it directly to Voice Mail

TIP: Need to silence the ringer but still want to answer the call?

Just **rolling the trackball up/down** will give you a few more seconds in which to answer the call before the caller is sent to voice mail.

2. Ignoring a call will immediately send the caller to your voice mail.

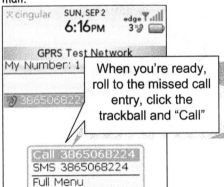

When you're ready, roll to the missed call entry, click the trackball and "Call"

3. The "Missed Call" will be displayed on your Home Screen. Click on the "Missed Call" with the trackball and a small

menu pops up allowing you to do various things depending on whether or not this phone number is already in your Address Book. If you see only a phone number, not a name, then this number is not in your address book and you may only "Call or SMS" this number.

If you do see a name you will be able to:

a. Call them and any number for this person (that is entered into your address book)

b. Send them an email (if this person has an email address entered)

c. Send them an SMS text message

d. Send them an MMS Message (Multi-Media Message with pictures or other media like songs)

e. View the contact information

Muting a Call

If you would prefer not send the call immediately to voicemail and simply let it ring a few times on the caller's end, but you don't want to hear the ring (perhaps you are in a movie theatre or a meeting) just:

1. When the call comes in, press the "Mute" key on the top of the phone. All this will do is silence the ring.

2. You may still pick up the call or let the caller go to voicemail.

Click the Mute button at the top here to Mute the Ringing phone call

Using the Call Log

The Call Log is an especially useful tool if you make and receive many calls during the day. Often, it is hard to remember if you added that individual to your **Address Book** or not - but you definitely remember that they called yesterday. Here is a perfect situation to use your Call Log to access the call, add the number into your Address Book and place a return call.

Checking your Call Log

1. The easiest way to view your call logs are to just tap the

   Green Phone key .

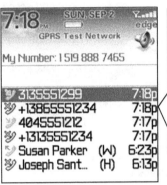

Click here to see Call Logs

My Number: 1 519 888 7465

313555 1299   7:18p
+13865551234   7:18p
4045551212   7:17p
+13135551234   7:17p
Susan Parker   (W) 6:23p
Joseph Sant... (H) 6:13p

Here are your Call Logs sorted by most recent first. Just click on any entry to call it.

You can also see call logs by rolling to and clicking on your **Phone** or **Call Log** icon. If you don't see this icon on your Home Screen, then press the **Menu key** to list all the applications.

2. The default setting is to show the most recent calls made and then move sequentially backwards showing calls made and received listed by date and time.

Placing a Call from the Call Log

1. Go to the Call Log as you did above and scroll through the list.
2. Find the number or name you wish to call and click the trackball. If you clicked on a name instead of number in the

call logs, and that person has more than one phone number, you will then be asked to select which number you wish to call.

3. Choose the option from the menu – Call, Email, PIN, SMS or MMS (depending on what numbers or email addresses you have for that individual in your Address Book.)

4. Click on "**Call**" to place the call.

To show your Call Logs in the Messages icon (Inbox)

It might be useful to show calls made, received and missed in your message list for easy accessibility.

1. Press the **Green Phone key** to see your call logs.
2. Press the **Menu key** and scroll down to "**Options**" and click.
3. Scroll to "**Call Logging**" and click.
4. Under "**Show These Call Log Types in Message List**" select either:
   a. **Missed Calls** (see only missed calls)
   b. **All Calls** (see all placed, missed, received)
   c. **None** (this is the default, don't see any calls)
5. Press Menu and select "**Save.**"

To Add a Note to a Call Log
1. Press the **Green Phone key**.
2. Press the **Menu key** and scroll to "**View History**" and click.
3. Press the Menu key again and click "**Add Notes.**"

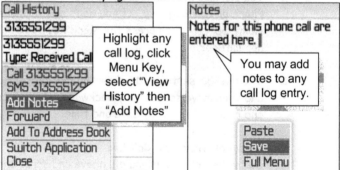

4. When you are done typing your notes, click the trackball and select save.

5. TIP: You can even "**Add Notes**" when you are still talking on the phone. You may want to use the Speakerphone or your headset so you can hear while typing.

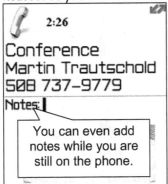

To Forward a Call Log
1. Go to your Call Log and highlight the log entry you wish to forward.
2. Press the **Menu Key** and click "**View History**" just as you did above.
3. Press the **Menu key** again and select "**Forward.**"
4. Input the Forwarding information.

To Delete or Edit your Call Log Notes
1. Follow steps 1-3 under "Add a Note to Call Log."
2. Press the Menu key and select "**Edit Notes**.
3. Enter your changes to the note or press the Menu key and select "Clear Field" to delete the note.
4. Click the trackball and select "**Save.**"

Adjusting the Volume on Calls

There may be times when you are having trouble hearing a caller. The connection may be bad (because of their old fashioned phone) or you may be using a headset. Adjusting the volume is easy. While on the phone call, simply use the two volume keys on the right hand side of the Pearl to adjust the volume up or down.

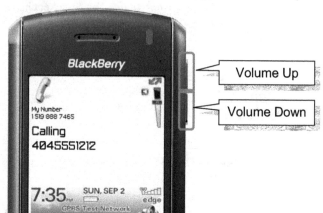

Setting up Speed Dialing

Speed dialing is a great way to call your frequent contacts quickly. Just assign them a one digit number key (or character key) that you hold, and their number is automatically dialed. There are a couple of ways to set up Speed Dialing on the Pearl.

Option #1: Setting up Speed Dial from the Call Log
1. Press the **Green Phone key** to see your call logs.
2. Highlight the call log entry (either phone number or name) you want to add to speed dial and press the **Menu key**.

3. Select "**Add Speed Dial**" and click. Confirm that you do want to add this call to Speed dial.

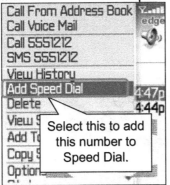

4. You may be asked to confirm you want to add this speed dial number with a pop-up window looking something like this:

5. In the Speed Dial menu use the trackball and move the phone number into a vacant slot.

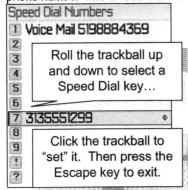

6. Once the correct speed dial key is chosen, just click the **trackball**. The number or symbol you selected is now set as the speed dial key for that phone number. In the image above, when you press and hold the "7" key you will start to dial the assigned phone number (313-555-1299).

7. TIP: You may want to reserve the number "5", which is also the "H" key to be your "Home" number.

Option #2: Press and hold a key from your Home Screen

1. If you press and hold any number key or the symbols "!", "?", "." Or "," from your Home Screen that have not already been assigned to a speed dial number, then you will be asked if you want to assign this key to a speed dial

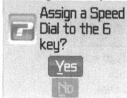

   number.

2. Select "Yes" to assign it. Then you will be shown your Address Book to select an entry or select "[Use Once]" to type in a new phone number that is not in your Address Book.

3. Once you select an entry or [**Use Once**] and type a phone number, you will see the same "**Speed Dial Numbers**" list. Press the **ESCAPE key** to back out.

4. Give your speed dial a try by pressing and holding the same key you just assigned.

Option #3: Setting a Contact Phone Number as Speed Dial

1. Press the Green Phone Key and start entering a contact name or number.

2. When you see the contact listed, scroll to it and highlight it.

3. Press the Menu key and follow steps 3-5 from above.

Using Voice Dialing

One of the powerful features of the Pearl is the Voice Command program for voice dialing and simple voice commands. Voice dialing provides a safe way to place calls without having to look at the Pearl and navigate through menus. Voice Command does not need to be "trained" like on other SmartPhones – just speak naturally.

Using Voice Dialing to call a Contact:

1. The left-hand convenience key is (usually) set for Voice Command simply press this key. It may be set as "Push-to-Talk" Walkie-talkie feature, depending on your particular BlackBerry phone company.

   TIP: We show you how to set or change your convenience keys on page 48.

Usually, this convenience key will start voice dialing. You may change it in "Options" > "Screen / Keyboard"

2. The first time you use this feature, the Pearl will take a few seconds to scan your Address Book.
3. When you hear "**Say a Command**" just speak the name of the contact you wish to call using the syntax "**Call Martin Trautschold**"
4. You will then be prompted with "Which number." Again, speak clearly and say "Home," "Work" or "Mobile"

5. Say "Yes" to confirm the selection and the Pearl will begin to dial the number.

Using Voice Dialing to Call a Number:

1. Press the Left Hand Convenience Key as you did above. (Assuming your convenience key is set to voice dialing, if it's not, you can change it by reading page 48)

2. When you hear "Say a command" say "Call" and the phone number itself. Example: "Call 386-506-8224"

3. Depending on your settings, you may be asked to confirm the number you just spoke or it will just start dialing.

Advanced Phone Topics

Chapter Contents:

Advanced Phone Topics

For many of us, the basic phone topics covered in the previous chapter will cover most of our phone needs with the BlackBerry Pearl. For others of us, however, we need to eek out every possible phone feature. This chapter will help you do just that.

More with Voice Command

Last chapter concluded with an Overview of Voice Command. Voice Command is a powerful tool for enabling not only basic phone calls, but other functions of the Pearl without having to push buttons or input text.

Other Commands

You can use the Voice Command Software to perform other functions on the Pearl. These are especially useful if you are in a position where you can't look at the screen (while driving) or in an area where coverage seems to fade in and out.

The most common are:

1. "**Call Extension**" will call a specific extension.
2. "**Call Martin Home**" will call the contact at their home number.
3. "**Check Battery**" will check the battery status.
4. "**Check Signal**" will let you know the strength of your wireless signal and whether or not you have "No Signal", "Low Signal", "High Signal" or "Very High Signal"
5. "**Turn Off Voice Prompts**" will turn off the "Say a command" voice and replace it with a simple beep.
6. "**Turn On Voice Prompts**" turns the friendly voice back on.

Changing Your Voice Dialing Options

You can control various features of Voice Dialing by going into your **Options** icon and selecting "**Voice Dialing**"

Options		Voice Dialing	
Custom Wordlist	▲	Choice Lists:	Automatic
Date/Time		Sensitivity:	Normal
Localisation		Audio Prompts:	Enabled
Network		Digit Playback:	Enabled
Owner		Name Playback:	Enabled
Screen/Keyboard		Name Playback Speed:	Normal
Security Options		Name Playback Volume:	Normal
SMS			
Status			
Theme			
Voice Dialing			

Click any of these settings to customize your Voice Dialing.

1. Change the "**Choice Lists**" – if you do not want to be confronted with lots of choices after you say a command. Your options here are "**Automatic**" (default), "**Always On**" or "**Always Off**".

2. **"Sensitivity"** – you can adjust the acceptance/rejection ratio of voice commands by adjusting the field that initially reads **"Normal."** You can go up to "**3 (Reject More)**" or down to "**-3 (Reject Less)**"

3. "Audio Prompts" – can be enabled or disabled from this screen or by saying "Turn Prompts On/Off."

4. **"Digit playback"** which repeats the numbers you say and **"Name playback"** which repeats the name you say, can also be enabled or disabled.

5. Finally, you can adjust the "**Playback Speed**" and "**Playback Volume**" of the Voice Dialing program.

Voice Command Tips and Tricks

There are a few ways to speed up the voice command process. You can also customize the way that Voice Dialing works on the Pearl.

To make Voice Dialing calls quicker

1. When using Voice Command, give more information when you place the call. For example, if you say "**Call Martin Trautschold, Home,**" the Voice Dialing program will only ask you to confirm that you are calling him at home.

2. The call will then be placed.

Give your Contacts Nick Names

1. Make a "Short Cut" entry for a contact – especially one with a long name.

   a. In addition to my "**Gary Mazo**" contact, I might also make a contact with the same information, but put "**GM**" as the name.

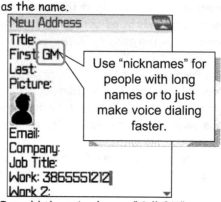

Use "nicknames" for people with long names or to just make voice dialing faster.

b. I would then simply say: "Call GM"

Call Waiting - Calling a 2nd Person

Like most phones these days, the BlackBerry supports call waiting, call forwarding and conference calling - all useful options in the business world and in your busy life.

Enabling Call Waiting: (This may already be "on")
1. Press the **Green Phone key** to get into the Phone screen.
2. Press the **Menu key** and scroll to "options" and click the trackball.
3. Scroll to "Call Waiting" and make sure the "Call Waiting Enabled" field is set to "Yes."

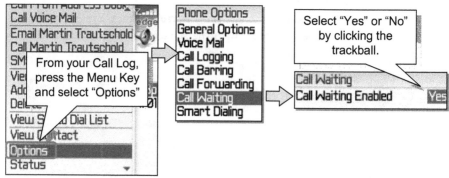

From your Call Log, press the Menu Key and select "Options"

Select "Yes" or "No" by clicking the trackball.

4. Press the **Menu key** and select "**Save**."

5. To turn off Call Waiting just repeat steps 1-3 and set the field to "No."

Using Call Waiting:

1. Make a phone call as usual.
2. Press the **Green Phone key** while on a call to dial a second phone number or call someone else from your BlackBerry Address Book. This will put the previous caller on "Hold"

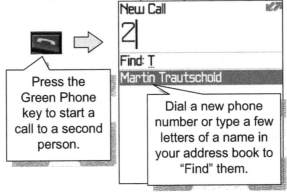

Press the Green Phone key to start a call to a second person.

Dial a new phone number or type a few letters of a name in your address book to "Find" them.

3. TIP: If a second person calls you while you are speaking to a first caller, just press the Green Phone key to answer the second caller - the first caller will still be waiting for you "On Hold".
4. Press the **Green Phone key** to toggle between calls.

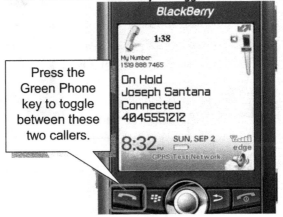

Press the Green Phone key to toggle between these two callers.

Working with a Second Caller

When you are speaking to a person on the phone and your phone rings again with a second caller you can do a number of things, it just takes a little practice to get "smooth" doing it.

Option 1: Answer and put the 1ˢᵗ caller on hold
This is probably the easiest option - just press the Green Phone key. (This is **"Answer - Hold Current"**)

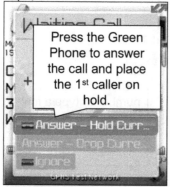

Then to swap between the callers, just press the Green Phone key again.

With two callers on the phone, pressing the Menu key allows you to do a number of other things including conference calling:

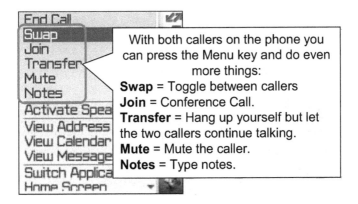

With both callers on the phone you can press the Menu key and do even more things:

Swap = Toggle between callers
Join = Conference Call.
Transfer = Hang up yourself but let the two callers continue talking.
Mute = Mute the caller.
Notes = Type notes.

Option 2: Hang up with the 1st Caller and Answer the 2nd Caller

Roll the trackball down and select the middle option to hang up on the first caller while answering the second. You would select "**Answer-Drop Current**"

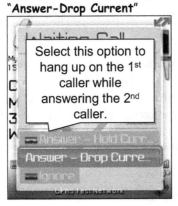

Select this option to hang up on the 1st caller while answering the 2nd caller.

Option 3: Send the 2nd Caller to Voicemail (Ignore them)

Pressing the Red Phone key or just simply doing nothing will send the 2nd caller to voicemail. You are selecting "**Ignore**."

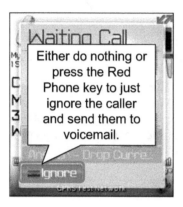

Call Forwarding

Call Forwarding is a useful feature when you are traveling or plan on leaving your BlackBerry at home. With Call Forwarding, you can send your BlackBerry calls to any other phone number you choose.

WARNING: Make sure you know how much your wireless carrier will charge you per Call Forwarding connection, some can be surprisingly expensive. Also, make sure that your SIM card has been set up by your service provider for this feature.

NOTE: Not all BlackBerry phone companies (service provider) offer this feature.

To Forward Calls Received by Your BlackBerry:
1. Press the **Green Phone key** and then press the **Menu key**.
2. Scroll to "**Options**" and click and then scroll to "**Call Forwarding**" and click.

3. You have two options: "**Forward All Calls**" or "**Forward Unanswered Calls.**"

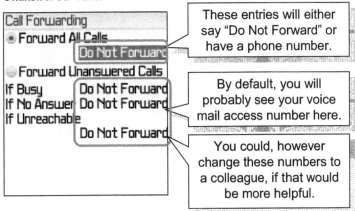

These entries will either say "Do Not Forward" or have a phone number.

By default, you will probably see your voice mail access number here.

You could, however change these numbers to a colleague, if that would be more helpful.

4. If you clicked "**Forward All Calls**," change the field to the Number you wish forwarded calls to be sent by pressing the Menu key and clicking **New Number**. This will forward every call received to the number you specify.

5. In the "**Forward Unanswered Calls**" fields click and edit the numbers (Just like you did above) for Call Forwarding in the "**If Busy**," "**If no Answer**" and "**If Unreachable**" fields.
   a. NOTE: the default set up is to send these calls to your voicemail – that is the phone number that is most likely already in these fields.

6. To Delete a Call Forwarding number, repeat steps 1-4 and click "Delete" after you have clicked "Edit Numbers."

7. Press the **Menu Key** and select "save."

Conference Calling

Conference Calling is a very useful option so that you can talk with more than one person at a time.

Take the recent scenario of one of the author's, where conferencing together two parties was faster (and safer) way to transfer needed information.
-   The author was leasing a new car

- The car dealer left a voicemail to call the insurance company to "Approve" the proof of insurance being faxed to the dealer
- The author called the insurance company, expecting they already had received the dealer's fax number.
- Unfortunately, the insurance company did not have the fax number.
- Instead of hanging up and calling the dealer, asking for the fax number and calling the insurance company back, the author used the **BlackBerry conference call feature**.
- Once the conference call between the dealer and insurance company completed, the dealer's fax number was immediately relayed along with any special instructions.

To Set Up a Conference Call
1. Place a call as you normally would.
2. While on the call, press the **Green Phone key** (or if this does not show you a "**New Call**" screen, then press the Menu key and select "**New Call**") and either choose a contact from your Address Book or type in a phone number and place the

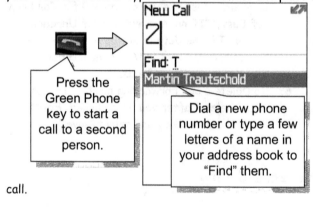

Press the Green Phone key to start a call to a second person.

New Call

2|

Find: T

Martin Trautschold

Dial a new phone number or type a few letters of a name in your address book to "Find" them.

call.

3. While on the second call, press the Menu Key and scroll to "**Join**" and click.

Once you have both parties on the phone, press the Menu key and select "Join"

4. If you add more than two callers to the conference call, just repeat the process starting with another "**New Call**" (press the **Green Phone key**).

5. "**Join**" the calls as you did above. Repeat as needed.

To speak with only one of the callers on a Conference Call
Press the **Menu key** while on the Conference Call.

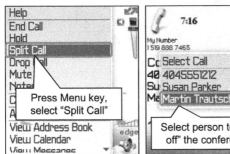 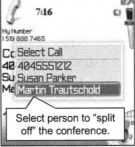 

Press Menu key, select "Split Call"

Select person to "split" off" the conference.

Now you may talk privately to this person.

Scroll to "**Split**" and click – the calls are now "**Separate**" and you can speak privately with just one of the callers.

To End or Leave a Conference Call

To hang up on everyone and end the conference call for all, press the Red Phone key or press the Menu key and select "Drop Call"

How can I see missed calls on my Home Screen?

Many of the Themes, will show you your missed calls with an icon with a phone and an "X" next to it as shown below. The "Zen" Theme and "Today" Themes both show this. See page 41 for help on how to change the "Theme" or look and feel of you BlackBerry. Below is an image with a missed call showing on the Home Screen.

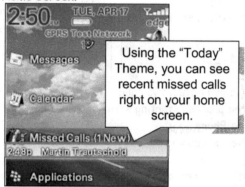

Using the "Today" Theme, you can see recent missed calls right on your home screen.

TTY or "TELETYPE" Support

The TTY or Teletype is a common name for the telecommunications device for the deaf ("TDD"). The BlackBerry Pearl is designed in such a way that is can convert received calls into text that can be read on a TTY device. You need to connect the Pearl to the TTY device and then enable that option.

1. Make sure that your Carrier supports TTY (Most do.)
2. Make sure that the TTY device operates at the universal standard of 45.45 BPS.
3. Connect the TTY device to the **Headset Jack** on the Pearl (There are other adapters, but this is the easiest way to connect the Pearl to a TTY Device.)

Enabling TTY Support on the Pearl
1. Press the **Green Phone key**.
2. Press the **Menu key** and scroll to "**Options**" and click.
3. Scroll to "**TTY**" and click.

4. Set the TTY field to "**Yes.**"
5. Press the **Menu key** and select "**Save.**"

Adding Pauses and Waits in Phone Numbers

There are times when you are entering phone numbers in your address book that require either a pause or a wait. These might be when you are dialing a conference call number, entering your password/PIN number for a voice mail access system, or want to auto-dial an extension at the end of a number, but need the extra pause. If you need more than a 2-second pause, just add a few more pauses--you can put as many pauses together as you need.

"**Pause**" = 2 second pause, then continues dialing automatically

"**Wait**" = Waits until for you to click the trackball, then continues dialing

Add pauses and waits when you by pressing the Menu key (or sometimes the trackball works) and select "Add Pause" or "Add Wait" from the menu.

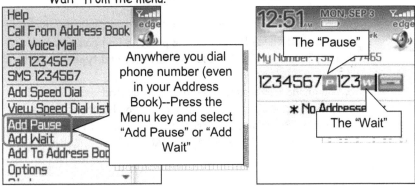

Dialing Letters in Phone Numbers or On the Phone

You can dial letters when you are **on a phone call** or even put phone numbers with letters in your **Address Book**. To do this

Dialing while on the phone: Just press the **ALT key** (lower left-most key with the up/down arrow) and type the letters using the "**Multitap**" typing mode. In other words, to type the first letter on the key, press it once, to type the second letter press the key twice. To type an "E", press the "ER" key once, to type an "R" press it twice.

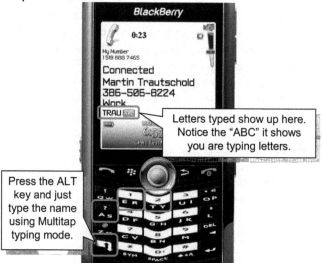

So when you hear "In order to use this phone directory, please dial the first three letters of the person's last name to look them up"... now you just press the **ALT key** and **type the letters!**

Typing phone numbers with letters in your Address Book or in the phone: Use the same technique. If you had to enter **1-800-CALLABC** into your address book, you would type in 1 800 then press the ALT key and type "**CALLABC**" with Multitap.

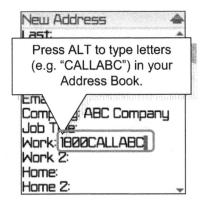

More Phone Tips and Tricks

Like most features on the Pearl, there is always more you can do with your Phone. These tips and tricks will make things go even quicker for you.

1. To place an active phone call on hold and answer a second incoming phone call, press the **Green Phone key**.
2. To view and dial a name from your **Address Book**, press and hold the **Green Phone key**.
3. To insert a "**plus**" sign when typing a phone number, hold the number "0."
4. To add an extension to a phone number, press the "X" key, then type the extension number. It should look like this: **8005551212x1234**.
5. To check your voice mail, press and hold the number "1."
6. To view the last phone number that you dialed, scroll to the top of the Phone screen, then press the **ENTER key**. Press the **Send** key to dial the number.

SMS Text and
Multi-Media Messaging

Chapter Contents:

Text & Multi-Media Messaging

As you may be aware, a key strength of all BlackBerry devices is their Messaging abilities. We have covered Email extensively and now turn to SMS and MMS Messaging. SMS stands for **"Short Messaging Service"** (text messaging) and MMS stands for "**Multi-Media Messaging**" Service. MMS is a short way to say that you have included pictures, sounds, video or some other form of media right inside your email (not to be confused with regular email when media is an attachment to an email message.) The Pearl is beautifully equipped to use both of these services - learning them will make you more productive and make your Pearl that much more fun to use.

12
SMS text, MMS

SMS Text Messaging on the Pearl

Text messaging has become one of the most popular services on cell phones today. While it is still used more extensively in Europe and Asia, it is growing in popularity in North America.

The concept is very simple; instead of placing a phone call - send a short message to someone's handset. It is much less disruptive than a phone call and you may have friends, colleagues or co-workers who do not own a BlackBerry - so email is not an option.

One of the authors uses text messaging with his children all the time - this is how their generation communicates. "R u coming home 4 dinner?" "Yup." There you have it - meaningful dialogue with a seventeen year old - short, instant and easy.

Composing SMS Text Messages
Composing an SMS message is much like sending an email. The beauty of an SMS message is that it arrives on virtually any handset and is so easy to respond to.

Option #1: Sending an SMS message from the message list
1. Use the trackball and navigate to your "Messages" list and press the Menu key. (Shortcut: Roll to a date row separator

– e.g. "Mon, Sep 3, 2007" and click the trackball).

2. Select "**Compose SMS Text**".
3. Begin typing in a contact name (as you did when selecting an Email recipient in chapter 7.) When you find the contact, click on the trackball.
4. If the contact has multiple phone numbers, the Pearl will ask you to choose which number – select the Mobile number you desire and click.
5. In the main body (where the cursor is) just type your message like you were sending an email. Remember: SMS messages are **limited to 160 characters** by most carriers. If you go over that in the Pearl, two separate text messages will be sent. When you are done typing, just click the trackball and choose "**Send**." That's all there is to it.

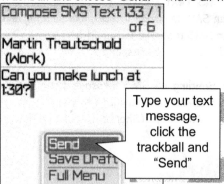

Option #2: Sending SMS message from your Address Book or Contact List

1. Click on your Address Book icon (it may say Contacts, instead). Type a few letters to "Find" the person to whom you want to send your SMS message.

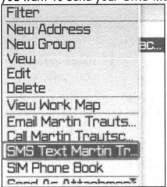

2. With the contact highlighted from the list, press the Menu key and you will see one of your menu options is "**SMS Text**" followed by the contact name. Select this option and follow the steps from above to send your message.

Basic SMS Menu Commands

As with the Email feature, there are many options via the menu commands in SMS messaging.

Menu Commands from Main SMS screen

1. On the "Compose SMS Text" screen, when you are typing your text message, press the Menu key. The following options are available to you:
   - **Help** – Gives you contextual help with SMS messaging (See page 51 for more tips on this Help feature)
   - **Send** – Sends your SMS message
   - **Save Draft** – Keeps a copy of SMS for later referencing
   - **Add Recipient** – Allows you to send SMS to more people contacts

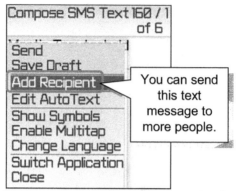

- Edit AutoText - Takes you to AutoText Menu - see page 60 for details on AutoText.
- Show Symbols - Calls up the Symbols menu
- Enable Multitap - Changes from SureType™ to Multitap typing mode (See page 54 for more information on typing.)
- Change Language - Allows you to send SMS in another language
- Switch Application - Jump over to another icon so you can Multi-Task (learn more about this on page 192)
- Close - The same as pressing the ESCAPE key - this closes your SMS text window and asks if you want to save changes.

Advanced SMS Menu Commands

There are ways to personalize and customize your SMS messaging. These settings are found in your "Options" menu.

1. Click on your Options icon, it may be inside the Applications, Settings or other icon, if you don't see it from your Home Screen.
2. Scroll down to "SMS Text" and click with the trackball. TIP: Press the letter "S" on your keyboard a few times to jump down to this entry - it's usually faster than scrolling.
3. The following options are available to the user

- **Disable AutoText** – generally this is set to "No" (This means you want to use the AutoText when typing SMS messages)
- **Leave messages on SIM card** – change to "Yes" if you want to keep copies of your messages on the SIM card and not have them deleted.
- **Delivery reports** – Change to "On" if you want delivery confirmation for your SMS messages.
- **Data Coding** – generally kept at "7 bit"

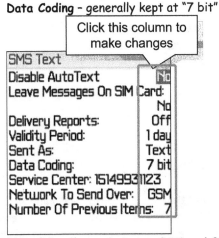

Click this column to make changes

SMS Text
Disable AutoText   No
Leave Messages On SIM Card:
                          No
Delivery Reports: Off
Validity Period: 1 day
Sent As: Text
Data Coding: 7 bit
Service Center: 15149931123
Network To Send Over: GSM
Number Of Previous Items: 7

- **Network** – Choose between GSM and GPRS
  - o GSM will ensure that your messages will be sent over any GSM signal.
  - o GPRS means that you need to have access to a GPRS data signal – while this is a "faster" delivery option, it can limit your SMS ability in rural areas.
  - o You may see other settings here such as "1X," "1XEV," "Wi-Fi" or more depending on the networks available to your BlackBerry.
- **Number of previous items** – default setting is "7," but can be adjusted if you like to keep more messages on your device.

Opening and Replying to SMS Messages

Opening your SMS messages couldn't be easier - the Pearl makes it simple to quickly keep in touch and respond to your messages.

1. Navigate to your waiting messages from either the message icon on the Home Screen or your messages screen and click on the new SMS message.
2. If you are in the midst of a dialogue with someone, your messages will appear in a "threaded" message format which looks like a running discussion.
3. Just press the **Menu key** or click the **trackball** and select "**reply.**"
4. The cursor appears in a blank field - type in your reply, click the **trackball** and select "**Send.**"

Searching for Messages

You might find that you use SMS messaging so often, since it is so easy and fun, that your messages start to really collect on the Pearl. Sometimes, you need to find a message quickly, rather than scroll through all the messages in your in box. There are three primary ways to search through your messages; searching the entire message through any field, searching the sender and searching the subject.

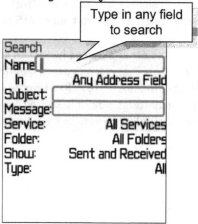

The General Messages Search Command
This is the easiest way to search for a message if you are not sure of the subject or date.

1. Click on your **Messages icon** and press the **Menu key**.
2. Scroll down to "**Search**" and click.
3. Enter in information in any of the fields available to you. When you are done, click the trackball.
4. The corresponding messages are then displayed on the screen.

Using the "Search Sender" or "Search Recipient" Command

TIP
The "**Search**", "**Search Sender**", "**Search Recipient**" and "**Search Subject**" work on SMS messages, Email, MMS – anything in your Messages Inbox!

Sometimes, you have many messages from one particular sender and you only want to see the list of your communication with that particular individual.

1. From the messages list, scroll to any message from the person you wish to search and press the Menu key - (Say that you want to find a specific message from Martin and you have 50 messages from Martin on your device – just highlight one of the messages and then press the Menu key.)

2. Only the list of messages from that particular sender (in this case, Martin) are now displayed. Just scroll and find the particular message you are looking for.

Using the "Search Subject" Command

You might be having an SMS conversation with several people about a particular subject and now you want to see all the messages about those subject that are on your device.

1. Navigate to any message which has the subject displayed that you are searching for. The subject is displayed right under or next to the sender's name.
2. Press the Menu key and scroll to "Search Subject" and click.
3. All the corresponding messages are now displayed – just navigate to the one you wish to read.

SMS Mailbox Housecleaning

It is possible for your SMS mailbox to get a little unwieldy, just follow these suggestions to manage and clean your mailbox.

> **TIP**
>
> ALT + "S" will show you only your SMS text messages in your Inbox.

To View and clean a particular SMS folder:

1. Start your **Messages icon** and press the **Menu key**.
2. Scroll down to "**View Folder**" and click. You will then see a list of your available message folders.
3. To clean up your inbox, just click on SMS Inbox and only your SMS inbox messages will now be displayed.
4. Highlight the date row separator (e.g. "Mon, Sep 4, 2007") under the most recent message you desire to keep, press the Menu key and select "**Delete Prior**."
    *   All "older" messages will then be deleted

Click on your SMS Inbox or Outbox

5. To delete an individual message, just click on the message, press the Menu key and choose "**Delete.**"
6. Choose the SMS Outbox folder to do the same with sent messages.

SMS Tips and Tricks

There are some quick Key strokes you can use to navigate quickly through your messages.

These Shortcuts are entered when in the Message List

1. Press the comma (,) key to compose a message from the message list,
2. Press the exclamation point (!) key to reply to a message
3. Press the question mark (?) key to reply to all
4. Press the period (.) key to forward a message

> **TIP**
>
> Most of these same shortcuts work for Email messages as well.

5. Push and hold the **Alt** key and press "**I**" to view Incoming (received) messages
6. Push and hold the **Alt** key and press the "**S**" key to view all SMS text messages
7. Press the ESCAPE key to view your message list once more
8. Push **2** to move up a message in the list
9. Push **8** to move down a message in the list

MMS Messaging on the Pearl

MMS stands for Multi-Media Messaging which includes Pictures, Video and Audio. **NOTE**: <u>Not all BlackBerry devices or carriers support MMS messaging</u>, so it is a good idea to make sure that your recipient can receive these messages before you send them.

BE AWARE: Some carriers (phone companies) charge extra for sending MMS message, some charge the same rate as SMS text messaging – which could be US$0.25 or more per message, even if you have an "unlimited" BlackBerry data plan – SMS and MMS are usually charged separately. One good note, many carriers offer unlimited SMS/MMS messaging for between US$5.00 and US$10.00 per month.

Sending MMS from the Message List

Perhaps the easiest way to send an MMS message is to start the process just like you started the SMS process earlier:

1. Click on the **Messages icon** and press the **Menu key**.
2. Scroll down to "**Compose MMS**" and click the trackball
3. Depending on the phone company that supplied your BlackBerry, you may be prompted to find the MMS file you desire to send (these are often stored in your "templates" file)
   - Some BlackBerry devices have a pre-loaded "Birthday.mms" in this folder.
   - Click on the Birthday MMS, if you have it

4. Then type in the recipient in the "To:" field and scroll to the appropriate contact and click.
5. You can add a subject and text in the body of the MMS. When finished, just click the trackball and send.
6. There are lots of template MMS files you can download on the web and put into this folder to be selected in the future.

Sending a Media file as an MMS from the Media Screen

This might be the more common and easier way for you to send Media files as MMS messages.

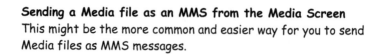

1. Use the trackball and navigate to your **Media** icon and click. You will be brought to the Media screen.

12
SMS text, MMS

2. Click on "**Pictures**" and find the picture either on your device or Media Card that you wish to send.
3. Just highlight the picture (no need to click on it) and press the Menu key.
4. Scroll down to "**Send As MMS**" and click. You will then be directed to choose the recipient from your contacts. Find the contact you desire and click.

TIP: If you do not have an MMS or SMS Text Messaging service plan from your phone company, you can usually "**Send As Email**" for no additional cost. The only other thing to be aware of is whether or not you have an 'unlimited BlackBerry data plan.' If you don't have this 'unlimited data plan' then you will want to send pictures only very rarely because they can eat up your data much faster than a plain-text email.

5. Type in a subject and any text in the message, click the trackball and send.

Basic MMS Menu Commands

You can personalize your MMS message even more through the MMS menu.

1. When you are composing the MMS message, press the Menu key.

2. Scroll through the menu to see your options; you can easily add more recipients "To:" "Cc:" "Bcc:"

3. You can also attach addresses from your Address Book. To add an Address – just click "**Attach Address**" and find the appropriate address on the next screen.

4. If you had scheduled a Birthday Dinner together, then you might want add an appointment from your BlackBerry Calendar ("Dinner at the Fancy French Restaurant for Two"), click the "**Add Appointment**" option.

5. To add an audio file to accompany the picture, choose "**Attach Audio**" and then navigate to the folder that contains the audio file.

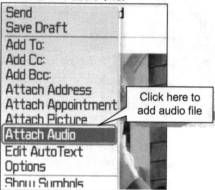

6. You can also attach another picture by choosing the appropriate option from the menu.

Advanced MMS Commands:

1. While you are composing your MMS message, press the Menu key and scroll down to "Options."

2. In the "Current Message Options" Screen you will see the estimated size of the MMS – which is important, because if the file is too big, your recipient may not be able to download it onto their device.

3. You can also set the importance of this MMS as well as set delivery confirmation options.

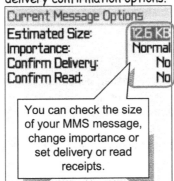

4. For additional Advanced MMS commands, navigate from the Home Screen to "Options" and click. Scroll to "MMS" and click.
   - From this screen you can set your phone to always receive multimedia files by setting the first line to say **"Always."**
   - You can also set your automatic retrieval to occur **"Always"** or **"Never"**.

- You can check each checkbox to set your notification and message filtering options as well.

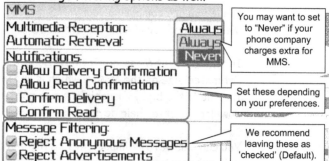

- "Allow Delivery Confirmation" means to allow you to send delivery confirmation messages when you receive MMS messages from others.

- **"Allow Read Confirmation"** means to allow your BlackBerry to send a confirmation message when you have opened an MMS message you received.

- **"Confirm Delivery"** means to request a delivery confirmation from people to whom you send MMS messages.

- **"Confirm Read"** means to request a 'read receipt' message when your MMS recipient opens the MMS message you sent them.

- We recommend leaving the filtering options checked as they are by default.

MMS Troubleshooting:

These troubleshooting steps will work for MMS, SMS, Email, Web Browsing - anything that requires a wireless radio connection. Please see page 413 for our entire chapter with more detailed steps on troubleshooting your wireless signal.

1. Click on the Options icon.
2. Scroll up to "**Advanced Options**" and click and then scroll to "**Service Book**" and click.
3. Scroll to "**Host Routing Table**"
4. Press the **Menu key** and then click on "Register Now."
5. While the Pearl is still on, do a "**Battery Pull**" - take off the back of the casing and remove the battery, wait 30 seconds and then re-install it. Once the Pearl reboots, you should be all set for MMS messaging.

PIN, BlackBerry and Other Instant Messengers

Chapter Contents:

TIP: PIN Messages Are Free

PIN Messages are always free, whereas other SMS text, BlackBerry Messenger and MMS (Multi-Media Messages) may be charged under an extra service plan by your phone company.

PIN Messaging

Martin Trautschold
Email: martin@blackberrymade
simple.com
Work: 3865068224
PIN: 240BB128

To easily "PIN" message someone, add their PIN number in your address book.

BlackBerry handhelds have a unique feature called PIN-to-PIN, also known as "PIN Messaging" or "Peer-to-Peer" Messaging. This allows one BlackBerry user to communicate directly with another BlackBerry user as long as you know that user's BlackBerry PIN number. We'll show you an easy way to find your PIN, email to your colleague and a few good tips and tricks.

1. Compose an email to your colleague. In the body type of the email type the code letters "mypin" and hit the SPACE key - you will then see your pin number in the following format "pin:2005xx11" where the 2005xx11 is replaced by your actual PIN. Click the trackball and select "**Send**".

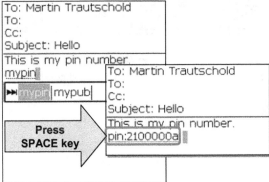

To: Martin Trautschold
To:
Cc:
Subject: Hello
This is my pin number.
mypin
▶▶ mypin | mypub |

Press SPACE key ⟹

To: Martin Trautschold
To:
Cc:
Subject: Hello
This is my pin number.
pin:2100000a

2. Ask your colleague to either copy/paste your PIN into your existing entry in their Address Book or, if you are not yet in

their Address Book, then ask them click on the underlined PIN number, click the trackball and "**Add to Address Book**".

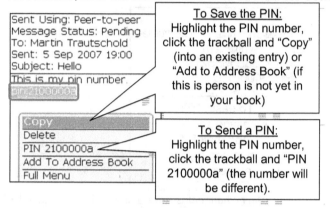

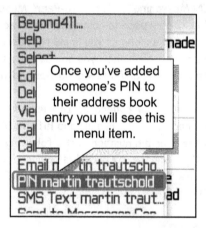

3. Your colleague could immediately send you a PIN message by clicking on the "pin:12345xx33" and selecting "PIN".

4. Once you receive your PIN message, you will see that it is highlighted in RED text in your Inbox.

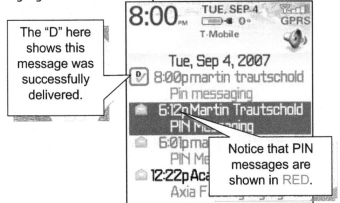

The "D" here shows this message was successfully delivered.

Notice that PIN messages are shown in RED.

5. To reply to a PIN message, simply click the trackball and select "**Reply**", just like with email and other messaging.

Adding Someone's PIN to your Address Book

1. After you receive a PIN message from someone you should roll up to their name or PIN number (either might be shown) in the "From:" field at the top of the message. Then click the trackball and select "**Add to Address Book**".

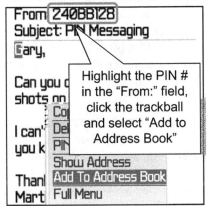

Highlight the PIN # in the "From:" field, click the trackball and select "Add to Address Book"

2. If the "**Add to Address Book**" did not work for you then follow the steps below.

3. After you highlight the name/PIN number, select "**Copy**" from the menu, then press the **Menu key** select "**Switch Application**".

4. Either click on the **Address Book** icon if it's running or go to the **Home Screen** and start the **Address Book**.
5. Open up the person's address book entry, "**Edit**" it and "**Paste**" the PIN number into the correct "**PIN**" field, which is just below all the phone number fields as shown.

Edit Address

Company:
Job Title:
Work:
Work 2:
Home:
Home 2:
Mobile:
Pager:
Fax:
Other:
PIN: 2004BB10

Or, you may copy and paste the PIN directly into someone's address book entry.

BlackBerry Messenger

So far, we have covered email, SMS text, MMS and BlackBerry PIN-to-PIN messaging. If you still need other ways of communicating with friends, family and colleagues you can try BlackBerry Messenger or any one of the most popular Instant Messaging programs like AIM (AOL Instant Messenger), Yahoo or GoogleTalk instant messengers. The Pearl is really the ultimate communication tool.

TIP: Don't Have BlackBerry Messenger?
Did you know that it is easy to download and install the BlackBerry Messenger icon. Go to "**mobile.blackberry.com**" from your BlackBerry Web Browser and follow the directions.

Many users have IM programs on their PC, or even their Mobile Phone. BlackBerry Includes a Messaging program just for fellow BlackBerry users called BlackBerry Messenger. You will find the BlackBerry Messenger icon in your applications menu.

Setting up BlackBerry Messenger

BlackBerry Messenger offers you a little more "secure" way of keeping in touch quickly with fellow BlackBerry users. Setup is very easy.

1. If you don't see the Blackberry Messenger icon, then press the Menu key (to the left of the trackball) and roll up or down to find it.

2. Click on the BlackBerry Messenger icon. You will be prompted to set your User Name.

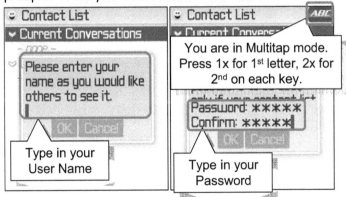

3. Type in your **User Name** and click OK. You will then be asked to set a BlackBerry Messenger password. Type in your password and confirm, then click OK.

Add Contacts to your BlackBerry Messenger Group

Once your User Name is setup, you need to add contacts to your BlackBerry Messenger Group. In BlackBerry Messenger, your contacts are fellow BlackBerry users who have the BlackBerry Messenger program installed on their handhelds.

1. Navigate to the main BlackBerry Messenger screen and press the Menu key. Scroll to "Add a Contact" and click.

2. Begin typing the name of the desired contact. When the desired contact appears, click on the trackball.

The BlackBerry generates a message stating: "X would like to add you to his/her BlackBerry Messenger. Click OK and the message is sent to your contact.

3. The Message request shows up in your Pending group, under Contacts.

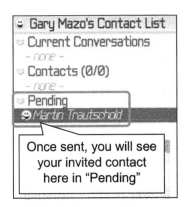

4. The contact will be listed under "**Pending**" until the recipient responds to your invitation.

5. If you do not get a response, then click on their name and use another communications method to ask your colleague to "hurry up."

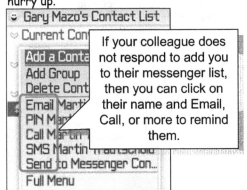

Joining a Fellow User's BlackBerry Messenger Group
You may be invited to join another BlackBerry user's Messaging group. You can either **Accept** or Decline this invitation.

1. You will receive your invitations via email or you can see them directly in BlackBerry Messenger.

2. Click on your BlackBerry Messenger icon.

3. Scroll to your "**Requests**" group and highlight the invitation and click.
    - A menu pops up with three options: Accept, Decline, Remove.
    - Click on "**Accept**" and you will now be part of the Messaging group. Click Decline to deny the invitation or "**Remove**" to no longer show the invitation on your BlackBerry.

BlackBerry Messenger Menu Commands

The Menu of the BlackBerry Messenger is very feature rich and straight forward.

1. Navigate to your main BlackBerry Messenger screen and press the Menu key.
2. The following options are available to you:

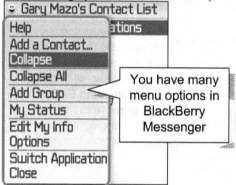

- "**Add a Contact**" - Use this to add people to your conversations and groups.
- "**Expand**" - simply expands the dialogue screen - if screen is already open. The menu command reads "**Collapse**." (TIP: Clicking your trackball on the main conversation screen does the same thing.)
- "**Collapse All**" - Hides all group members.
- "**Add Group**" - Click to add a new messaging group such as "Work", "Family" or "Friends."

- **"Rename Group"** – Use this to rename your messaging groups.
- **"My Status"** – Click to make yourself "Available" or **"Unavailable"** to your Messaging Buddies
- **"Edit My Info"** – Change your Name and/or Password
- **"Options"** – Click to bring up your Options screen (see below for details)
- **"Switch Application"** – Press this to "multi-task" or jump to another application while leaving the messenger application running.
- **"Close"** – Exit the Messenger application.

13
PIN, BB & Other IM

Your BlackBerry Messenger Options Screen

If you wanted even more control of your Messenger, you would press the Menu key and select "Options." On the Messenger Options screen, you can set the following:

- Whether or not your BlackBerry will vibrate when someone "**PINGs**" you (the default is "Yes").
- Have the BlackBerry force you to enter your password every time you send a "new contact" request – would be a good security measure if your BlackBerry was lost.
- Set whether or not your requests can be forwarded by other people – the default it "Yes".
- Finally, you may choose to display your Messenger conversations in your Messages (Email Inbox) – the default is "Yes" If you change it to "No" then none of your Messenger conversations will show up in your email inbox.

```
Options
Vibrate When Receiving a Ping
                          Yes
Ask Password Question When
Adding Contacts
                           No
Allow Forwarding of Requests
                          Yes
Show Conversations in
Message List
                          Yes
```

Starting/Continuing Conversations

While Messaging is a lot like Text Messaging, you actually have more options for personal expression and the ability to see a complete conversation with the Messaging program.

1. Your Conversation List is in your Main Screen. Just highlight the individual with whom you are conversing and click the trackball. The conversation screen opens.

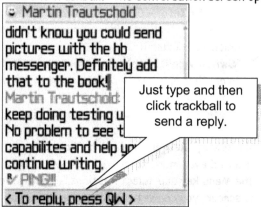

Just type and then click trackball to send a reply.

2. Just type in the new message and click the trackball to "**Send**".

3. To add an Emoticon to your message, press the "Symbols" button three times and navigate to the emoticon you wish to use. Just click on the desired emoticon (or press the corresponding key - shown under the emoticon) and it will appear in the message.

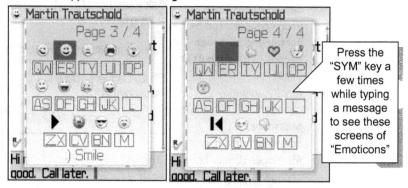

Press the "SYM" key a few times while typing a message to see these screens of "Emoticons"

Sending Files to a Message Buddy

In the midst of your conversation, you can send a file very easily (At the time of publishing of this book, you are limited to sending only files that are images, photos or sound files - ringtones and music).

1. Click on the contact in your conversation screen and open the dialogue with that individual.
2. Click the trackball and select "**Send a File.**" Choose whether you wish to send an image or an audio file.

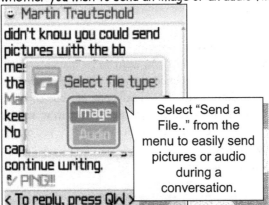

13
PIN, BB &
Other IM

3. Using the trackball, navigate to where the image or audio file is stored on your BlackBerry and click when it is located
    - Selecting the file will automatically send it to your message buddy.

NOTE: Some BlackBerry providers (phone companies) may limit the size of file you can send via Bluetooth to a small size, such as 15 kilobytes (kb). Most pictures maybe 300kb or more and full songs might be 500kb or more.

Pinging a Contact

Let's say that you wanted to reach a BlackBerry Messenger contact quickly. One option available to you is to "**PING**" that contact. When you Ping a BlackBerry user, their device will vibrate once to let them know that they are wanted/needed immediately. (TIP: You can set your BlackBerry to vibrate or not vibrate when you receive a "PING" in your BlackBerry Messenger Options screen.)

1. Open up a conversation with a contact from the contact screen.

2. Press the Menu key and scroll down to "Ping Contact"
3. The dialogue screen will reflect the Ping by showing "PING!!!" in capital red letters. The Ping recipient will notice that their BlackBerry vibrates and indicates that you have "pinged" them.

Using the "Status" options

Sometimes, you might now want to be disrupted with Instant Messages. You can change your status to "Unavailable" and you won't be disturbed. Conversely, one of your contacts might be "Offline" so to speak and you want to know when they become "Available." You can set an alert to notify you of their availability.

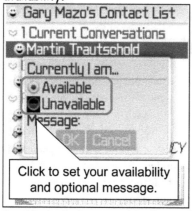

Gary Mazo's Contact List
1 Current Conversations
Martin Trautschold
Currently I am...
• Available
Unavailable
Message:
OK   Cancel

Click to set your availability and optional message.

1. Navigate to your main Messaging screen and press the Menu key.
2. Scroll to "**My Status**" and click. Choose either "**Available**" or "**Unavailable.**"
3. To set an alert, just highlight an "**Unavailable**" contact from your Contact List screen and press the Menu key.
4. Scroll to "**Set Alert**" and you will be notified as soon as he/she becomes available.

Using AIM™, Yahoo™ and Google Talk™ Messaging

After you get used to BlackBerry Messenger you will begin to see that it is a powerful way of quickly keeping in touch with friends, family and colleagues. Realizing that many are still not in the "BlackBerry" world, you can also access and use popular IM programs like AOL Instant Messenger ("AIM"), Yahoo Messenger and Google™ Talk™ Messenger right out of the box on the Pearl. Individual carriers do have some restrictions, however, and you will need to check your carrier web sites to see which services are supported.

13
PIN, BB &
Other IM

To Install Instant Messenger Applications on the Pearl

1. First see if your carrier has placed an "IM" icon in your applications directory – this may be
   - Navigate to "Applications" and scroll for an icon that simply is called "IM."
   - If you have an IM icon, click and follow the on screen prompts.
2. If there is no IM icon, start your **Web Browser** on the Pearl.
3. Press the **Menu key** and select "Go To..." then type in www.mobile.blackberry.com or "**mobile.blackberry.com**" to get to the BlackBerry "Home" page which may look something like the image below (Please forgive us if this page looks very different by the time your get to it – web sites can change on a monthly basis!)

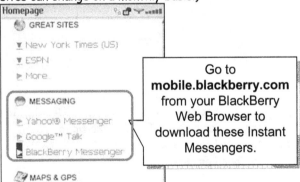

Go to **mobile.blackberry.com** from your BlackBerry Web Browser to download these Instant Messengers.

4. Locate the "**Messaging**" group, you need to scroll down a bit, then click on the Instant Messenger application you want to download and install.
5. Under Applications you will see a link for downloading both Yahoo Messenger and Google™ Talk.

- Yahoo messenger allows you to IM all of your AIM buddies as well as Yahoo Messenger buddies.

TIP: Other excellent 3rd party messaging programs like "Jivetalk" are available for download on the web. The benefit of "Jivetalk" is that it can access multiple Instant Messenger Networks like AOL, Google Talk, ICQ, Jabber, Windows Live Messenger, and Yahoo! Messenger (as of September 2007).

To find and download "Jivetalk" or other instant messengers:
(1) Open your BlackBerry Web Browser
(2) "Go To..." your favorite search engine: (e.g. Google.com, Yahoo.com)
(3) Type in a search string to find what you need (e.g. "blackberry jivetalk") and "Search" for it. Follow the instructions to download and install the software.

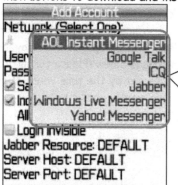

Like some other competitors, the "JiveTalk™" Instant Messenger allows you to communicate across multiple networks in one application.

For more help to download and install Third Party software, please check out our entire chapter devoted to software starting on page 503. Our specific instructions showing how to install software "Over the Air" ("OTA") or wirelessly can be found on page 480

Connecting with Bluetooth

Chapter Contents:

Bluetooth

The BlackBerry Pearl ships with Bluetooth 2.0 Technology. Think of Bluetooth as a short range, wireless technology which allows your Pearl to "connect" to various peripheral devices without wires.

Bluetooth is believed to be named after a Danish Viking and King, Harald Blåtand (which has been translated as *Bluetooth* in English.) King Blåtand lived in the 10th century and is famous for uniting Denmark and Norway. Similarly, Bluetooth technology unites computers and telecom. His name, according to legend, is from his very dark hair which was unusual for Vikings. Blåtand means dark complexion. There does exist a more popular story which states that the King loved to eat Blueberries, so much so his teeth became stained with the color Blue.

Sources:

http://cp.literature.agilent.com/litweb/pdf/5980-3032EN.pdf
http://www.cs.utk.edu/~dasgupta/bluetooth/history.htm
http://www.britannica.com/eb/topic-254809/Harald-I

Understanding Bluetooth

Bluetooth allows your Pearl to communicate with things like headsets, GPS devices and other hands-free systems with the freedom of wireless. Bluetooth is a small radio that transmits from each device. The Pearl gets "paired" – connected to the peripheral. Most Bluetooth devices can be used up to 30 feet away from the Pearl.

Using Bluetooth on the Pearl

In order to use Bluetooth on the Pearl, it must first be turned on. This is done through the application menu.

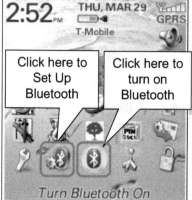

Turning On Bluetooth

1. Scroll through the application icons and click on "**Turn Bluetooth On**", or you may need to go to the radio tower icon (if it's called **Manage Connections**)
2. The small Bluetooth icon will now be showing next to the battery meter in the Home Screen.

If you don't see a "**Turn On Bluetooth**" or "**Setup Bluetooth**" icons, then click on the "**Manage Connections**" icon.

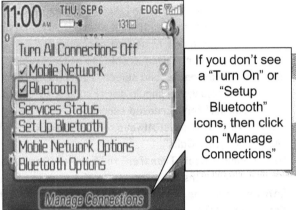

If you don't see a "Turn On" or "Setup Bluetooth" icons, then click on "Manage Connections"

Configuring Bluetooth
Once Bluetooth is enabled, you will want to follow the steps below to take full advantage of the Bluetooth capabilities of the Pearl.

There can sometimes be two or three ways to get into the Bluetooth setup and options screens. This depends a bit on your BlackBerry software version and BlackBerry carrier (cell phone) company.

1. Navigate to the Bluetooth Option screen with one of the methods below:
   Method 1: Click on the **Options** icon. Then scroll to "**Bluetooth**" and click, then click the Menu key and select "**Options**"
   Method 2: Scroll to the "**Set Up Bluetooth**" icon and click on it, then click the Menu key and select "Options"
   Method 3: Scroll to the "**Manage Connections**" icon, click on it then select "**Bluetooth Options**" at the bottom, then click the Menu key and select "**Options**"

2. If you have already paired your Pearl with Bluetooth devices, you will have seen those devices listed (we will cover pairing below.)

3. To change your Device name (the way other Bluetooth devices will see your Pearl) click where it says "**Device Name**" and type a new name (not necessary).

4. To make your Pearl "Discoverable" to other devices click next to "**Discoverable**" and select "**Yes**" (the default is "**No**") As we note below, you should set this back to "**No**" after you finish "pairing" for increased security.

5. Make sure that it says "**Always**" or "**If Unlocked**" after "**Allow Outgoing Calls**"

6. Set "**Address Book Transfer**" to "**Enable**" (Depending on your software version, you may see the options of "All Entries" - same as "Enable", "Hotlist Only" or "Selected Categories Only" - depending on your preferences). This option allows your address book data to be transferred to another device or computer using Bluetooth.

7. To see a blue flashing LED when connected to a Bluetooth Device, make sure the LED Connection Indicator is set to "On."

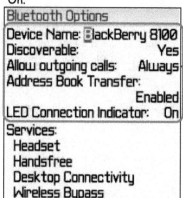

These are settings for Pairing.
Security Note: For higher Bluetooth security, after you have "paired" your device , set "Discoverable" to "No" and "Address Book Transfer" to "Disabled"

Bluetooth Security Tips:

Here are a few security tips from a recent BlackBerry IT Newsletter. These will help prevent hackers from getting access to your BlackBerry via Bluetooth:

- **Never pair** your BlackBerry when you are **in a crowded public area.**
- **"Disable"** the **"Discoverable"** setting after you are done with pairing your BlackBerry.
- **Do not accept** any "pairing requests" with "unknown" Bluetooth devices, only accept connections from devices with names you recognize.
- **Change the name of your BlackBerry** to something other than the default "BlackBerry 8100" - this will help avoid hackers from easily finding your BlackBerry.

Source: http://www.blackberry.com/newsletters/connection/it/jan-2007/managing-bluetooth-security.shtml?CPID=NLC-41

14
Bluetooth

Supported Devices

The BlackBerry Pearl should work with most Bluetooth headsets, car kits, hands free kits, keyboards and GPS receivers that are Bluetooth 2.0 and earlier compliant. At publishing time, Bluetooth 2.1 was just coming on the scene; you will need to check with the device manufacturer of newer devices to make sure they are compatible with the Pearl. At publishing time, the Pearl did not support Bluetooth stereo streaming, so Bluetooth Stereo Headphones did not yet work with the Pearl. Future releases of BlackBerry handheld system software may correct this issue.

How to Pair the Pearl with a Bluetooth Device

Think of "Pairing" as establishing a connection between your Pearl and a peripheral (Headset, Global Positioning Device, external keyboard, Windows™ or Mac™ computer, etc.) without wires. Pairing is dependent on entering a required **"Pass key"** which "locks" the Pearl into a secure connection with the peripheral. Similar to getting into the "Bluetooth options" screens, there could be several ways to get into the "Bluetooth Setup" screen to "pair" the Pearl and establish this connection.

1. First, put your Bluetooth device (e.g. Headset, GPS unit, computer or other peripheral) already in "Pairing" mode as

recommended by the manufacturer. Also, have the "Pass key" ready to enter.

After your Bluetooth device is "Found" it will appear in this window.

2. Navigate to the Bluetooth Setup screen with one of the methods below:

   Method 1: Click on the **Options** icon. (May be inside the "Settings" icon). Then scroll to "Bluetooth" and click.

   Method 2: Scroll to the **Set Up Bluetooth** icon and click on it.

   Method 3: Scroll to the **Manage Connections** icon, click on it then select "**Bluetooth Setup**"

3. The Pearl will ask you to make sure your Bluetooth device is in Pairing mode - click "**OK**".

   IMPORTANT: If you are pairing your Pearl with your computer, then you need to make sure that both your Pearl and your computer are in "**Discoverable**" mode. Set this in the "**Bluetooth Options**" screen by setting "**Discoverable**" to "**Yes**" or "**Ask**". (The default setting is "No" which will prevent you from pairing.)

4. When the Device is found, the Pearl will display the Device name on the screen. Click on the device name to select it.

5. You will then be prompted to enter the 4 digit Pass Key provided by the manufacturer of the Bluetooth peripheral.

Enter in the Passkey and then click the trackball. (Many default passkeys are just "0000" or "1234")

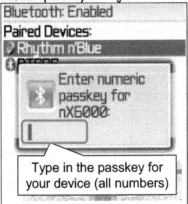

14
Bluetooth

6. You will then be prompted to accept the connection from the new Device (TIP: If you check the box next to **"Don't ask this again"** you will only have to do this once.)

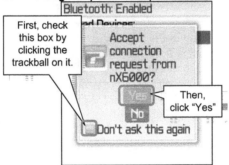

7. Your device should now be connected and paired and ready to use.

Answering and Making Calls with the Headset

Some Bluetooth headsets support an "**Auto Answer**" protocol which will, as it sounds, automatically answer incoming calls and send them right to the headset. This is very helpful when driving or in other situations where you should not be looking at the Pearl to answer the call. Sometimes, you will need to push a button – usually just one – to answer your call from the headset.

Option #1: Answer Directly From the Headset Itself

1. When the call comes into your Pearl, you should hear an audible beep in the headset. Just press the multi-function button on your headset to answer the call.
2. Press the Multi function button when the call ends to disconnect.

Option #2: Transfer the Caller to the Headset

1. When the phone call comes into the Pearl, press the Menu key.
2. Scroll to "**Activate Handset**" and the call will be sent to the headset.

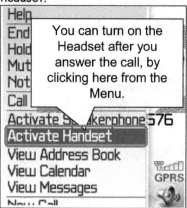

You can turn on the Headset after you answer the call, by clicking here from the Menu.

Bluetooth Setup Menu Commands

There are several options available to you from the Bluetooth menu. Learn these commands to be able to take full advantage of Bluetooth wireless technology on the Pearl.

Bluetooth Menu Options

1. Navigate to the **Options** icon and click.

2. Scroll to "**Bluetooth**" and click. You will now see the list of paired devices with your BlackBerry.

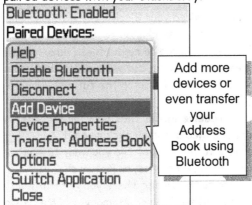

Bluetooth: Enabled

Paired Devices:

Help
Disable Bluetooth
Disconnect
Add Device
Device Properties
Transfer Address Book
Options
Switch Application
Close

Add more devices or even transfer your Address Book using Bluetooth

14
Bluetooth

3. Highlight one of the devices listed and press the Menu key. The following options become available to you:

a. **Disable Bluetooth** - another way to turn off the Bluetooth radio - this will help to save battery life if you don't need the Bluetooth active

b. **Connect / Disconnect**- clicking this will immediately connect/disconnect you to/from the highlighted Bluetooth device

c. **Add Device** - to connect to a new Bluetooth peripheral

d. **Delete Device** - removes the highlighted device from the Pearl

e. **Device Properties** - To check whether the device is trusted, encrypted and if "Echo control" is activated

f. **Transfer Address Book** - If you connected to a PC or another Bluetooth Smartphone, you can send your address book via Bluetooth to that device

g. **Options** - Shows the Options screen (covered above)

Send and Receive Files with Bluetooth

Once you have paired your BlackBerry with your computer, you can use Bluetooth to send and receive files. At publishing time, these files were limited to media files (videos, music, pictures) and address book entries, but we suspect that you will be able to transfer more types of files in the future.

To send or receive media files on your BlackBerry:
1. Start the Media icon by clicking on it.
2. Navigate to the type of file you want to send or receive – Music, Video, Ringtones, or Pictures
3. Navigate to the folder where you want to send or receive the file – either "**Device Memory**" or "**Media Card**"
4. If you are **sending a file** to your computer, then roll to and highlight the file, select "**Send using Bluetooth**". Then you will need to follow the prompts on your computer to receive the file. NOTE: You may need to set your computer to be able to "**Receive via Bluetooth**".
5. If you are **receiving a file** (or files) on your BlackBerry, then you need to select "Receive via Bluetooth". Go to your computer and select the file or files and follow the commands to "**Send via Bluetooth**". You may be asked on the BlackBerry to confirm the folder which is receiving the files on your BlackBerry.
6. TIP: You can send (transfer) only media files that you have put onto your BlackBerry yourself. The "Pre-Loaded" media files cannot be transferred via Bluetooth.

Bluetooth Troubleshooting

Bluetooth is still an emergent technology and, sometimes, it doesn't work as well as we might hope. If you are having difficulty, perhaps one of these suggestions will help.

1. My Pass key is not being accepted by the device?

a. It is possible that you have the incorrect pass key.
    Most Bluetooth devices use either "0000" or "1234" –
    but some have unique pass keys.
b. If you lost your manual for the Bluetooth device, many
    times you can use a web search engine such as Google or
    Yahoo to find the manufacturer's web site and locate
    the product manual.

2. I have the right passkey, but I still cannot pair the device?
    a. It is possible that the device is not compatible with the
        Pearl. One thing you can try is to turn off encryption.
        Click Options, then Bluetooth and then highlight
        the problem device and click. In "Device
        Properties" Then disable Encryption for that
        device and try to connect again.

14
Bluetooth

3. I can't share my Address Book?
    a. Inside the **Bluetooth setup screen**, press the **Menu key**
        and select "**Options**". Make sure that you have enabled
        the "**Address Book Transfer**" field.

Section 4: Web Browsing

Web Browsing on the Pearl

Chapter Contents:

- Locating the Web Browser from the Home Screen
- Browser Menu Options
- Using the Address Bar
- Setting and Managing Bookmarks
- Security Options for the Web Browser
- Web Feeds and streaming Web Video
- Carrier Specific Web Sites
- "Pushing" Web Content to the Pearl
- Search with Yahoo! Mobile and Google
- Web Browser Tips and Tricks

15
Web
Browser

Web Browsing on the Pearl

One of the amazing features of SmartPhones like the BlackBerry Pearl, is the ability to browse the web with ease and speed right from your handheld. More and more web sites are now supporting mobile browser formatting. These sites "sense" you are viewing them from a small mobile browser and automatically re-configure themselves for your Pearl so they load quickly – some, even quicker than a desktop browser.

Locating the Web Browser from the Home Screen

Web browsing can actually start with a few of the icons on your Home Screen. The easiest way to get started is to find the "Browser" icon – it looks like a globe.

1. Use the Trackball and navigate to the Browser icon and click. It might say "BlackBerry Browser" or "Internet Browser" or even something different like "mLife" or "T-Zone".

To start the web browser, highlight and click on the "Browser" icon

2. You will either be taken to directly the "Home" screen of your particular carrier or to your list of Bookmarks. (You can change this by going to your "Browser > Options" Screens" – learn more on page 321)

The Browser Menu

Like most other applications, the Heart of the Browser, and its capabilities, lies in the Menu options available to you. One push and one click and you are off to specific sites, bookmarked pages, recent pages, your internet history and more.

Menu Options:
1. While in the Browser application, press the **Menu key**
2. The following options are available to you:
   a. **Help** – See on-screen text help for the Web Browser, useful when you forget something and need quick help
   b. **Select Mode** – to allow "selecting text" to copy and paste into another application such as email or your MemoPad
   c. **Preview Mode** – changes the view to a web preview of the page with a bar along the side show the area of the web page you are currently viewing
   d. **Find** – search for text in the current web page – can be very useful when you don't want to scroll around looking for something specific
   e. **Home** – takes you to the Browser Home Page – You can set or change the Home Page inside the "Browser > Options" screen (See page 321 for details)
   f. **Go To...** – allows you to type in a specific web address for browsing (See page 314 for details)
   g. **Back** – goes back to the previous web page
   h. **Recent Pages** – allows you to view the most recent web pages browsed
   i. **History** – shows your entire web browsing history
   j. **Refresh** – updates the current web page
   k. **Set Encoding** – This is an advanced feature to change character encoding of web browsing. (Probably won't need to change this).
   l. **Add Bookmark** – sets the current page as a "Favorite" or "Bookmark." **(Extremely useful)** (See page 317 for details)
   m. **Bookmarks** – lists all your Bookmarks **(Extremely useful)** (See page 322 for details on using Bookmarks, Page 320 for details on organizing Bookmarks with folders)
   n. **Page Address** – Shows you the full web address of the current page (See page 316 for details)
   o. **Send Address** – Send the current page address to a contact (See page 316 for details)
   p. **Options** – Set Browser Configuration, Properties and Cache settings.

15
Web
Browser

q. **Save Page** - Save the page as a file and puts it in your Messages icon (your Email inbox)

r. **Switch Application** - Jump or multi-task over to other applications while leaving the current web page open.

s. **Hide** - Hide this menu.

t. **Close** - Close the Web Browser and exit to the Home Screen.

Web Browser Shortcut Keys

Here are a list of shortcut keys that will work when you are viewing a web page.

NOTE: They do not work in the Bookmark list. In the Bookmark list, when you start typing letters, your BlackBerry will try to "Find" a Bookmark matching the letters you typed.

1 Top of Web Page	, Connection Information	Space - Page Down
7 Bottom of Web Page		ALT + Roll Trackball
2 Up 1 Link (or line)	. Go To... Web Page	- Page Up/Down
8 Down 1 Link (or line)	! Show/Hide Top	ENTER - Select
5 Go to your Home Page (Set in Browser Options > Browser Configuration)	Status Bar	("click-on")
		highlighted link
	@ Show (Hide) Page Thumbnail in right column.	
DEL / 4 Go Back 1 page		3 Page Up
		9 Page Down
	? Add New Bookmark	

Using the "Go To" Command (Your Address Bar)

Really the first thing you will want to know how to do is get to your favorite web sites. In one of the author's cases, it is Google.com. On your desktop computer, you simply type the web address or ("URL") into your browser's "Address Bar". You won't see an Address Bar on the BlackBerry. Instead you have to use the "Go To…" menu command or "." (period) shortcut key to type in your web address.

Using the "Go To" Command (Shortcut key: ".")

1. Open the Browser by clicking with the trackball on the Browser icon.
2. Press the Menu Key and select "Go To…"

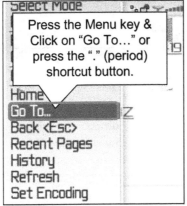

3. The Address bar comes up with the http://www. In place waiting for you to type the rest of the address.
   a. Simply type in the web address (remember, pushing the SPACE bar will put in the "dot" (.)

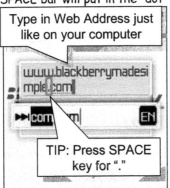

   b. Press the Trackball when you are done and the Browser will take you to the web page entered.

Once you have typed in a few web addresses using the "Go To…" command, you will notice that they appear in a list below the web address next time you select "Go To..." You can select any of these by rolling the trackball down and clicking on them.

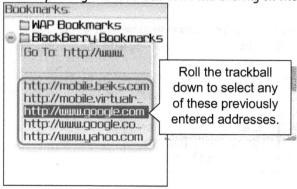

TIP: You can save time by "Editing" a previously entered address. If you want to enter a web address that is similar to one that you entered previously, you should highlight the previously entered address, press the Menu key and select "Edit"

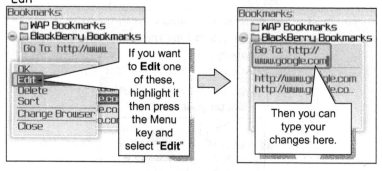

To Copy or Send the Web Page you are Viewing

1. Open the **Browser icon** and press the **Menu key**.
2. Scroll down to "**Page Address**" and click.
3. The web address is displayed in the window. Scroll down with the trackball for options.
   a. Scroll to "**Copy Address**" and click. This will copy the Web address to the clipboard and can easily be pasted into a Contact, an Email, a Memo or your Calendar.

b. Alternatively, scroll to "**Send Address**" and click. This will allow you to send the particular Web Address information via Email, MMS, SMS or PIN messaging. Just select the form and then the contact.

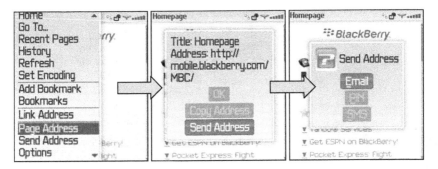

Setting and Naming Bookmarks (e.g. Local Weather)

One of the keys to great Web Browsing on your Pearl is the liberal use of Bookmarks. Your BlackBerry Pearl will come with a couple of bookmarks already set. It is very easy to customize your bookmarks to include all your web favorites for easy browsing.

TIP

You can instantly "**Find**" bookmarks by typing a few letters of the bookmark name – just like you lookup contacts in your Address Book. *Keep this in mind as you add new bookmarks.*

Adding And Naming Bookmarks

1. Open the Browser and use the "**Go To...**" command (or "." Shortcut key) to input a favorite Web Page. In this

example, we will choose www.weather.com

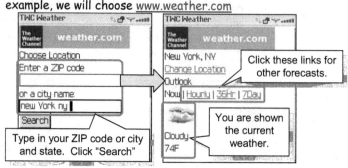

Type in your ZIP code or city and state. Click "Search"

Click these links for other forecasts.

You are shown the current weather.

2.   Once the page loads, press the Menu key and select "Add Bookmark" (or use the "?" Shortcut key).

3.   The Full name of the Web address is displayed. In this case you will probably see "TWC Weather" - you will want to re-name it (see below).

Edit the bookmark name here. Then click "Add"

4.   In this case (and most cases) we recommend changing the bookmark name to something short and unique.

(Note: if you bookmarked 4 different weather forecasts for NY, the 'default' bookmark names would all show up as "TWC Weather" - sort of useless if you want to get right to the "NY - 7 Day" forecast).

To rename the bookmark, you can press the "DEL" key to erase the entire thing. You can roll the trackball back to edit a particular section and save part of it. In this case, you could want to keep the word "Weather", but it might make the bookmark name too long to easily see on your screen. You'll need to experiment a little to find what works best.

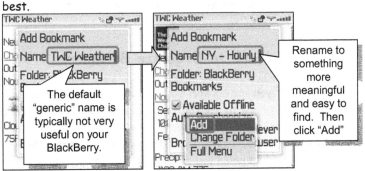

Keep these things in mind as you rename your bookmarks:

(a) **Make all bookmark names fairly short.** You will only see about the first 10-15 characters of the name in your list (because the screen is small).

15
Web
Browser

(b) **Make all bookmark names similar but unique.** For example if you were adding 4 bookmarks for the weather in New York or your area, you might want to name them:

"NY - Now",
"NY - 7 day",
"NY - 36 hour",
"NY - Hourly".

When you're done, you just type "NY" and instantly see all your weather bookmarks!

This way you can instantly locate all your forecasts by typing the letters "NY" in your bookmark list. Only those bookmarks with the letters "NY" will show up. (See image).

Using Folders to Organize Bookmarks

If you are careful about how you name your bookmarks, you may not need to use folders, but just use the "**Find**" feature in the bookmark list. However, if you like using folders to organize your bookmarks, we will show you how to use them. You can set folders when you are adding new bookmarks or change folders of bookmarks already on your list.

Setting a Folder when Adding A New Bookmark

1. First, navigate to the web page you want to add using the "**Go To...**" command ("." Shortcut key) as described above.
2. Then press the Add New Bookmark Shortcut key "?" to see the "**Add a Bookmark**" pop-up window.
3. Now, press the (after you have selected Press the Menu key and select "**Change Folder**" and click.

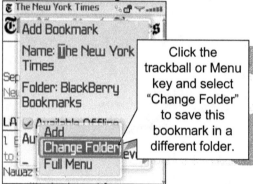

4. The available Web Folders will now be displayed.
5. Highlight the desired Folder and click the trackball.
6. You can either "**Select Folder**" to use the highlighted folder or "**Add Subfolder**" if you want to create a new folder.

Type your new Subfolder name and click "OK".

Then click the trackball on your new Subfolder name.

Notice your new folder is shown here.

Moving Existing Bookmarks to Different Folders

1. Highlight a bookmark in your list you wish to move to a different folder and then click the Menu key.
2. Select "Move Bookmark"
3. Roll the trackball up/down to move the bookmark to the correct folder.

Select the bookmark you want to move to a different folder and press the Menu key.

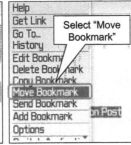

Select "Move Bookmark"

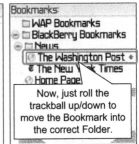

Now, just roll the trackball up/down to move the Bookmark into the correct Folder.

15
Web
Browser

Browser Options: See Bookmark List or Home Page

You might prefer to see the bookmark list rather than a "home page" when you open the Browser. The reason is simple: this will allow you to use the **"Find"** feature in the bookmark list to instantly locate the bookmark and click on it.

Benefits: It ends up being much faster to get to favorite web pages that are bookmarked like local weather (hourly, 7 day) or your favorite search engine ("Google").

Your Pearl may automatically open up to your Bookmarks list, but you may prefer to see a selected home page instead. You can use these instructions to make that change as well.

1. Click on the **Browser** icon.
2. Press the **Menu key** and select "**Options.**"
3. Click on "**Browser Configuration**"

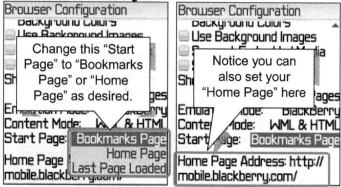

4. Roll all the way down to the "**Start Page**" near the bottom and click on the options. You will most likely see three options "**Bookmarks Page**" (list of bookmarks), "**Home Page**" (the web site you have listed as your home page, which you do on this screen) or "**Last Page Loaded**" (keeps the last web page in memory and brings it back up when you re-enter your Browser).

5. To select bookmark list, choose "**Bookmarks Page**" and make sure to "Save" your settings.

Using Your Bookmarks to Browse the Web

1. Click on your **Browser icon.**

2. If you don't see your Bookmark list automatically when you start your browser, press the **Menu key** and scroll down to "**Bookmarks**" and click.

3. TIP: Want to see your Bookmark List automatically? See the section called "Browser Options: See Bookmark List Or Home Page"

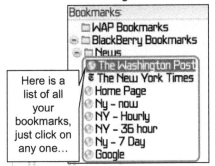

Here is a list of all your bookmarks, just click on any one...

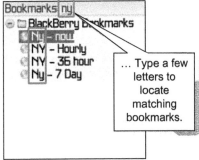

... Type a few letters to locate matching bookmarks.

4. All of your Bookmarks will be listed, including any 'default' bookmarks that were put there automatically by your phone company.

5. You might want to click on a particular folder to open all the bookmarks contained within or if you see the bookmark you need, just click on it.

6. However, if you have a lot of bookmarks, then you should use the "Find:" feature and type a few letters matching the bookmark you want to find.

7. See the image above – typing the letters "ny" will immediately "**Find**" all bookmarks with "ny" in the bookmark name.

8. Once you get familiar with your bookmark names, you can type a few letters and find exactly what you need.

Security Options for the Web Browser

Today, web security is a concern for anyone who browses the web on any kind of device.

The Pearl uses TLS (Transport Layer Security) or SSL (Secure Socket Layer) – two security protocols that jumble or encrypt your data. WTLS (Wireless Transport Layer Security) is another security option available.

Besides these settings here, if your BlackBerry is connected to a BlackBerry Enterprise Server ("BES"), you will also have the

15
Web
Browser

added security of Triple DES encryption (very strong encryption). There are ways, if necessary, to increase the security levels of the browser.

A full description of each of these security protocols is beyond the scope of this book. There are many great descriptions of security you can find by entering these security acronyms into your favorite web search engine. ("TLS, WTLS, Triple DES, SSL," etc.)

To change between TLS and WTLS security

1. Click on the "Options" icon from your Home Screen or applications menu.
2. Roll down and click on "Security Options"

3. Scroll first to "**TLS**" and click
4. Set the "**TLS Default**" to either "**Proxy**" (default) or "Handheld" and then click the trackball. If you are connected to a BlackBerry Enterprise Server, you should leave this as "**Proxy**" which allows you both Triple DES encryption and TLS or SSL.
5. Choose whether to allow HTTPS redirections or not by setting the available field to either "**Yes**" or "**No**." (The

default is "**No**.")

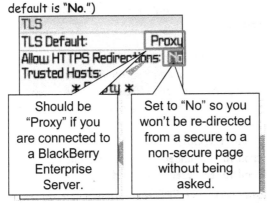

TLS

TLS Default:	Proxy
Allow HTTPS Redirections:	No
Trusted Hosts:	

* Security *

Should be "Proxy" if you are connected to a BlackBerry Enterprise Server.

Set to "No" so you won't be re-directed from a secure to a non-secure page without being asked.

6. To change WTLS options, save your settings for TLS and then select "**WTLS**" from the "**Security Options**" Screen follow step 1 and scroll to WTLS and click

7. Highlight "**Encryption Strength**" and click and change setting to "**Strong Only**" or "**Allow Weak**."

8. Select "**Yes**" in the "**Prompt for Server Trust**" field.

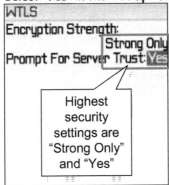

WTLS

Encryption Strength:

Strong Only

Prompt For Server Trust: Yes

Highest security settings are "Strong Only" and "Yes"

"Pushing" Web Content to the Pearl

There are two main ways of viewing web content on the Pearl. You can go visit a site and "**Pull**" content into your browser by visiting a page and loading the most current content. Or, you can set the Pearl to periodically poll various web sites and "**Push**" content directly to your device. With "**Push**" content, just click on an icon in your desktop to view the content that was "Pushed" to the Pearl.

Enabling "Browser Push"

NOTE: You may not need to change these push settings. Often the default settings from your phone company will work. Only follow these steps if the Browser Push applications are not working.

1. Click on the **Options** icon.
2. Scroll to "**Advanced Options**" and click.
3. Scroll to "**Browser Push**" and click.
4. Either click the trackball or press the **SPACE key** to check the first three checkboxes to enable Push content to be sent to the Pearl. Depending you your carrier (phone company), most of these settings shown should be default settings.

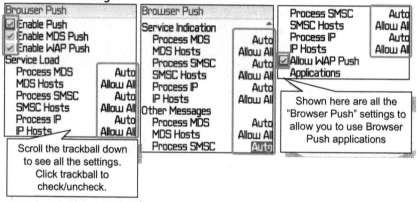

Adding Push Content to your Device
(NOTE: Each Carrier/Phone Company is slightly different)

WEB SITE DISCLAIMER: As with all web sites, they change frequently. The web site images you see below may look the same on your BlackBerry, or may look totally different. If they look different, please try to look for links with approximately the same name.

1. Start your **Web Browser** on the Pearl as you normally would.

2. Press the **Menu key**, select **"Go To..."** and enter http://mobile.blackberry.com/ (TIP: This may be set as your home page.)

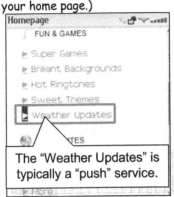

The "Weather Updates" is typically a "push" service.

3. Scroll down and click on **"Weather Updates"**

4. Accept the Push services Data Disclaimer and click the trackball.

15
Web
Browser

5. If you see an error message saying something about "This service is only available with the BlackBerry Internet Browsing Service...", then you need to press your ESCAPE key and look for an **"Internet Browser"** and try step 1 again.

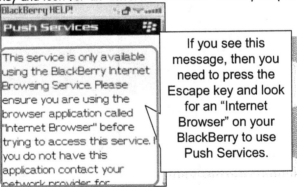

If you see this message, then you need to press the Escape key and look for an "Internet Browser" on your BlackBerry to use Push Services.

6. Various Push serviced will be available to you. Click **"Add"** on the service you wish to subscribe to.

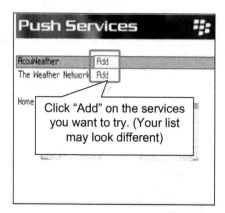

7. Click "**Subscribe**" on the next screen and the data will automatically begin being "Pushed" to your Device.

8. Below is an example of the "**AccuWeather**" site once it's configured to work on your BlackBerry.

Search with Yahoo! Mobile

Yahoo!, like most of the other big search engines, does have a mobile version of its search site. The web site 'senses' you are viewing it from your small BlackBerry browser adjusts to a 'scaled-down' version that gives you most of the functionality on a smaller screen.

How to get access? Go to www.yahoomobile.com from your BlackBerry web browser.

What is the pricing? Free

Search with Google

Google also has a mobile version that loads quickly and is quite useful on your BlackBerry. To get there, just go to www.google.com in your BlackBerry web browser. We highly recommend creating easy-to-use bookmarks this and all your favorite web sites (Learn more on page 317). Just like on your computer, type in your search string and hit the ENTER key (saves time from rolling and clicking on the "Search" button). If you wanted to find and even call pizza restaurants in a certain zip code or city, then you would type in "pizza (and your zip code or city)" See below.

15
Web
Browser

Type in your search and hit the ENTER key.

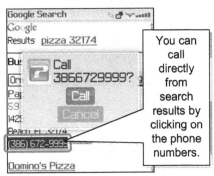

You can call directly from search results by clicking on the phone numbers.

Finding Things Using Google Maps

Later in this book, we describe in detail how to obtain and use Google Maps on your BlackBerry. Please go to page 382.

Web Browser Tips and Tricks

There are some helpful shortcuts to help you navigate the Web faster and easier. We have included a few for you below:

1. To insert a **period "."** in the web address in the "**Go To...**" dialog box, press the **SPACE key**.

2. To insert a **forward slash "/"** in the "Go To" dialog box, hold the **SHIFT key** and press the **SPACE key**.

3. To open the **Bookmark list** from a web page, press 5.

4. To **Add a Bookmark** from a web page, press the **question mark "?"** Key.

5. To view a thumbnail version of a web page, press "**X**." To return to the normal view, press any key.

6. To stop loading a web page, press the **ESCAPE key**.

7. To "**Go To...**" to a specific web page, press the **period "."** key.

8. To hide the banner on a web page, press the exclamation point "! " key. To view the banner on a web page, press the exclamation point "! " key again.

9. To close a browser, press and hold the **ESCAPE key**.

Section 5: Multi-Media Features of the Pearl

Working with the Camera and Pictures

Chapter Contents:

- Camera Features and Buttons
- Setting the Flash Mode
- Setting the Size of the Picture
- Adjusting the Picture Quality
- Adjusting White Balance
- Using the Zoom
- Managing Picture storage
- Using the Optional Media Card
- Viewing Pictures Stored in Memory
- Transferring pictures using Desktop Manager

Using the Camera

Your BlackBerry Pearl is the first ever BlackBerry to come equipped with a camera. A camera might be problematic for security reasons for the business user - but for consumers, a camera is a great feature. The Pearl includes a feature-rich 1.3 or 2.0 mega pixel camera (depends on which BlackBerry Pearl model you have). At publishing time the camera resolution for the 8100 BlackBerry Pearl is 1.3 mega pixels, but the new 8130

Pearl with 2.0 mega pixels was just being released. There may even be further improvements to camera resolution over time.

Camera Features and Buttons

You can get as involved as you want in your picture taking with the Pearl. Every feature of your photo is configurable. Before we do that, however, let's get familiar with the main buttons and features.

Starting the Camera Application
The Camera can be started in one of two ways:

Option #1: The right side convenience key
1. Unless you have re-programmed your convenience key (See page 48 for details), then pressing the right side key will start your camera – the one directly below the volume control buttons.
2. Push this button once, and the Camera should be started.

Press this right convenience key to start the Camera. (Unless you re-programmed it.)

16
Camera &
Pictures

Click on your
Camera Icon

Option #2: The Camera Icon

1. Navigate to your "Applications" Menu and click. Scroll to the Camera Icon and click.
2. The Camera application is now active.

Icons in the Camera Screen

Usually, when you open the Camera application either the last picture you took is in the window or the Camera is active. Underneath the picture window are five icons.

The "Take a Picture" icon

1. Click on the picture of a Camera
   - Frame your subject in the viewfinder (the screen) and Click the trackball to take a picture.

The Trash Can

Sometimes, the picture you take might not be what you want. Simply scroll to the Trash Can and click. The last picture taken will then be deleted.

1. Click on the Trash Can with the picture you wish to delete on the screen.
2. Confirm that you desire to delete the picture.

Click to Take **New Picture**

Click to **Delete**

Click to **Set as Caller ID** or **Home Screen Image**

Click to **Save** or **Change Name** of picture

Default **Picture Name**

Click to **Email, MMS,** or send to **BlackBerry Messenger Contact**

The "Save" Icon

1. With the picture you desire to save on the screen, click on the folder under the Camera icon.

2. In the dialogue box, click "Save" or "Cancel" or click on the folder icon to specify a new location. We recommend using the Media Card if you have one installed.

16
Camera & Pictures

The "Set as" or "Crop" Icon

1. Next to the Trash Can is a "Set As" Icon. Click on it and a dialogue box pops up.

Here is an image as background for the **Home Screen**

Go, Dog, Go!

2. You can use the picture in the main window as a picture caller ID for one of your people in your Address Book by

selecting the "Set as Caller ID" button.

3. You can also set that picture as a background image for your Home Screen (Like "desktop background image" on your computer) by clicking "**Set as Home Screen Image**."

Sending Pictures with the "Email" Envelope Icon

There are several ways to send your pictures via email. The Camera application contains this handy Icon which lets you email the picture on your screen quickly to one of your contacts.

1. Click the "Envelope" Icon which brings up the email dialogue box.

2. Click one of the three options:
    *   Send as MMS – Multi Media Message (as body of email) – Learn all about MMS on page 277
    *   Send to Messenger Contact (This option may not be available if you have not yet setup BlackBerry Messenger – see page 288 for details)
    *   Send as Email (Attached to an email as an image file)

3. Navigate to the contact you desire and click the trackball. Continue sending the message.

Setting the Flash Mode

One of the nice features of the BlackBerry Pearl Camera is the inclusion of a Flash. Just like with most digital cameras, you can adjust the properties of the Flash.

Changing Flash Mode for current Picture

1. With your subject framed in the **Camera** window, press the **SPACE key**.

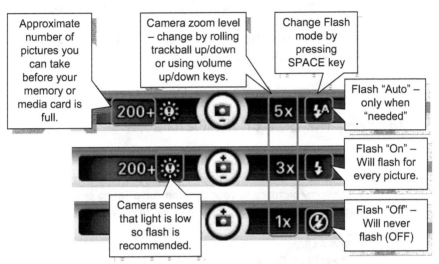

2. Look in the lower right hand corner of the screen and the current flash mode will be displayed.
3. The three available modes are:
   a. "Automatic" indicated by an "A"
   b. "On" indicated by the Flash symbol
   c. "Off" indicated by the No Flash symbol

16
Camera & Pictures

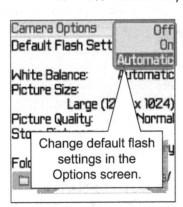

Changing the Default Flash Mode

1. When in the **Camera**, press the Menu key and select "**Options**"
2. Use the trackball and highlight the **Default Flash Settings** in the upper right hand corner.
3. Select from "**Off**", "**On**" or "**Automatic**" (the default).
4. Press the **Menu key** and "**Save**" your settings.

Adjusting the Size of the Picture

The size of your pictures corresponds to the number of pixels or dots used to render the image. If you tend to transfer your BlackBerry pictures to your desktop for printing or emailing, you might want a bigger or smaller picture to work with.

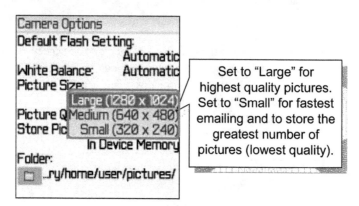

1. From the camera screen press the Menu key and select "Options."
2. Scroll down to Picture Size and select the size of your picture; Small, Medium or Large.
3. Press the Menu key and "Save" your settings.

TIP: If you email your pictures, then you will be able to send them faster if you set your picture size to Small.

Adjusting the White Balance

Usually the automatic white balance works fairly well, however, there may be times when you want to manually control it. In this case you would select from the manual options for White Balance in the same Camera Options screen.

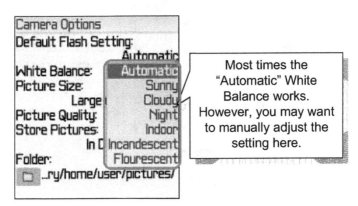

Most times the "Automatic" White Balance works. However, you may want to manually adjust the setting here.

Adjusting the Picture Quality

16
Camera & Pictures

While the Pearl is not meant to replace a 7 or 8 mega pixel camera, it is a very capable photo device. There are times when you might need or desire the change the picture quality. Perhaps you are using your Pearl camera for work and need to capture an important image. Fortunately, it is quite easy to adjust the quality of your photos. Realize, however, that **increasing the quality or the size will increase the memory requirements for that particular picture.**

In one "non-scientific" test, changing the picture quality resulted in the following changes to the file size of the picture at a fixed size setting of "Large (1280 x 1024)":
    Normal: 32.2k image file size
    Fine: 38.7k (20% larger than "Normal")
    Superfine: 47.2k (47% larger than "Normal")

1. Start your **Camera**.

2. Press the **Menu key**, select "**Options**"
3. Scroll to "**Picture Quality**."
4. The choices "**Normal**," "**Fine**" and "**Superfine**" will be available. Just click on the desired quality, press the Menu key and save your settings.

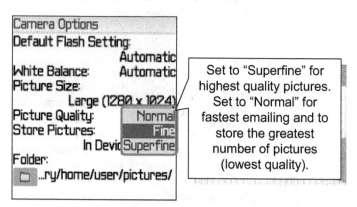

Set to "Superfine" for highest quality pictures. Set to "Normal" for fastest emailing and to store the greatest number of pictures (lowest quality).

Using the Zoom

As with many cameras, the Pearl gives you the opportunity to zoom in or out of your subject. Zooming on the Pearl could not be easier.

1. Frame your picture and gently roll up on the trackball. The Camera will **Zoom** in on the subject.

Roll trackball up / down to change zoom level between 1x, 3x and 5x.

2. The Zoom level will be displayed to the right of the "camera" icon with a **1x**, **3x** or **5x** indicating the power of

zoom chosen.

3. To Zoom back out, just roll the trackball down.

Managing Picture Storage

The authors strongly recommend buying a MicroSD Media Card
for use in your Pearl. Prices are under US$20 for a 1.0 GB card
(and may be under $50 for a 4.0 GB card) which is very low
compared to the price of your Pearl. For more information on
inserting the media card, please see page 49. See below for help
on storing pictures on the media card.

If you do not have a media card, then you will want to carefully
manage the amount of your BlackBerry's main "Device Memory"
that is used for pictures.

Selecting Where Pictures are Stored

The default setting is for the Pearl to store pictures in main
Device Memory, but if you have a Media Card inserted, we
recommend selecting that instead.

1. To confirm the default picture storage location, press the
    Menu key from the main **Camera** screen and scroll to
    "**Options**" and click.
2. Scroll down to the "**Store Pictures**" and select "**On Media
    Card**" if you have one, or "**In Device Memory**" if you do not
    have a media card.

16
Camera &
Pictures

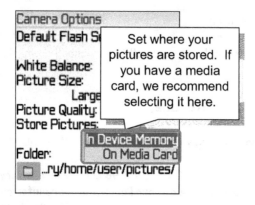

3. Look at the folder icon at the bottom and make sure the folder name ends in the word "**/pictures**". This will help keep pictures together with pictures, videos with videos, music with music, and make it easier when you want to transfer pictures to and from your computer.

To limit memory storage for pictures in the Device Memory:
It is a good idea to set a limit for how much of your BlackBerry's internal "Device Memory" is reserved for picture storage. NOTE: This does not affect how much memory you can use on your media card.

1. From your Home Screen, click on the **Media** icon.

2. Click on "**Pictures**" then press the Menu key and select "**Options**".

3. The bottom line should read "Reserved Pictures Memory" and can be adjusted from 0mb to 12mb. Just choose the amount of space you would like to reserve for pictures. Generally, 2mb should be sufficient and will allow additional memory to be freed up for your other needs like, email,

contacts, calendar, and important things like games.

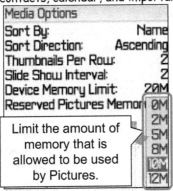

Using the Optional Media Card

At publishing time, your BlackBerry can support up to a 4.0 GB "gigabytes" Micro SD Media Card. Rumors are around that this may increase to 16 or 32 MB sometime in 2008. To give you some perspective, a 4.0 GB card can store over 60 times the 64MB ("megabytes") of memory that comes with the device. This is equivalent to several full length feature films and thousands of songs. At this beginning of this book we detailed how to install the Media Card. Verify your card is installed as described in Chapter 1 on page 49. Since program files can only be stored in Main memory, we recommend putting as much of your Media files on the Micro SD card as possible.

16
Camera &
Pictures

To store Pictures on the Media Card
1. Navigate to the main screen of the **Camera** application and press the **Menu key** and scroll to "**Options**" and click.
2. Change the option in the "**Store Pictures**" field to "**On Media Card**."
3. The folder below should change automatically to the Pictures folder on the Media Card.

To see available storage space on Media Card

1. Click on the **Options** icon from your Home Screen, Settings or Application menu.
2. Click on "Advanced Options", then click on "Media Card" and you should see a screen similar to the one below.
3. The bottom line tells you how much free space remains on the Media Card.

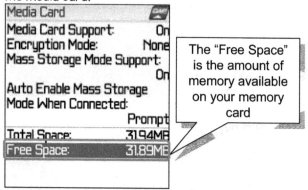

Encryption of Your Media Card (.rem file extension)

Very Important: If you have turned on encryption of your Media in your Options Screen (either device or password security or both), then every new picture you take with your BlackBerry camera will have a **.jpg.rem** file extension indicating that file is encrypted.

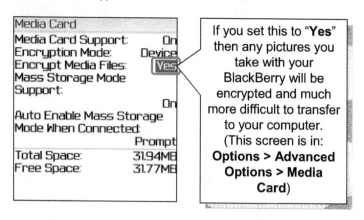

How do you view the encrypted picture files?
You can view them any time from your Pearl.

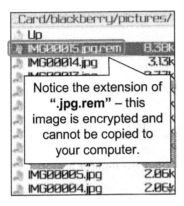

Notice the extension of ".jpg.rem" – this image is encrypted and cannot be copied to your computer.

How do you transfer these ".rem" encrypted files?
You can send these files via Bluetooth one-by-one or you can email them one-by-one, but you cannot (as of publishing time) transfer them using Mass Storage Mode – drag and drop to your computer, nor can you transfer them using the Windows™ Desktop Manager Software nor any of the Apple Mac™ software for transferring media. These files are "Locked" to the media card for security purposes.

16
Camera &
Pictures

<u>Warning</u>: Be aware that enabling your Media Card encryption and Media encryption will make it much more difficult to share the pictures that you take with your BlackBerry camera.

Viewing Pictures stored in Memory

There are two primary ways one would view their stored pictures.

Option #1: Viewing from the Camera program

1. Open up the Camera application and press the Menu key

2. Scroll down to "View Pictures" and navigate to the appropriate folder to view your pictures.

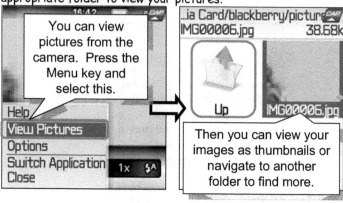

Option #2: Viewing from the Media menu

1. Navigate to the Media icon and click.
2. Scroll to **"Pictures"** and click. Your initial options will be **"Media Card," "Preloaded Media"** and **"Device Memory."**

Click on the Media icon.

Click her to locate your pictures.

Then click on the folder icons to find your pictures.

3. Click the appropriate folder and navigate to your pictures.

To view a Slide Show

1. Follow the steps above and press the **Menu key** when you are in your picture directory.
2. Scroll to **"View Slideshow"** and click.

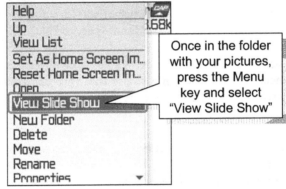

Once in the folder with your pictures, press the Menu key and select "View Slide Show"

16
Camera & Pictures

Adding Pictures to Contacts for Caller ID

As discussed previously, you can assign a picture as a "Caller ID" for your contacts. Please check out our detailed explanation on starting on page 153.

Transferring Pictures To or From Your Pearl

There are a few ways to get pictures you have taken on your Pearl off it and transfer pictures taken elsewhere onto the Pearl.

Method 1: Send via Email, Multi-Media Messaging, or BlackBerry Messenger. You can email or send pictures immediately after you take them on your camera by clicking the "Envelope" icon as shown on page 336. You may also send pictures when you are viewing them in your Media application. Click the Menu key and look for menu items related to sending pictures.

Method 2: Transfer using Bluetooth. If you want to transfer pictures to/from your computer (assuming it has Bluetooth capabilities), you can. We explain exactly how to get this done in the Bluetooth chapter on page 308.

Method 3: Transfer to your computer using desktop software Transferring pictures and other media to your computer is handled using the Media section of your desktop software. On a Windows computer, this software is called "BlackBerry Desktop Manager" on an Apple computer, the software may be called "PocketMac for the BlackBerry™" or "The Missing Sync for BlackBerry." To learn how to use these programs, please see instructions that start on page 351.

Method 4: Transfer using "Mass Storage Mode" This assumes you have stored your pictures on a media card. (What's a media card? See page 49.) The first time you connect your BlackBerry to your computer, you will probably see a "Turn on Mass Storage Mode?" question. If you answer "Yes", then your Media Card looks just like another hard disk to your computer (just like a USB Flash Drive). Then you can drag and drop pictures to/from your BlackBerry and your Computer. For more details see page 357.

"Mass Storage Mode" and the Media Manager

IMPORTANT: "Mass Storage Mode" must be "On" for the Media Manager in BlackBerry Desktop Manager to view the files that are stored on your BlackBerry Media Card. You can turn on or off Mass Storage mode by going into your "Options" Icon, Selecting "Media Card" (If you don't see it, then click on "Advanced Options" to find it). Inside the Media Card settings you need to set "Mass Storage Mode Support" to "On." TIP: Select "Yes" for "Auto Enable Mass Storage Mode When Connected" to avoid being asked every time.

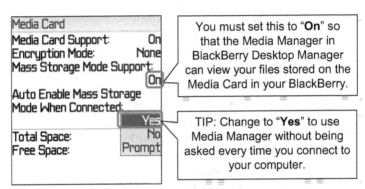

You must set this to "On" so that the Media Manager in BlackBerry Desktop Manager can view your files stored on the Media Card in your BlackBerry.

TIP: Change to "Yes" to use Media Manager without being asked every time you connect to your computer.

16
Camera &
Pictures

Camera Tips and Tricks

1. To see how many remaining pictures you can store in memory, just look at the lower left hand corner in the main

   Approximate number of pictures you can take before your memory or media card is full.

   Camera screen.

2. To take a picture, press the right "**Convenience**" key.
3. To zoom the camera in, press the "**Volume Up**" key.
4. To zoom the camera out, press the "**Volume Down**" key.

Working with Music and Videos

Chapter Contents:

Working with Music and Videos

One of the things that sets the Pearl apart from earlier BlackBerry devices is the inclusion of Multi-Media capabilities and the ability to expand memory with the use of a media card. The Pearl comes pre-loaded with a capable music and video player. We expect RIM, BlackBerry's maker, to continue to improve the Pearl's media capabilities. In fact, during the writing of this book, some improvements have already been made with the media transfer capabilities in the Media Manager software within BlackBerry Desktop software. At time of publishing, media software from Roxio (a well known name in the media industry) was already included as the Media Manager component in Desktop Manager software.

While some of the most popular formats of digital media are supported, you may have to take some steps to get all your music and videos working on the Pearl.

With a 4.0 GB media card, the media capabilities of the Pearl, one might even suggest:
Why do I need an iPhone or iPod?
I've got a BlackBerry Pearl!

Adding Music, Videos, and Pictures to the Pearl

The Pearl makes it possible for you to leave your iPod or other MP3 player at home and load your BlackBerry instead with lots of your favorite music and videos. As mentioned previously, we strongly recommend buying a Micro SD storage card – at least 1.0 GB of storage space, but 2.0 GB or 4.0 GB is even better. You can certainly add music without a storage card, but you will be extremely limited in the number of songs you can transfer.

Transferring Media using BlackBerry Desktop Manager (Windows™)

Why use Desktop Manager instead of the drag and drop with "Mass Storage" mode (page 357) or Bluetooth file transfer? Two main reasons:
(1) It's easier to use, especially for more than one file
(2) The Media Manager in Desktop Manager has an automatic file conversion feature that will convert and/or re-size many media files (songs, videos, images) so that they will be viewable and playable on your BlackBerry Pearl.

Microsoft Windows™ computer users, need to use BlackBerry Desktop Manager Software to transfer media – pictures, songs, videos and ringtones - to and from the BlackBerry Pearl.

If you need help getting the latest version of BlackBerry Desktop Manager installed, then please see our instructions on page 127.

NOTE: If you have enabled Password Security for your device and/or Password Security for your Media Card, then you will have to type your password on your BlackBerry and on your computer in order to connect to it from your computer.

1. Connect your BlackBerry to your computer with the USB cable or Bluetooth and start the Desktop Manager program. If your Desktop Manager does not looks like image below, then you will need to upgrade to the latest version by following the steps found on page 95. (Unless you work at an organization that supplied your BlackBerry to you - then please contact your **Help Desk** before you try to install any software on your computer.)

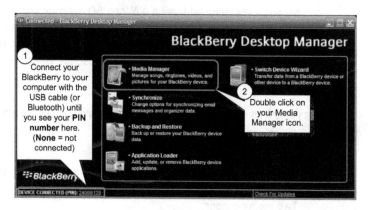

2. Double click on the **Media Manager** icon.

    If you see an error message like the one below "**ERROR: BlackBerry not ready.**" and you do have a Media Card (Micro SD Card) inserted, then you need to turn on "Mass Storage Mode" on your BlackBerry. See how to turn on "**Mass Storage Mode**" on page 357.

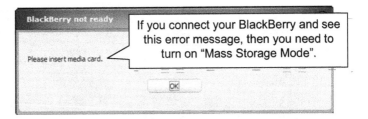

If you connect your BlackBerry and see this error message, then you need to turn on "Mass Storage Mode".

Your **Media Manager** should look similar to this image below.

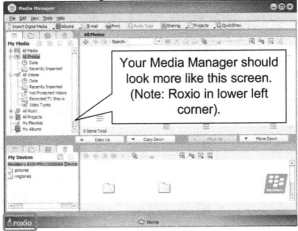

Your Media Manager should look more like this screen. (Note: Roxio in lower left corner).

3. In the default layout, the first time you open up the Media Manager, the top portion of the screen, called the top "window pane" shows files on your PC and the bottom "pane" shows media files on your BlackBerry.

17
Music &
Video

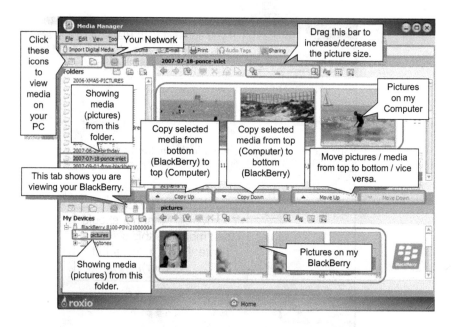

To change what is shown on the top or bottom panes in your Media Manager, just click the 4 tabs in the left column: "**Media (on your PC)**", "**Folders (on your PC)**", "**Network (Shared media on your local network)**", and "**Mobile Device (Media on Your BlackBerry)**"

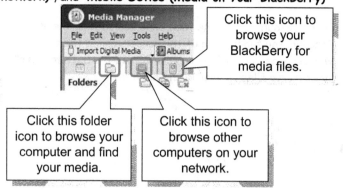

You can drag the slider bar above the pictures/media to increase or

decrease their size

Select multiple pictures/media files in a group by dragging a box around them with your mouse.

Select individual pictures/media files by holding down the Control key on your Windows™ computer keyboard and clicking on individual files.

Click to select pictures/songs /video. Selected pictures are shown with a yellow border around them.

This picture is not selected.

2007-07-18-ponce-...012.jpg   2007-07-18-ponce-...013.jpg

To move or copy media files (music, pictures or videos) from your computer to your BlackBerry.

1. Select the media files in the "Computer" folder (usually the top 'pane') by clicking on individual files, dragging a box around a group or holding the Control key and clicking on individual files.

2. Make sure the bottom pane is in correct folder for the type of media you are copying (e.g. "Music", "Ringtones", "Videos" or "Pictures".) If you have a Media Card Installed, navigate to the media folder under the **[Media Card]** folder. If you don't have the media card installed then you will go to the media folder under **[Device Memory]**.

3. Click on the "Copy Down" button as shown.

4. Select whether or not the media (pictures) should be converted, usually the default is fine, and click OK.

17
Music &
Video

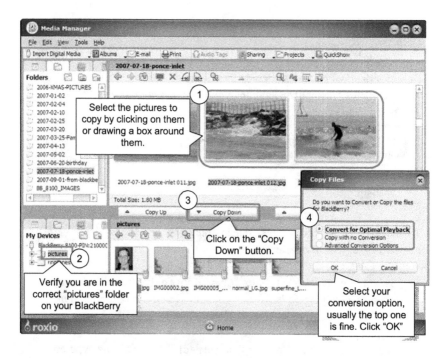

NOTE: You have the choice of "**COPY**" or "**MOVE**"
"**COPY**" will place a copy of the files to the destination pane, and leave them alone in the source pane.
"**MOVE**" will copy the files then erase them from the source pane.

Once you have completed the copy to your BlackBerry, you will see the media files in the BlackBerry pane. And, once you disconnect your BlackBerry, you will also see the media files on your BlackBerry Pearl in the Media icon under the "pictures" folder.

When completed, you see your media copied down here.

... and it's now available for you in the Media icon in your BlackBerry!

You can use a similar technique to copy or move pictures that you have taken on your BlackBerry to your Computer.

Transfer Media using "Mass Storage Mode" (Windows or Mac)

This works whether you have a Windows or a Mac computer. We will show images for the Windows computer process, and it will be fairly similar for your Mac.

17
Music & Video

This transfer method assumes you have stored your media on a MicroSD media card in your BlackBerry. (What's a media card? See page 49.)

1. Make sure your Media Card "**Mass Storage**" mode support is "**On**" and other settings are as shown below. To get to this screen, go into your **Options** icon, then "**Advanced Options**",

then "**Media Card.**"

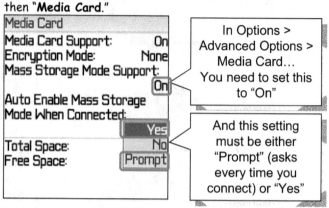

In Options >
Advanced Options >
Media Card…
You need to set this
to "On"

And this setting
must be either
"Prompt" (asks
every time you
connect) or "Yes"

2. Now, connect your BlackBerry to your computer with the USB cable. If you selected "Prompt" above, you will see a "Turn on Mass Storage Mode?"

question. Answer that "**Yes**" (You may want to check the box that says "Don't Ask Me Again"). When you answer "Yes", then your Media Card looks just like another hard disk to your computer (similar to a USB Flash Drive). If you set the "Auto Enable Mass Storage Mode" setting to "Yes" – then you won't be asked this question, the media card on the BlackBerry will automatically look like a "Mass Storage" device.

IMPORTANT

For the newest version of BlackBerry Desktop Manager (v4.3 at publishing time) you need to have "**Mass Storage Mode**" enabled or turned **ON**, otherwise you cannot see the files on your BlackBerry media card using BlackBerry Desktop Manager's Media Manager. *NOTE: This was not the case with some previous versions of Desktop Manager.*

3. After your BlackBerry is connected and in "Mass Storage" mode, just open up your computer's file management software. On your Windows™, press the Windows key + "E" to open Windows Explorer or on your Mac™ start your Finder.

4. Look for another hard disk that has been added. In the image below you see "**Removable Disk (G:)**" – that is the BlackBerry media card. Then navigate to the media type you want (movies, pictures, etc.) and just drag and drop or copy the pictures between your BlackBerry and you computer as you normally do with other files on your computer.

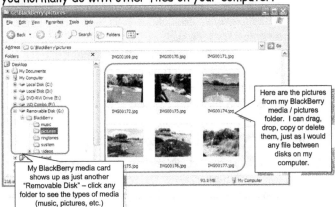

Here are the pictures from my BlackBerry media / pictures folder. I can drag, drop, copy or delete them, just as I would any file between disks on my computer.

My BlackBerry media card shows up as just another "Removable Disk" – click any folder to see the types of media (music, pictures, etc.)

17
Music & Video

5. To copy pictures from your BlackBerry, select the files from the "**BlackBerry / pictures**" folder. Then draw a box around the pictures, or click on one and press "**Ctrl+A**" to select them all. Or hold the Ctrl key down and click on individual pictures to select them. Once selected – right click on one of the selected pictures and select "**Cut**" (to move) or "**Copy**"

(to copy).

6. Then click on any other disk/folder - like "My Documents" and navigate to where you want to move / copy the files. Once there, right click again in the right window where all the files are listed and select "**Paste**"

7. You can also delete all the pictures / media / songs from your BlackBerry in a similar manner. Navigate to the BlackBerry / (media type) folder like "BlackBerry / videos" - Press "**Ctrl + A**" on your computer keyboard to select all the files then press the Delete key on your keyboard to delete all the files.

8. You can also copy files from your computer to your BlackBerry using a similar method. Just go to the files you want to copy, select (highlight them). Then right-click "Copy" and paste them into the correct "BlackBerry / (media type)" folder.

IMPORTANT: Not all media (videos), pictures (images), or songs will be playable/viewable on your BlackBerry - if you use a desktop software such as Desktop Manager (for Windows) to transfer the files, they will be automatically converted for you. (See page 351 for details) You can use the "Missing Sync for BlackBerry" software for the Mac to transfer files (but we are not certain that this software does Media 'auto' conversion.)

Transferring Media using Bluetooth and Mass Storage Mode on a Windows™ Computer

There are two ways to transfer files using Bluetooth to a Windows PC: (1) "Mass Storage Mode" - where your BlackBerry Media Card looks just like another hard disk and you can drag and drop files or (2) Transfer one file at a time using the Bluetooth "Send and Receive" mode.

IMPORTANT: Your Windows PC must have Bluetooth capabilities to accept the connection from the BlackBerry.

Transfer a group of files with Bluetooth

When transferring media files using Bluetooth and Mass Storage Mode, you can only transfer files to and from your media card in your BlackBerry. This is usually not a problem, because typically you would store all your media on the card since they take up too much space on the main memory of the BlackBerry. To do this, you need to "Pair" or establish a Bluetooth connection between your BlackBerry and PC. (See page 303). Once your BlackBerry is connected or "paired" with your computer, then just follow the same directions as shown on page 357, except your connection to the BlackBerry is via Bluetooth instead of the USB cable.

Transfer A Single File with Bluetooth (Mac or Windows)

You can transfer files between your Mac™ or Windows™ computer and your BlackBerry, or between BlackBerry devices using **Bluetooth file transfer**. Note that some Bluetooth file transfer capabilities may be turned off altogether by your BlackBerry administrator or limited to only certain file types (ringtones).

IMPORTANT: If you are transferring a file using Bluetooth, the receiving device (computer or BlackBerry) must be in "**Receive using Bluetooth**" mode, otherwise the file transfer will fail. This is not intuitive and causes problems for most people the first time they try to transfer files using Bluetooth. Unlike a 'drag and drop' file transfer, you have to do a second step to accept the file being transferred. This is done for security purposes.

17
Music &
Video

First, Pair your BlackBerry with the device with which you want to transfer files. (See page 303)

To transfer from your computer to your BlackBerry:

1. Go into the correct media type folder on your BlackBerry media card – e.g. "videos" for videos, "music" for music, "pictures" for pictures. Now press the menu key and select "Receive using Bluetooth" from the menu.

TROUBLESHOOTING: If you don't see this menu item, then you need to turn on Bluetooth (page 303) and then pair your BlackBerry to your computer (page 303).

2.   Select the media file on your computer and right click on it and "Send using Bluetooth" or on a Mac follow the commands to send a file using Bluetooth.

TROUBLESHOOTING: If you see a "**file transfer error**" message on your computer, then it is likely that you may have forgotten to set the "**Receive using Bluetooth**" on the destination device where you are copying your files (either your computer or your BlackBerry).

3.   Finally, you may be asked to confirm the receipt of the files on your BlackBerry.

To transfer from your BlackBerry to your Computer:
1.   After pairing your BlackBerry with your Computer (see page 303), you need to set your computer in "Receive Using Bluetooth" mode.

2.   Go into the correct media type folder on your BlackBerry media card – e.g. "videos" for videos, "music" for music, "pictures" for pictures. Select the media file you want to transfer to your computer by highlighting it with the trackball. Now press the menu key and select "Send using Bluetooth" from the menu.

TROUBLESHOOTING: If you don't see this "**Send using Bluetooth**" menu option, then you may not have Bluetooth turned on or your device "paired" (see page 303).

3.   Finally, you may be asked to confirm the receipt of the file on your computer and where you want to save it.

Storing Music on the Micro SD Card

The BlackBerry Pearl comes with 64 MB of memory, and some of that is taken up with the OS and other pre-loaded programs. Since program files must be stored on the device itself, your storage card is really only for music, picture and video. Putting all your music on the Memory Card or Media Card will help keep your program memory free on the Pearl. Follow the steps above to transfer your music from your PC to the Pearl.

Finding your Music when you use a Memory Card

Assuming you have followed the steps above, your music is now on your Micro SD card. Now, you want to play your music – so what do you do?

1. From your Home Screen of icons, press the **Menu key** to see your "**Applications**" menu and click on the **Media** icon.

2. Click on the "**Music**" icon to view your songs.

3. The available music folders are now displayed. Click on the appropriate folder (if your music is on a Media Card, click that folder) and all of your music will now be displayed.

4. Click on any song to start playing it.

Using Playlists (Folders)

Many MP3 players utilize playlists to organize music and allow for a unique "mix" of songs. On the Pearl, the playlist function is handled through the creation of "Folders." Each folder can have a unique name and contain a grouping of songs just like a playlist.

What types of music are supported on the Pearl? See page 366.

To create unique music folders using Desktop Manager or Mass Storage Mode

1. Connect your Pearl to your computer using either the **Desktop Manager** (Windows only) or **"Mass Storage Mode"** (Windows or Mac) if you are using a Mac as shown earlier in this chapter.

2. Navigate to the BlackBerry in the Media Manager (Desktop Manager) or the BlackBerry "Removable Disk" in your File Manager software on your computer.

3. Create new folders in the BlackBerry/Music folder by right-clicking the mouse and selecting "New Folder" or using the "New Folder" command on your Mac - name this folder your playlist name. Repeat this for how many folders you would like to create.

To move music into your new folders

1. Simply highlight the music you want and either "cut and paste" into the new folder or "copy and paste" if you want the music files to be part of more than one folder

To create unique music folders from the Pearl itself

1. Open your **Media** icon on the Pearl. Click on Music and navigate to the folder where you want to create new 'sub-

folders.'

2. When you see the list of your music, press the Menu key and scroll to **"New Folder"** and click.

3. Type in a name for the new folder.

To Move Music into the new folder
1. Scroll through your music on the Pearl and **highlight the song you wish to move.**
2. Press the **Menu key** and scroll to "**Move**" and click.
3. In the next window, navigate to the new folder you wish to move the song into and click the trackwheel to complete the "**Move**."

Playing your Music

Once your music is in the right place, you are ready to start enjoying the benefit of having your music on your Pearl – with you at all times.

Playing an individual song
1. Navigate to your **Media** icon and click. Then, click on the **Music** icon and find the song you desire to play and click.

2. The Music Player will open and your song will begin to play.

3. Clicking the trackball will pause the player or continue playback.

   TIP: Pressing the **MUTE key** will also pause or resume playback.

4. The volume keys on the side of the Pearl control the song volume.

Playing all your music or an entire folder
1. Navigate to your music as above and highlight the first song in the folder you wish to play. If you have not set up individual folders, just highlight the first song – then press the **Menu key**.
2. Scroll down to either "**Play All**" or "**Play Folder**" and the music player will begin to play all the songs in that particular folder.

To "Shuffle" your songs in that folder
1. Navigate to the first song in your folder and press the menu key. Click on "Play all."

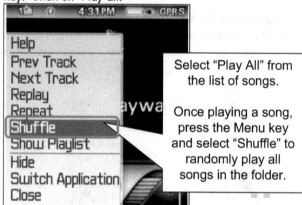

Select "Play All" from the list of songs.

Once playing a song, press the Menu key and select "Shuffle" to randomly play all songs in the folder.

2. The Music Player will launch. Press the Menu key again and scroll to "Shuffle" and click.

Supported Music Types

The BlackBerry Pearl will play most types of music files. If you are an iPod user, all music except the music that you purchased on iTunes should be able to play on the Pearl.

The most common audio/music formats supported are:

1. ACC - audio compression formats AAC,

2. AAC+, and EAAC+ AMR - Adaptive Multi Rate-Narrow Band (AMR-NB) speech coder standard
3. MIDI - Polyphonic MIDI
4. MP3 - encoded using MPEG
5. WAV - supports sample rates of 8 kHz, 16 kHz, 22.05 kHz, 32 kHz, 44.1 kHz, and 48 kHz with 8-bit and 16-bit depths in mono or stereo.

Note: At time of publishing, playback of WAV files received as email message attachments requires BlackBerry Enterprise Server software version 4.1 Service Pack 2. However, the authors believe this may change with future releases of the BlackBerry software as the BlackBerry Curve 8300 running version 4.2.2.89 BlackBerry software supports WAV file attachments today.

TIP: MUTE Key for Pause & Resume

You can pause (and instantly silence) any song or video playing on your BlackBerry by pressing the **MUTE key** on the top of your BlackBerry. Press **MUTE** again to resume playback.

Using your Music as Ringtones (Phone Tune)

The Pearl supports using any type audio file listed above as a Ringtone. You can set one 'general' ringtone ("**Phone Tune**") for everyone or set up individual tones for your important callers.

17
Music & Video

IMPORTANT: Place Ringtones in 'Ringtone' Folders

In some BlackBerry handhelds, when you are attempting to set a Ringtone for a specific person in the Address Book or in Profiles, you can only browse to the 'Ringtone' folder, not the 'Music' folder. If this is the case, then you must copy your ringtones to the 'Ringtone' folder using the methods to transfer media found in this book.

To set one Song (MP3) as your general "Phone Tune"

1. Navigate to your list of music as you did above.
2. Find the MP3 file you wish to use as the general "Phone Tune."

3. Press the Menu key and scroll to "**Set As Phone Tune**" and click.

TIP: Unique Ringtones for Callers

Set up unique ringtones for each of your important callers, this way you will know when each of these people is calling without looking at your BlackBerry screen.

To set one MP3 as an Individual Person's Ringtone

1. Start the **Address Book** icon.
2. **Find** the contact you wish to edit by typing a few letters of their first and last name.
3. After you have the cursor on the correct person, press the **Menu key** and select "**Add Custom Phone Tune**".
4. Click the Trackball again and the list of available Phone Tunes is displayed. If you need to navigate a different directory, just select "browse" at the top of the screen and choose the ringtone folder in which you MP3 files are stored. NOTE: You may not be able to browse to your 'Music' folder. (It depends on the version of BlackBerry system software you are running on your handheld).

NOTE: If you have already assigned a custom tune to this person, then it will ask you if you want to overwrite the existing tune.

5. Find the file you wish to use and click on it.
6. Press the **Menu key** and "**Save**" your changes.

Music Player Tips and Tricks

1. To Pause a Song or Video, press the **MUTE key**.
2. To Resume playing, press the **MUTE key** again.
3. To move to the next item, press "**6**."
4. To move to a previous item (in your playlist or Video library,) press "**4**."

Converting DVD's and Videos to Play on the Pearl

The process for getting the videos onto your Pearl are just like the ones used for adding audio files. The one important difference is that many videos need to be converted to a format (and screen size) that is playable on your Pearl.

Please Respect Copyright Laws

As people who make our living from intellectual property (BlackBerry books, videos, etc.), we strongly encourage you to respect the copyrights of any material you are attempting to copy to your BlackBerry.

17
Music &
Video

For security and copyright reasons, many DVDs cannot be copied onto a device like the BlackBerry Pearl. Many DVDs can, however, be converted to work and play on the Pearl. Make sure before you buy a video encoder or converter program that it supports the file formats that will play on the Pearl. Many of the User Enthusiast Forums like www.pinstack.com, www.crackberry.com or www.blackberryforums.com offer tutorials for Video Conversion.

Converting Videos using a Windows™ computer

Use the same procedures as outlined in the pictures sections earlier in this book to add or remove videos from your Pearl. Videos can be transferred in a way similar to images, and songs. The only major difference compared to images or music is that videos that may run just fine on your computer, might not play on your BlackBerry. This is because the BlackBerry Media Player only accepts a limited number of video formats. (See page 373) The Media Manager that comes with BlackBerry Desktop Manager can re-format many of the 'standard' video formats to play on your Pearl. Give your favorite videos a try in the Media Manager or check the documentation on accepted formats.

Roxio Media Manager in BlackBerry™ Desktop Manager
See page 373. Price: **Free.**

IMPORTANT NOTE: Below are a few products available at time of publishing; however, we strongly recommend doing a web search for something like "blackberry video converter windows".

Amerisoft BlackBerry Converter Suite
http://www.aimersoft.com/blackberry-converter-suite.html
Pricing: **Free Trial** - Full Price is **$35.00**

Seabyrd Technologies - Blackberry Video Converter
http://www.seabyrdtech.com/bbvideo Pricing: **Free**

Converting Videos using a Mac™

We have not used the following products, but notice that they indicate they are able to convert non-copy protected DVDs and videos to run on BlackBerry handhelds from a Mac™.

IMPORTANT NOTE: Below are a few products available at time of publishing, however, we strongly recommend doing a web search for something like "blackberry video converter apple mac".

ImTOO video converter
http://www.imtoo.com/video-converter-mac.html Pricing is
$49.00

Xilisoft Video Converter for Mac.
http://www.xilisoft.com/video-converter-mac.html. Pricing
is **$49.00**

Supported Video Formats for the BlackBerry Pearl

The following are the video formats that are supported by the
BlackBerry Pearl™

- MPEG-4 Part 2 (Simple Profile and bvop, including DivX 4)
  - File formats - .avi, .3gp, .mp4, .mov
  - Video – Up to 240 x 180 pixels, up to 800 kbps,
  up to 30 frames per second
- H.263 (Profile 0 & Profile 3)
  - File formats - .avi, .3gp, .mp4, .mov
  - Video – Up to 240 x 180 pixels, up to 800 kbps,
  up to 30 frames per second
- Windows Media® Video (Simple Profile)
  - File formats - .wmv
  - Video – Up to 240 x 180 pixels, up to 800 kbps,
  up to 24 frames per second

Note: Windows Media Video is supported in BlackBerry Device
Software 4.2.1 and above.

17
Music &
Video

Source: BlackBerry Knowledgebase
http://www.blackberry.com/btsc/articles/216/KB05419_f.SAL_Public.h
tml#7

Video Conversion Best Output Settings

For all you techies, we listed below the output conversions if you
have to manually set either your Windows or Mac software.
Most often, you will never see this settings, but we put them

here just in case.   Typically, you will just select "Pearl" or
"BlackBerry Pearl" as the output format.

> Video format: **MPEG-4**
> Video file extension: **.AVI**
> Resolution (4:3): **240x180**
> Resolution (16:9): **240x135**
> Video bitrate: **400 kbps**
> Frames per second: **24**

Source: BlackBerry Knowledgebase
http://www.blackberry.com/btsc/articles/216/KB05419_f.SAL_Public.h
tml#7

Viewing Videos on the Pearl

The Pearl contains a very sharp screen which is perfect for
watching short Videos. The Video player is as easy to use as the
Audio player.

Playing a Video
1.   Click on your **Media** icon.
2.   Click on the "**Video**" icon and choose the folder where your
     video is stored.
3.   The video player screen looks very similar to the Audio
     Player screen – just click the trackball to pause or play and
     use the volume controls on the side of the Pearl.

Supported Video Formats

The Pearl will play many types of Videos typically found on PC's or the Web. Other types of Video files will need to be converted to work with the Pearl.

Supported Video types

1. MPEG-4 Part 2 - Simple Profile + bvops (including DivX files in this format)
2. H.263 Profile 0 and Profile 3
3. AVI (.avi) containing MPEG4 Part 2 and H.263
4. QuickTime (.mov) containing MPEG4 Part 2 and H.263
5. 3GP (.3gp) containing MPEG4 Part 2 and H.263
6. MP4 (.mp4) containing MPEG4 Part 2 and H.263
7. M4V (.m4v) containing MPEG4 Part 2 and H.263
8. MPG (.mpg) containing MPEG4 Part 2 and H.263

17
Music &
Video

Section 6:
Your Pearl
as Traveling
Companion

Mapping with Your BlackBerry & BlackBerry As Tethered Modem

Chapter Contents:

- Using a Bluetooth Global Positioning System ("GPS") Device
- Using Third Party GPS enabled Software
- Pairing the Pearl and the GPS
- Using BlackBerry Maps
- Getting Directions with BlackBerry Maps
- BlackBerry Map Menu Commands
- Downloading Google Maps
- Google Map Menu Commands and Shortcuts
- Finding and Address or Business
- My Location and Switching Views in Google Maps
- Current Traffic on Google Maps
- BlackBerry as a Tethered Modem for Your Laptop

BlackBerry Maps, Google Maps, Bluetooth GPS

In addition to the myriad of possibilities in which your BlackBerry Pearl can manage your life, it can also literally "take you places." With the aid of software that is either pre-loaded on the Pearl or easily downloaded on the web you can find just about any location, business, or point of attraction using your Pearl.

18
Maps &
Modem

Unless you have a newer Pearl with built-in GPS, you will need to add a Bluetooth GPS receiver to and your Pearl so it will literally "tell you where to go." Locate your exact position and navigate your way to your destination – all from that little gem of a Smartphone.

Using Your Built-in GPS or Bluetooth GPS

Whether you have built-in GPS in your Pearl or you need to add GPS capabilities with a Bluetooth GPS receiver, the functionality will be identical.

With GPS capabilities, the BlackBerry Pearl will help you navigate you around your neighborhood, around town, from coast-to-coast and around the world.

Purchasing a Bluetooth GPS
If your Pearl did not come with GPS built-in, then you will need an add-on Bluetooth GPS units are sometimes called "Bluetooth Pucks" or "Bluetooth GPS Receivers." The concept is that your position is captured by the receiver's antenna and transmitted via Bluetooth wirelessly to your Pearl. These are the things to look for in a Bluetooth GPS receiver:

1. **SiRF Star III Chipset** (give you the fastest lock and strongest signal available)
2. **WAAS capable** (Wide Area Augmentation System which give you better accuracy)
3. **Multiple channel availability** (helps for a quick and strong satellite lock)
4. **High capacity rechargeable battery**

Using Third Party GPS Enabled Software

Once a Bluetooth GPS Receiver (sometimes called a "Bluetooth GPS Puck") is purchased, your BlackBerry Pearl can be used as a full-functioning navigation system. You just need some software to get going.

Most Wireless Service Providers offer a subscription to the **TeleNav** system. TeleNav is a "real time" GPS guidance program.

Maps are continually downloaded to track your position and guide you via voice prompts to your destination.

In addition to **TeleNav**, at publishing time we heard that Alk Technologies is developing a version of their popular **Co-Pilot Live™** software for the BlackBerry Pearl.

Pairing the Pearl and the Bluetooth GPS

NOTE: If your Pearl comes with GPS built-in, then you can skip this section. All you will need to do is "Enable GPS"

No matter which Bluetooth GPS receiver you choose and which software to accompany it, you will need to "Pair" your GPS receiver to the Pearl. The "Pairing" process might alter slightly depending on the manufacturer, but most the steps are fairly consistent.

1. Click on the **Set Up Bluetooth** icon in the Applications menu. If you don't see this icon, then you may instead see a **Connections Manager** icon, click on that.

2. Make sure your Bluetooth is in "Pairing" mode as per the manufacturer's instructions.

3. Click "OK" on the Pearl screen to begin to search for a GPS.
4. Once GPS is found, click on its name and enter the Passkey provided.

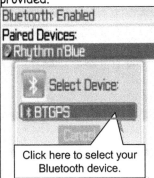

Click here to select your Bluetooth device.

Enter your Bluetooth GPS passkey Here

18
Maps & Modem

5. The Pearl will confirm that the connection has been established.

Using BlackBerry Maps

The BlackBerry Pearl ships with the BlackBerry Maps software – a very good application for determining your current location and tracking your progress via your GPS (Bluetooth or built-in) receiver.

Click here to start BlackBerry Maps.

To Enable GPS use on BlackBerry Maps (Use either Bluetooth GPS Receiver or a Built-In GPS)

1. Click the **BlackBerry Map** icon in the applications menu and then press the **Menu key**.

2. If you use a Bluetooth GPS, then you will need to click on "**Options**" and click in the first field "**GPS Device**." Select your Bluetooth GPS receiver that you just paired with your BlackBerry Pearl and the GPS commands will now be available to you.

   In the Mapping screen, press the **Menu key** and select "**Start GPS**."

To start GPS tracking on the Map, click the Menu key and select this.

3. The BlackBerry Map software will now display your current location.

To view a particular map from an address book contact

1. You can get to this function from either the **Map** icon or directly in the **Address Book** icon. From the **Map** icon, press the **Menu key** from the main map screen and select "**Map From Address Book**". This just jumps you directly into the **Address Book** icon.

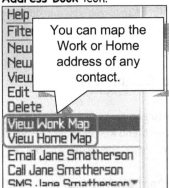

You can map the Work or Home address of any contact.

2. Now, in the Address Book, navigate or "**Find**" the contact you want to map, then press the Menu key and select either "**View Work Map**" (shows "Work" address) or "**View Home Map**" (shows "Home" address).

To Get Directions

1. Press the Menu key from the map screen and select "**Directions.**"
2. Input the starting address (if you have saved an address as a "Favorite" it will be listed below.
3. Input the **destination address**.
4. When done, click on the Trackball and select "**Search**" and the BlackBerry Map program will create a route for your trip.

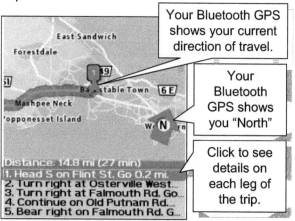

Your Bluetooth GPS shows your current direction of travel.

Your Bluetooth GPS shows you "North"

Click to see details on each leg of the trip.

5. If you have enabled GPS use, the GPS will track you along the route but it will not give you voice prompts or turn-by-turn voice directions.

BlackBerry Maps Menu Commands

There is a great deal you can do with the BlackBerry Map application. Pressing the Menu key offers you many options with just a scroll and a click. From the Menu you can do the following:

1. **Pan** – lets you "Pan" or move the map.
2. **Zoom** – takes you from street level to the stratosphere (Keyboard Shortcut Keys: "L" = Zoom In, "O" = Zoom Out)
3. **North Up** – places the North Arrow straight up and keeps the map oriented so up is always north (only with GPS enabled)

4. **Stop GPS** – to end GPS tracking (only with GPS enabled)
5. **Go To** – Type in an address to jump to that address.
6. **Directions** - Find directions by using your location history or typing in new addresses.
7. **Map From Address Book** – jump to the Address Book so you can map any contact's Work or Home address.
8. **Zoom to Fit** – Fit the entire map from Directions on the screen at once. (Only when viewing directions.)

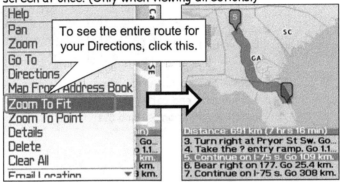

9. **Zoom to Point** – Show the map detail around the currently selected point in the directions. (Only when viewing directions.)

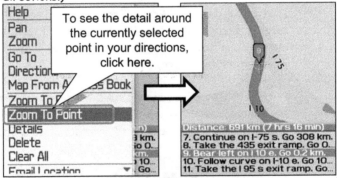

10. **Email Location** – Send your map location via email
11. **Copy Location** – To add your current location to your address book or another application.
12. **Add to Favorites** – To all your current location as a "Favorite" for easy retrieval on the Map.
13. **Options** – Change GPS Bluetooth device, Disable Backlight timeout settings, Change Units from Metric (Kilometers) to Imperial (Miles), enable or disable tracking with GPS and

18
Maps &
Modem

show or hide title bar when starting.

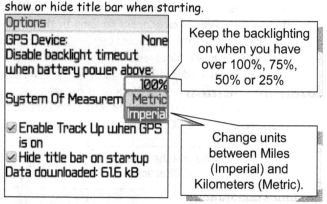

14. **About** - Show information about the current provider of the mapping data and software.
15. **Switch Application** - Jump over to any other application (Multi-Task).

Google Maps: Downloading & Installing

If you have ever used Google Earth you have seen the power of satellite technology in mapping and rendering terrain. Google Maps Mobile brings that same technology to handheld devices including the BlackBerry Pearl.

With Google Maps you can view 3-D rendered satellite shots of any address - anywhere in the world. To get started with this amazing application, you need to first download it onto your Pearl.

1. Click on the **Browser** icon from the application menu.

2. Press the Menu key and scroll to the "**Go To**" command and click.
   TIP: Use the shortcut hotkey of "." (period) for "**Go To**"

3. Enter in the address to perform an "Over the Air" ("OTA") download right onto the Pearl: http://www.google.com/gmm

4. Click on "**Download Google Maps**" and the installation program will begin.

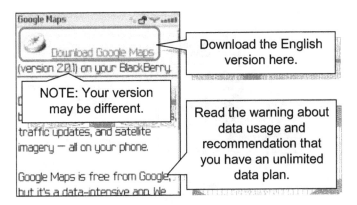

5. Then click the "**Download**" button on the next screen and "**Yes**" on the "**Not Trusted Source**" screen as shown.

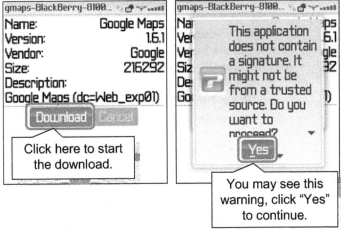

6. Finally you will see a screen that the application was successfully installed. Select "**OK**" to close the window or "**Run**" to start Google Maps right away.

18
Maps &
Modem

Google Map Menu Commands

Google Maps is full of great features – most of which are accessed right from the menu. Press the Menu key to see it.

Search – Find Business or Address
My Location – Use GPS or Cell Tower to find your current location.
Directions – Driving Directions
Satellite/Map View – Show Satellite image or map.
Favorites – Add key points to map.
Show Traffic – Show/Hide traffic (some cities only)
Bluetooth GPS – Turn on GPS tracking.

Finding an Address ("Location") Or Business

Finding an Address or Business is very easy with Google Maps.

1. Start the Google Maps application by clicking on the icon.
2. Press the Menu key and choose "**Search**", Click on "**Enter new search**" or roll down to click on a **recent search** below.

   TIP: You can EDIT saved (recent) searches by rolling the trackball down to the search and then rolling it to the right.

3. Select "**Enter new search**" to type just about any search string – an address, type of business and zip code, business name and city/state, etc. If we wanted to find bike stores in Winter Park, Florida, we would enter "**bike stores winter park fl**" or "**bike stores 32789**" (if you know the zip code).

4. Your search results will show a number of matching entries, just roll the trackball up/down to select an entry then click the trackball to see details.

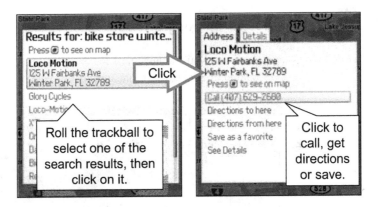

5. Press the "#" key to see the search results on the map.

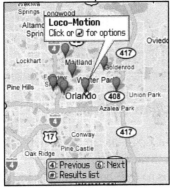

Google Map Shortcut Keys

4 – Previous search results

6 – Next search results

\# – Toggle between Map View and Search Results List

2 – Toggle between Satellite and Map Views

1 – Zoom Out

3 – Zoom In

5 – Move Up

* – Favorites List / Add a New Favorite Location

7 – Pan left / Show Traffic

9 – Pan right

0 – Show / Hide Location (if available)

18
Maps &
Modem

Switching Views in Google Maps

Google Maps give you the option of looking at a conventional Map grid or looking at real satellite images.

To Switch between Views (Shortcut Key = "2")
1. Press the Menu key and select "**Satellite View**" (or "2")
2. Press the Menu key and select "**Map View**" (or press "2")

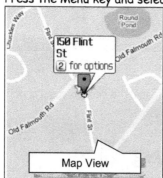

Map View

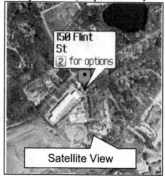

Satellite View

See Your Current Location (beta)

Just released in version 2.0 of Google Maps is the ability to show your location as a little blue dot, even when you do not own a GPS device or there is no GPS built-into your BlackBerry. Without GPS, your approximate location is determined by using the cell phone towers. If cell towers are used, there will be a shaded circle around the blue dot to show that the location is approximate (usually within about $\frac{1}{4}$ mile or 1,500 meters).

This is a great feature and very easy to access using the shortcut key of zero "0". Pressing "0" or selecting "**My location**" from the Menu will show you the blue dot.

NOTE: In some places, the software cannot find enough information to show your location, so it will tell you.

See Current Traffic in Google Maps

One other cool thing you can do in major metropolitan areas (this does not work everywhere) is to view current traffic with Google Maps. First, map the location you want to view traffic.
Press the Menu key and select "**Show Traffic**".

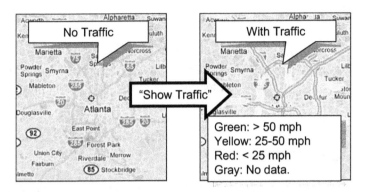

To Enable GPS use in Google Maps
(Use either built-in GPS if your Pearl has it or use a separate Bluetooth GPS Receiver)

1. Start Google Maps and press the Menu key. Then select "**Bluetooth GPS**" Or "**Enable GPS**" depending on how you are accessing the GPS signal in your Pearl.

2. In the next screen select the GPS device that you paired with your BlackBerry and the GPS commands will now be available to you.

18
Maps & Modem

3. Once GPS is enabled, your location will be shown with a little blue dot. If you press the SPACE key ("0"), then the map will move and follow your location.

Tethered Modem with a Mac™ Computer

NOTE: If you are a Windows™ computer user, please see page 391.

If you're out and about with your BlackBerry and computer anywhere with a fairly strong (usually 3 bars or higher) cellular network signal, you can connect to the Internet on your computer using your BlackBerry as a modem. Many times, this is called a "Tethered Modem" setup because your BlackBerry is connected to your computer (either with a USB cable, or Bluetooth connection).

Since you are a Mac™ user, you'll need to follow these steps. We want to sincerely thank Grant Goodale who gave us permission to use these instructions which are posted on Fibble.org. Link: http://www.fibble.org/ (Look for Modem Scripts for OS X or Leopard or BlackBerry) You can also try these links: http://www.fibble.org/archives/2007/10/updated-modem-s.html and http://www.fibble.org/archives/2006/09/use-your-blackb.html

One other link you might be interested in is one put together by Dave Taylor with good screen shots, and it can be found here: http://www.askdavetaylor.com/blackberry_pearl_as_bluetooth_modem_with_mac.html

VERY IMPORTANT: Many carriers charge an extra fee to allow you to use your BlackBerry as a "Tethered Modem" or "Dial Up Networking" or "Phone as Modem." You may be able to connect using your BlackBerry as a modem, however, unless you have specifically signed up for the "BlackBerry as Modem" or similar data plan. We have heard of users getting a surprise phone bill in the hundreds of dollars, even when they had an "unlimited BlackBerry data plan" (This carrier did not include BlackBerry modem data in the unlimited plan.)

NOTE: This solution for the Mac is highly dependent on the BlackBerry operating system and may not work correctly with all different (especially newer) operating systems. At publishing time, it appeared as if the T-Mobile BlackBerry OS v4.2 latest update for the Pearl™ was causing the tethered modem to lose connection after the first successful try. Check for any updates on the www.fibble.org site and forum.

1. Download the Modem Scripts from the www.fibble.org links:

    For Mac OS X:
    http://www.fibble.org/archives/2006/09/use-your-blackb.html

    For Mac Leopard:
    http://www.fibble.org/archives/2007/10/updated-modem-s.html

2. Unzip the downloaded file into your Macintosh HD: Library: Modem Scripts folder. If you are successful, then you will see a new directory named "BlacKBerry.ccl" there.

3. Pair your BlackBerry with your Mac (see detailed instructions on page 303).

    IMPORTANT: Make sure you set your BlackBerry Bluetooth Options "**Discoverable**" to "**Yes**" - the default is "No"

4. If you've already paired your Pearl™ with your Mac™, open Bluetooth Preferences, select your Pearl from the list of devices and press 'Configure...'. (If you haven't, please choose '**Set up Bluetooth Device**' - the following dialogs will be shown after you've paired your phone with your Mac. Make sure your Pearl doesn't require a password for your Mac to connect to it - the '**Trusted Connection**' option for the pairing should be set to '**Yes**' on your phone, not '**Ask**'.)

5. Make sure '**Access the Internet with your phone's data connection**' is checked. Also, make sure '**Use a direct,**

18
Maps &
Modem

higher speed connection' is selected. Click **Continue.**

6. In the Modem Script pull down on the following screen, Select '**BlackBerry 8100**'. Use the following settings for the other fields, then click Continue:

> Username and Password: leave blank
> GPRS CID: *99***1#

Make sure to check the box next to "**Show Modem status in the menu bar**" so you can see a small phone icon in your menu bar.

7. Click on that phone icon in the menu bar and select "Open Internet Connection" from the drop down menu.

Click the Bluetooth icon at the top.

Under Phone Number, put your Access Point Name ("APN").

For T-Mobile USA, use wap.voicestream.com
For Cingular it's wap.cingular
For Other Carriers, please see the
APN/Username/Passwords listed on page 428.

Enter your username in the "Account Name" field and password.

For T-Mobile USA: username = (blank) or your T-Mobile web site login username, Password = (blank) or your T-Mobile web site login password

For Cingular: username = WAP@CINGULARGPRS.COM, Password = CINGULAR1

For all other carriers, please consult the chart in the section starting on page 428. NOTE: Telephone Number (="APN"), Account Name (="Username") and Password = ("password").

INACTIVITY / AUTO LOGOFF: Some BlackBerry phone company carriers seem to have implemented inactivity timeouts on their data services. While it seems like you are actively using your connection, if you stop to read a web page for a couple of minutes your provider (carrier) will assume you're done with your internet connection and disconnect you. There does not seem to be a good solution for this problem.

Tethered Modem with a Windows™ Computer

NOTE: If you are a Mac™ computer user, please see page 388.

AN EASIER WAY?
Some BlackBerry phone companies, such as Verizon in the USA, actually have simple setup script files ("Verizon Access Manager") that you can download and install on your computer to do all setup required to use your BlackBerry as a Modem. Many times, these files are contained on the CD that is in the box with your BlackBerry or can be downloaded from the phone company's web site. Please check with your BlackBerry Help Desk or BlackBerry Phone Company for such an 'easy' solution before you follow the steps in this book. You could save yourself a great deal of time!

THIS DOES COST EXTRA: Many carriers charge an extra fee to allow you to use your BlackBerry as a "Tethered Modem" or "Dial Up Networking" or "Phone as Modem." You may be able to connect using your BlackBerry as a modem, however, unless you have specifically signed up for the "BlackBerry as Modem" or similar data plan. We have heard of users getting a surprise phone bill in the hundreds of dollars, even when they had an "unlimited BlackBerry data plan" (This carrier did not include BlackBerry modem data in the unlimited plan.)

18
Maps & Modem

Pricing Examples: (At publishing time)
Verizon in the US charges a total of $60 / month for BlackBerry service plus the "BlackBerry as Modem" data plan. (Either $15 or $30/month extra)
Cingular in the US charges $69 for the same service. (About $40 / month extra).

TIP: TURN IT ON AND OFF WHEN YOU NEED IT
Some carriers allow you to turn this BlackBerry As Modem Extra Service on and off. Check with your particular carrier. Also, beware that changing turning this modem service on and off might extend or renew your 2 year commitment period. Ask your phone company for their policies. Assuming there are no extra hidden costs or commitments, you could just enable it for a scheduled trip and then turn it off when you return home.

THANKS: A special thanks to Mark Rejhon and other contributors from BlackBerry Forums who has spent a great deal of time putting together the details of how to connect your BlackBerry as a Modem to your Windows™ computer across different wireless carriers. You can see the latest updates to this information by going to his posting on BlackBerry Forums here: http://www.blackberryforums.com/blackberry-guides/2019-user-howto-use-blackberry-modem-laptop.html

GOOD RESOURCE: We also want to thank Research In Motion, Ltd. and BlackBerry.com for valuable information contained in their extensive "**BlackBerry Technical Solution Center**". We strongly encourage you to visit this site for the latest information on using your BlackBerry as a Modem and anything else! Visit: http://www.blackberry.com/btsc/supportcentral/supportcentral.do?id=m1 and search for "modem how to."

SEARCH TIP: When searching the knowledgebase, do not enter your specific BlackBerry model, but the series. For example, if you have an 8130, then enter 8100, or just leave that out of the search.

SEARCH TIP: To locate the modem instructions for your particular BlackBerry, you will need to know the network – EDGE, GPRS, CDMA, EVDO on which your BlackBerry operates. The 8100, 8120 models run on the EDGE/GPRS networks and the 8130 models are CDMA/EVDO networks.

NOTE: Not every BlackBerry wireless carrier supports using your BlackBerry as a modem. Please check with your carrier if you have any trouble.

"SLIGHTLY" COMPLICATED:

This procedure is a bit complicated to get setup the first time, however, once you get it setup, it is fairly easy to use. If you need assistance, you should check out our video tutorial on how to setup your BlackBerry as a modem at www.blackberrymadesimple.com, or contact your Help Desk.

FIRST TIME SETUP:

1. **If your organization supplied your BlackBerry to you, please first check with the Help Desk** to make sure that using your BlackBerry as a modem for your laptop is allowed, supported and included in your organization's cell phone data plan. NOTE: The central administrator can turn off this capability using what is called an "IT Policy" setting from the server called **"Disable IPModem."** If this is turned on, then you will not be able to use your BlackBerry as a modem.

2. **If you purchased your BlackBerry on your own**, then please contact your BlackBerry phone company to check with them about your "BlackBerry as Modem" or "Dial-up Networking" data plan, charges and the special configuration settings you will need to connect using your BlackBerry.

   You should also ask about:
   "**APN**" (Access Point Name): _____
   Your **username** for dial-up: _____
   Your **password** for dial-up: _____
   You will need this information later in the setup process.

3. **Download and install the latest version of BlackBerry Desktop Manager** using the steps we outline starting on page 95. The Desktop Manager installation process will install a modem driver and "**Standard Modem**" on your computer to allow you to use your BlackBerry as a Tethered Modem.

18
Maps &
Modem

UPGRADING: If you are upgrading from a version of Desktop Manager earlier than 4.0, then you may need to first install the newest version then re-install it again in "Repair" mode – because the modem and drivers may not be installed correctly on the upgrade process.

NOTE: If you are at an organization, you may be "locked out" of installing new software. If so, check with your Help Desk if you cannot install new software on your computer.

4. **Next you need to setup your Modem "Extra Initialization Commands."**

    In **Windows Vista**, you need to go to "**Start** > **Control Panel** > **Hardware and Sound** > **Phone and Modem Options**"

    In **Windows XP**, you need to go to "**Start** > **Control Panel** > **Network and Internet Connections** > **Phone and Modem Options**" (See image)

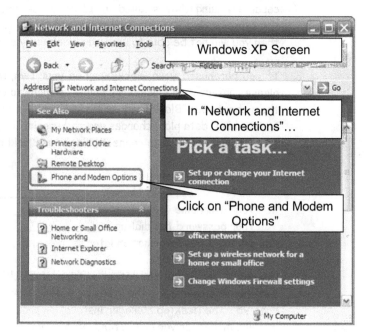

5. Then in the "**Phone and Modem Options**" window, click on the "**Modems**" tab at the top, click on the "**Standard Modem**" and then click on the "Properties" button. (See image)

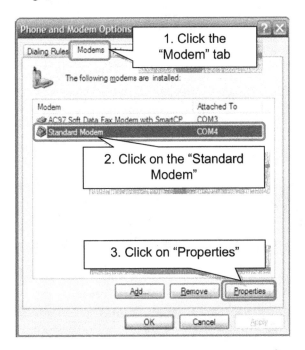

6. Now in the "**Standard Modem Properties**" window, type in the specific command text for your particular BlackBerry phone company. If you did not already get your APN from your BlackBerry phone company, please see information about APN – Access Point Name listed starting on page 428. If you cannot find your APN information, then please contact your BlackBerry phone company.

    This command text will be in the following format:

    +cdgcont=1,"IP","<your carrier's APN>"

    You will replace <**your carrier's APN**> with the **actual APN** for your BlackBerry phone company. (see Image)

18
Maps &
Modem

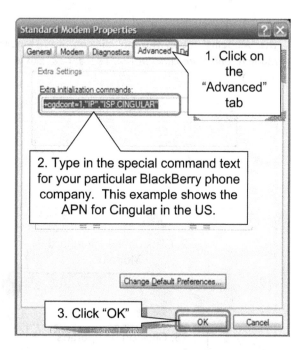

After you exit the above window, click "**OK**" again and close out of the **Phone and Modem Properties** and return to the "**Network and Internet Connections**" window from the **Control Panel**.

7. From the "**Network and Internet Connections**" window in the **Control Panel**, click on "**Setup or change your Internet Connection**" then click on the "**Add**" button in the "**Internet Properties**" window. (See image)

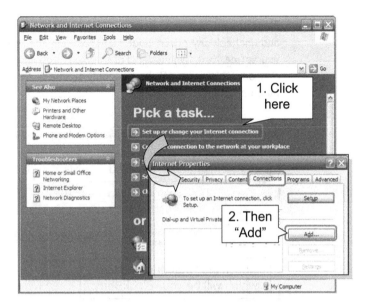

8. Now, make sure **"Dial Up to private network"** is selected and click **"Next"**

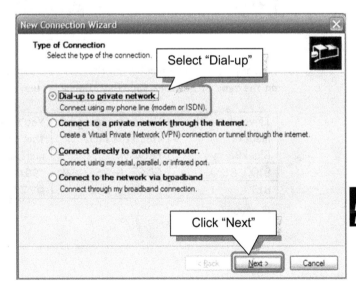

9. Please make sure to check the "**Standard Modem**" as shown and uncheck any other modems listed. On the image below, you notice that two modems are shown. You may only have only one or several. Make sure only to check the "**Standard Modem**," then click "**Next**"

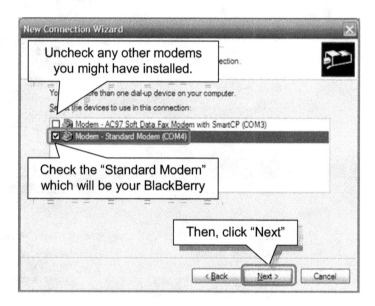

10. Now type the phone number on this next screen depending on the type of network your BlackBerry is running on.

If you have this model BlackBerry	You are running on this type of network...	You should use this phone number...
8100, 8120	EDGE, GPRS, GSM	*99#
8130	CDMA, EVDO	#777

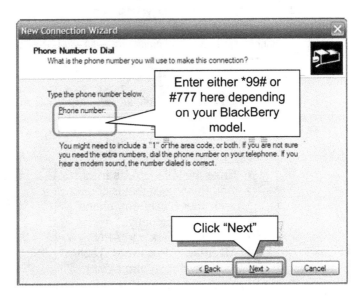

11. Now on the final screen, type a name for this modem connection – for example "**BlackBerry Modem**" and click the "**Finish**" button.

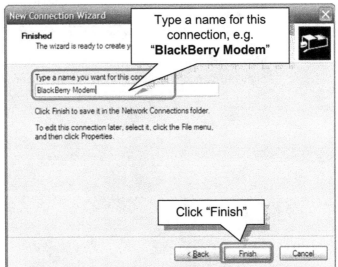

18
Maps &
Modem

12. Now you need to enter your username and password as described in our APN section starting on page 428. If you cannot find your username and password, then please contact your BlackBerry phone company.

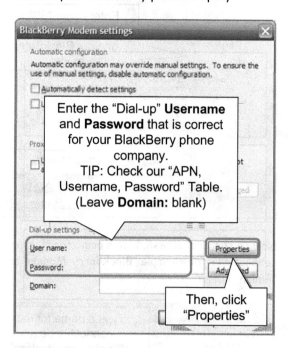

13. Now verify that the "**Modem – Standard Modem**" is highlighted and checked – then click the "**Configure**" button.

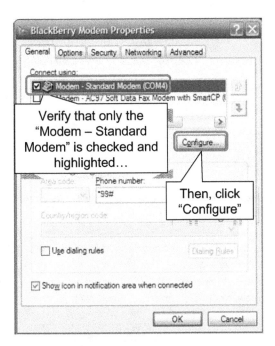

14. What you do in this next step depends on which model
    BlackBerry you are using and which network it runs on.

If you have this model BlackBerry	You are running on this type of network...	Hardware flow control checkbox is...
8100, 8120	EDGE, GPRS, GSM	**checked**
8130	CDMA, EVDO	**unchecked**

18
Maps & Modem

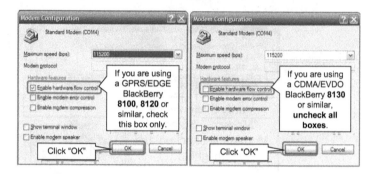

Make sure **none of the other boxes are checked**. Then click "**OK**."

15. Now click on the "**Networking**" tab at the top of the "**BlackBerry Modem Properties**" window. Click on the "Internet Protocol (TCP/IP)" row in the middle of the window, then click on the "Properties" button.

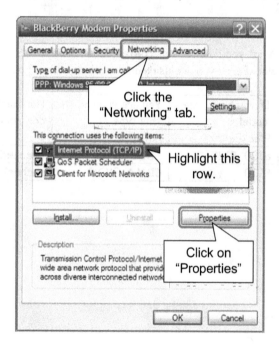

16. In the "**Properties**" window, click the "**Advanced**" button as shown.

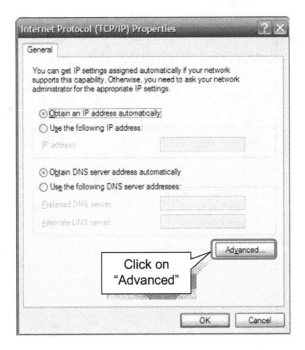

17. In the Advanced TCP/IP Settings window, make sure to **uncheck "Use IP header compression"** box is unchecked as shown.

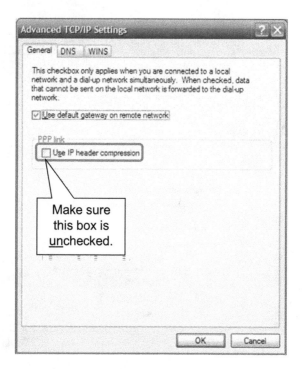

18. Now click "OK" enough times (probably 5 times) to close all the windows for your Modem and Network settings.

19. One final step is to make sure your Dial Up connection is only used when you do not have another Internet connection (e.g. WiFi, cable, etc.).

    In **Windows XP**: Start Menu > Control Panel > Network and Internet Connections > Internet Options

    In **Windows Vista**: Start Menu > Control Panel > Network and Internet > Internet Options

    Click on the **Connections tab** at the top and make sure to select the option in the middle of the page labeled: "**Dial whenever a network connection is not present**" Click on "Apply" to save your settings and close the window and Control Panel.

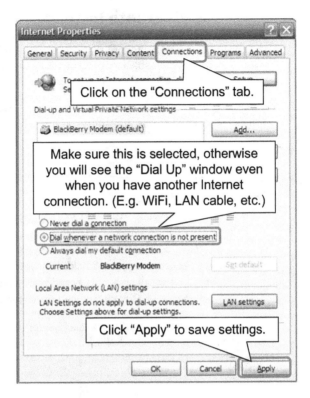

CONGRATULATIONS!

You're now done with the initial one-time setup of your BlackBerry as a Modem.

NOW YOU ARE READY TO TRY YOUR FIRST CONNECTION.

1. **Connect your BlackBerry to your computer.** Usually you would use the USB cable to connect by plugging it into your BlackBerry and a USB port on your computer. However, if you have a Bluetooth-enabled computer you could pair your computer with your BlackBerry (See page 303 for Bluetooth Pairing Help) If you have trouble getting the BlackBerry "connected" with your USB cable, then please see our USB connection troubleshooting tips on page 108.

18
Maps & Modem

Use Bluetooth Instead of USB?

If your BlackBerry and computer both have Bluetooth capabilities and your organization's administrator has not disabled this feature, you should be able to use a Bluetooth connection instead of the USB connection for your BlackBerry modem. See our Bluetooth Pairing section on page 299.

If you need additional help, please go to the **BlackBerry Technical Solution Center** (see page 388) and search for "**Bluetooth modem**"

2. **If asked, enter any passwords requested on both your BlackBerry and your computer.** If you use passwords on your BlackBerry or have enabled password security for your Media Card ("**Mass Storage Mode**"), you may see one or more password requests on your BlackBerry and your computer. Enter all passwords requested to complete the connection between your BlackBerry and your computer.

3. **Start your Desktop Manager software.** If you are using v4.3 or higher, you should see a screen similar to the one below.

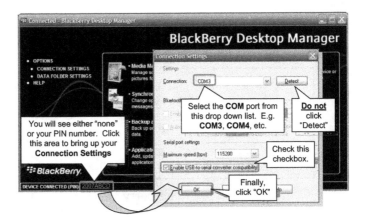

After you click OK, you may see an error message such as the one below. Click "**OK**" to close the error message and then you must click "**Cancel**" to exit the "**Connection Settings**" window.

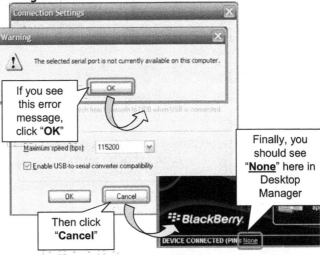

4. Finally, you will see "**None**" in the lower left corner of your Desktop Manager main window. This means your BlackBerry is not connected to your Desktop Manager, but it is connected to your computer to be used as a Modem.

18
Maps &
Modem

5. Next, go ahead and "Connect To" your "BlackBerry Modem" by clicking the **Start Button**, selecting **Connect To** and "**BlackBerry Modem**"

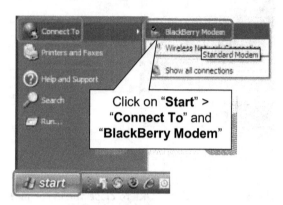

Next you will see a "Connect BlackBerry Modem" window, just click the "Dial" button. Leave the Username and Password fields alone – these were set by you during the setup process.

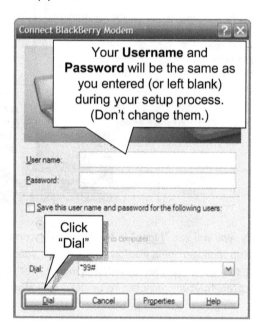

YOU ARE NOW CONNECTED!

If everything is setup correctly, and you have a good wireless connection (3-5 BARS on your BlackBerry), then you should be connected and see a message similar to this one below in the lower right portion of your computer screen.

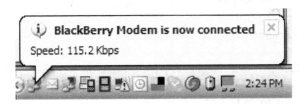

If you are on a high-speed "3G" network, then you might see speeds of 750 Kbps or even as high as 1,500 Kbps. Most "2G" networks ("EDGE") will have maximum connection speeds of 115.2 Kbps as shown.

NOT WORKING?

If you have any trouble, you will see various error messages, please check out our troubleshooting section below or call your Organization's Help Desk or BlackBerry Phone Company's technical support number.

Troubleshooting Your BlackBerry As A Modem

Below are some things you can try if your BlackBerry is not connecting as a modem for your Windows computer.

1. **Try re-tracing your initial setup steps earlier in this book.** It is easy to miss one step that could cause you problems.

18
Maps & Modem

2. **Try disconnecting and then re-connecting your BlackBerry to your Computer.** If you are using Bluetooth, instead try using the USB cable connection.

3. **Make sure Desktop Manager is running.** You cannot connect to your BlackBerry as a Modem unless Desktop

Manager is running.

4. **Try re-booting your BlackBerry and your Computer.**
Sometimes a simple reboot does wonders. To reboot your
BlackBerry, turn it off, then remove the back cover and
remove the battery. Wait 30 seconds and then replace the
battery and turn it back on. Then try re-connecting to the
BlackBerry modem.

5. **Contact your BlackBerry Help Desk or BlackBerry Phone
Company.** Depending on your level of frustration, you might
want to do this step now.

6. **Verify that the Modem Driver Files** were installed
correctly on your Computer. Go to c:\program files\common
files\research in motion\ and verify you see modem driver
files. Your files may have different names, dates and sizes
from those in the
image.

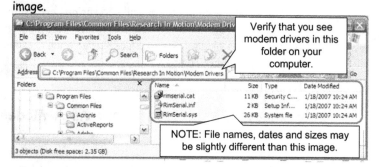

If these files are missing, then please re-install Desktop
Manager Software (page 95).
If you see these files, and you are still having trouble, then
delete these files and re-install Desktop Manager (page 95)
using the "**REPAIR**" option.

7. **Verify the Modem Exists.** From the Windows Start Menu,
select "Control Panel" > "Network and Internet Connections"
in the category view then look for "Phone and Modem
Options" in the Other Tasks listed in the left column on the
window. Then click on the "Modems" tab in the "Phone and

Modem Options" window and verify you see a "**Standard Modem**" listed. This will be your "BlackBerry Modem."

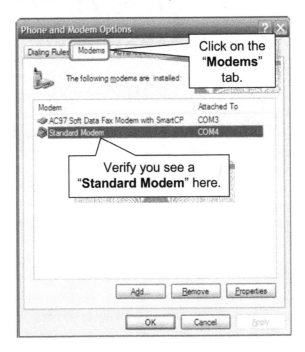

8. **Try out some of the BlackBerry discussion web sites.** Use some of the BlackBerry forum discussion sites listed on page 506.

9. **Try the BlackBerry Technical Solution Center.** Go to www.blackberry.com and click on the "Support" link. Look for the Technical Solution Center – their extensive online knowledgebase of technical solutions to all things BlackBerry.

18
Maps &
Modem

Section 7:
The Kitchen Sink-
Troubleshooting,
Backup and Utilities

Troubleshooting Your Wireless Signal

Chapter Contents:

Wireless: Your Connection to the World

Understanding how to monitor and troubleshoot your BlackBerry wireless connection is probably the most important things you'll learn about your BlackBerry. Your wireless signal provides many of the things you know and love including among other things: phone, email, web browsing, and if your organization has a BlackBerry Server, also wireless updates of your contacts, calendar, tasks and memos. And, if you installed other software like news readers and other applications, it's likely that they will require the wireless connection as well.

The "Layer Cake" of Voice and Data Connections

Your BlackBerry has two types of connections; one way to think
of them is as a layer cake: The bottom layer is always your voice
connection and the top layer (or layers) are your data
connections (low speed and high speed). Like a cake, you must
have the bottom layer in place in order to put on the top layers.

In a BlackBerry, you start with the voice connection layer on the
bottom then move up to the low-speed data connection layer and
finally on the top is the high-speed data connection layer.

As with a layer cake, you can have the bottom layer in place
without the top layers (BlackBerry: Phone "Voice" without Data),
but you can never have the top without the bottom layer first in
place (BlackBerry: You cannot have a data connection without
first having a phone "voice" connection.)

If you have a Pearl 8100 Series device, then the data connections will work like shown below. You will see GSM, GPRS, or EDGE in some combination of upper/lower case next to your wireless radio indicator.

"EDGE"
High Speed
Data Connection

"GPRS"
Low Speed
Data Connection

"GSM", "gprs", "edge"
Only Phone Calls
Voice Connection

19
Trouble-
Shooting

If you have a Pearl 8120 (with "WiFi") device, then the data connections work like shown below. When your wireless network "WiFi" is working, you will see that logo in addition to the GSM, GPRS, or EDGE upper/lower case letters next to your wireless radio indicator.

If you have a Pearl 8130 ("1XEV") CDMA device, then the data connections work like shown below. When your high-speed "EVDO" connection is working you will see the letters "1XEV" in the wireless network status. A "1X" shows lower speed data connection and finally a "1x" (x is lower case) shows only voice connection, no data connectivity (no email or web browsing).

Understanding When It Is Working

Normally, you never have to think about your wireless signal, it just works. The first time you notice that new email has not been received in a long time (In the BlackBerry world, "long time" = more than about 5 minutes).

If you see an hourglass or "X" instead of a check mark when you try to send an email, you know something is wrong. The BlackBerry makers were nice enough to give you a wireless signal status meter at the top of your BlackBerry screen (or it might be on the bottom, depending on your particular BlackBerry wireless carrier or "Theme").

19
Trouble-
Shooting

There are two components to your wireless status meter: The **Signal Strength Meter** and the **Data Connection Letters** which are usually right next to the Signal Strength.

Signal Strength Meter
This meter shows the strength of the wireless signal at your current location. Most times, you will see a number of "Bars" – usually from 1-5 bars with the higher number being the strongest. (Sometimes 4 bars is highest, it varies some depending on your wireless carrier and Theme.)

Data Connection Letters
Your "data connection" is what allows you to send/receive email, browse the web and send/receive data (addresses, calendar, and more). The confusing thing is that you may have very strong signal strength (e.g. 4-5 bars) but still not be able to send/receive email. The 3 or 4 letters (and maybe numbers) that are shown right next to the Signal Strength Meter (usually "EDGE", "edge", "gprs", "GPRS", "1XEV", "GSM", etc.) will tell you instantly if you have a "data connection". Take a look at the

table below to understand whether or not you have a data connection:

If you see ...	It means that...	What you should do...
OFF	Your radio is turned off	Turn your radio back on: Press the Menu Key > "Turn Wireless On"
GSM	No data connection, but Phone works	Start with Step 1 of our Troubleshooting Tips in this chapter.
EDGE, EVDO, 1X	High-speed data is working Phone is working	If email and web are not working, then start with Troubleshooting Step 2: Register Now
GPRS	Low-speed data is working Phone is working	If email and web are not working, then start with Troubleshooting Step 2: Register Now
edge, gprs, evdo, 1x, (any lowercase letters)	No data connection, Phone works	Start with Step 1 of our Troubleshooting Tips in this chapter.

Radio Turn Off by itself?
Travel away from Network Signal?

Thanks to the engineers at RIM (Research In Motion - BlackBerry's maker, if you travel away from a wireless signal for a significant amount of time (a few hours), your BlackBerry will automatically turn off the radio to conserve battery strength. This is because the radio consumes a lot of power when its trying to find a weak or non-existent wireless signal.

The nice thing is that all you need to do is turn your wireless radio back on by hitting the Menu key and selecting the "Turn Wireless On" icon. For pictures see "Step 1" Below.

Signal Strength Only 1-2 Bars?

You may have already figured this out, but signal strength is usually stronger above ground and near the windows, if you happen to be inside a building. It is usually best outdoors away

19
Trouble-Shooting

from large buildings. We once worked in an office building that was on the very edge of coverage, and we all had to leave our BlackBerry devices on the window sill to get any coverage at all! We're not sure why, but sometimes following the "Step 1" troubleshooting trick below will help increase your signal strength.

Step 1: Radio Off/On

Many times the simple act of turning your radio off and back on will restore your wireless connectivity.

1. To do this, first go to your Home Screen From your Home Screen, tap the **Menu** key and click the **"Turn Wireless Off"** icon (Your icon may look different from this one, but look for the words **"Turn Wireless Off"** when you highlight it)

2. Wait to see the "OFF" at the top of your screen:

Now, click the same radio tower icon to turn your radio back on:

3. Look for your wireless signal meter and upper case **EDGE or GPRS**. Check to see if your Email and Web are working.

If you do not see uppercase EDGE or GPRS, then proceed to Step 2.

Step 2: Register Now

1. From your Home Screen, tap the **Menu** key and click the "**Options**" icon. (Your icon may look different from this one, but look for the word "Options" when you highlight it)
2. Click on "**Advanced Options**"
3. Now select "**Host Routing Table**"
   In the HRT Editor you will see many entries related to your BlackBerry phone company. Press the Menu key and select "**Register Now**"
4. If you see this message:

   Look for your wireless signal meter and upper case **EDGE** or **GPRS** and check to see if your Email and Web are working. If not, go to Step 3 in troubleshooting.
5. If you instead see a message like "**Request queued and will be send when data connection is established**" then skip to Step 3.

Step 3: Hard Reset (Remove Battery)

1. Turn off your BlackBerry by pressing and holding the power button (the Red Phone Key).

2. **Remove the battery cover.** After your BlackBerry is off, then turn it over and press the little button at the bottom of the battery cover and slide it toward the top and off.

3. **Gently pry out and remove the battery** (look for the little indent in the upper right corner to stick in your finger tip).
4. Wait about **30 seconds**.

19
Trouble-
Shooting

5. **Replace the battery** – make sure to slide in the bottom of the battery first, then press down from the top.
6. **Replace the battery door**, by aligning the tabs then sliding it so it clicks-in and is flat.
7. **Power-on** your BlackBerry (it may come on automatically). Then wait for the hourglass – similar to a soft-reset wait.
8. Now, if it's not already turned on, tap the **Menu key** and click the **radio tower** icon which says "**Turn Wireless On**".

If email and/or the web browser are still not working, and you are using your BlackBerry with a BlackBerry Enterprise Server, please contact your organization's help desk or your wireless carrier's support number.

If email and web are not working and you do not use your BlackBerry with a BlackBerry Enterprise Server, then proceed to Step 4.

Step 4: Send Service Books (For BlackBerry Internet Service or "Personal Email" Users)

This step will work for you only if you have "Setup Internet E-Mail" or "Setup Personal E-mail" on their BlackBerry or using their wireless carrier's web site. [What is Internet/Personal Email? See page 77]

1. Click the Menu key and click on the "**Setup Internet E-Mail**" or "**Setup Personal E-Mail**" icon.

2. Note: If you have not yet logged in and created an account for your BlackBerry Internet Service, you may now be asked to create an account to login for the first time.

3. If you already have an account (or after you create your new account), you will be automatically logged in and see the screen below. Roll down and click on the "**Service Books**" link.

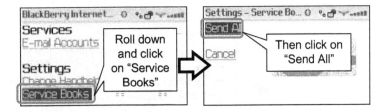

4. On the next screen, click the "**Send All**" link.

5. After clicking "**Send All**" you should see a "**Successfully Sent**" message:

19
Trouble-
Shooting

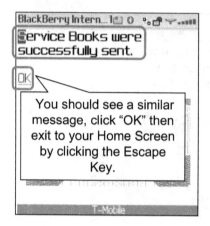

6. If you see any other message indicating the message was not sent, then you may want to verify that you have good coverage at your current location. You may also want to repeat some of other the troubleshooting steps described above.

7. After the service books have been sent, you will then see an "**Activation Message**" in your Messages email inbox for each one of your Internet Email accounts setup or integrated to your BlackBerry. Each message, when opened, will look similar to this one the one below.

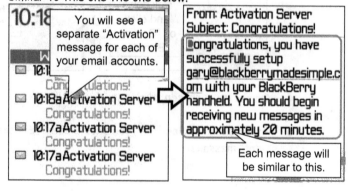

What Might Cause Data Connection Problems

Traveling away from your "Home" Network

When you travel with your BlackBerry away from your home network or to another country, the BlackBerry will have has to switch wireless networks to continue working. What happens is that sometimes the BlackBerry has trouble logging onto the new network in your new location. The troubleshooting tips, especially the "Register Now" will usually take care of this type of issue. Also, when you return to your home network, you may well need to repeat these steps if you have troubles.

Traveling to another Country?
Avoid a Phone Bill Surprise

Over the years, one thing that comes up over and over again is how people can be surprised by a very high phone bill, usually due to what's called "Data Roaming" charges. These data roaming charges are the charges levied by the foreign carrier on your particular phone bill to allow your BlackBerry data access on their network. You may be aware of "Voice Roaming," however data roaming can be quite a surprise because it can happen without you doing anything - simply by email flowing into your BlackBerry. The worse culprits are browsing the web or opening and viewing larger attachments – both can be quite data intensive.

How to avoid being surprised?

Before Your Trip:
Check with your wireless carrier about any data roaming charges – you can try searching on your carrier's web site, but usually you will have to call the help desk and specifically ask what the "Voice Roaming" and "Data Roaming" charges are for the country or countries you are visiting. If you use Email, SMS, Web Browsing and any other data services, you will want to ask

19
Trouble-
Shooting

about whether or not any of these services are charged separately.

After You Get There:
Try to contact the local phone company to find out any data roaming or voice roaming charges.
Worst case, if you are worried about the data roaming charges, and can do without your email and web, then you can keep on your voice connection but just turn off your data connection:

1. Start the **Options** icon.
2. Press the "N" key to select "Network" and click on it.

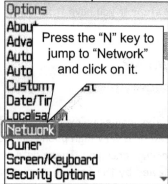

3. Your "**Data Services**" will most likely say "**On**", you should change that to "**Off When Roaming**" or "**Off**". We recommend "**Off When Roaming**" so that you can continue to receive data in your "**Home Network**"

4. Finally, save your settings by hitting the Menu key and selecting "Save"

Making this "**Off When Roaming**" change should help you avoid any potentially exorbitant data roaming charges. (You still need to worry about voice roaming charges, but at least you can control those by watching how much you talk on your phone).

Access Point or TCP Network Settings (Required for Some Third Party Software)

NOTE: If your BlackBerry is used together with a BlackBerry Enterprise Server, then you will not need to follow the steps here. Instead, you will want to contact your Help Desk for support.

This section is designed for BlackBerry Internet Service Users who have installed additional Third Party software that requires a special type of Internet connection to work correctly. Examples of such software include, but are not limited to:
- RSS News Readers
- Special Attachment Software (e.g. Software to open and view attachments or software to open and listen to audio attachments)
- Any other software that requires a connection from your BlackBerry to that software provider's web site.

1. Start the "Options" icon
2. Roll to "Advanced Options" and click on it.
3. Roll down (or hit the "T" key to jump down to it) and select "TCP"
4. Now, you need to enter the "**APN**", "**Username**" and "**Password**" for your particular wireless carrier (Phone

Company that supplied your BlackBerry) See the list below.

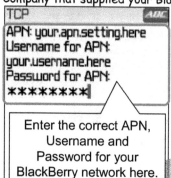

TCP `ABC`

APN: your.apn.setting.here
Username for APN:
your.username.here
Password for APN:
********|

Enter the correct APN,
Username and
Password for your
BlackBerry network here.

What are the APN ("Access Point Name") Settings for my BlackBerry?

Since the wireless carriers sometimes change their APN settings so the ones below will no longer work, we strongly recommend you do a web search (Google, Yahoo, other) for "apn settings blackberry" or "access point name settings" You will most likely come across a number of web sites listing APN settings. We found one that seems to be very complete from a company called "WebMessenger" an Instant Messaging company for BlackBerry and other handheld devices. (View the company's web site at: www.webmessenger.com) To view the most up to date APN list, please visit their web site http://www.webmessenger.com/support/APN.jsp -- at the time of publishing this book, the list included wireless carrier's APN settings in 65 countries!

Below is the APN settings list for the United States:
If the Username and password are blank, just leave them blank.
If there are several options, you may need to try each one.

IMPORTANT: After you change the APN settings, if they do not seem to start working right away, then you need to do a hard reset of your BlackBerry (Power off, remove the battery, wait 30 seconds, replace the batter, power on). Sometimes this "hard reset" will be required for the settings to take effect.

USA Carriers APN, Username and Password Settings courtesy
of WebMessenger. See over 65 different countries settings at
www.webmessenger.com

Carrier: AT&T (USA) APN: proxy User name: Password:	Carrier: AT&T (VPN) (USA) APN: public User name: Password:	Carrier: Bell Mobility (USA) APN:internet.com User name: Password:
Carrier: Cincinnati Bell (USA) APN:wap.gocbw.com User name:cbw Password:	Carrier: Cingular (USA) APN: blackberry.net User name: Password:	Carrier: Cingular Blue/former AT&T (USA) APN: proxy User name: Password:
Carrier: Cingular Orange/MediaWorks (USA) APN: wap.cingular User name: WAP@CINGULARGPRS.COM or blank Password: CINGULAR1	Carrier: Dobson/Cellular One (USA) APN:cellular1wap User name: Password:	Carrier: Nextel/Telus/Rogers Sprint CDMA (USA) APN: internet.com User name: Password:
Carrier: SunCom (USA) APN: internet User name: Password:	Carrier: T-Mobile VPN (USA) APN: internet3.voicestream.com User name: Password:	Carrier: Cingular (USA) APN: isp.cingular User name: ISPDA@CINGULARGPRS.COM or ISP@CINGULARGPRS.COM Password: CINGULAR1
	Carrier: T-Mobile/T-Zone (USA) APN: wap.voicestream.com User name: blank or your T-Mobile user name Password: blank or your T-Mobile password	Carrier: T-Mobile Internet (USA) APN: internet2.voicestream.com User name: Password:

19
Trouble-Shooting

BlackBerry
Security

Chapter Contents:

Why Use Password Security for my BlackBerry?

The best way to answer this question is by asking another:

What your BlackBerry was lost or stolen? (Would you be uncomfortable if someone found and accessed all the information on your device?) (Names, Addresses, Confidential Email, Calendar, Notes, etc.)

For most of us the answer would be "**YES!!**" In that case, you will want to enable or "turn on" the password security feature.

When you turn this on, you will need to enter your own password in order to access and use the BlackBerry. In many larger organizations, you do not have an option to turn off your password security, it is automatically 'turned on' by your BlackBerry Enterprise Server Administrator.

Email & Web Browsing Security Tips

If you work at an organization with a BlackBerry Enterprise Server, then you will have very secure email communication when you send email to others in your organization. Once you send email to someone outside of your organization, your email is typically lightly encrypted (Wireless Transport Layer Security) or totally unencrypted (not secure at all). This is true for BlackBerry Internet users as well - please exercise the same level of discretion as you would when you normally send email over the Internet.

Email Security Tips

Never send personal information or credit card information via email. Examples of information not to send are: Credit Card numbers, Social Security Number, Date of Birth, Mother's Maiden Name, Sensitive Passwords / PIN numbers (e.g. bank account ATM card). If you have to transmit this information, it's best to call the trusted source or, if possible, visit them in person.

Web Browsing Security Tips

Like email, if you are in an organization with a BlackBerry Enterprise Server, then when you use the "BlackBerry Browser" that is secured by the encryption from the Server, your communications will be secure as long as you are browsing sites within your organization's Intranet. Once you go outside to the Internet and are not using HTTPS connection, your web traffic is no longer secure.

Anyone that visits a site with HTTPS (Secure Socket Layer) connection will also have a secure connection from your

BlackBerry to the web site, like with your computer's web browser.

Whenever you are browsing a regular "HTTP" web site on the Internet (not your organization's secure Intranet) - then be aware that your connection is not secure (even if are using a BlackBerry Enterprise Server). In this case, please make sure not to type or enter any confidential, financial, or personal information. See "Email Security Tips" above.

Preparing for Worst Case Scenario (Lost BlackBerry)

There are a few things you can do to make this worst case scenario less painful.
Step 1: Backup Your BlackBerry to your Computer.
Step 2: Turn On ("Enable") BlackBerry Password Security, and
Step 3: Set your Owner Information with an incentive for returning your BlackBerry.

Step 1: Backup Your BlackBerry Data

Use the steps outlined in our chapter on Backing up your BlackBerry starting on page 455.

Step 2: Turn On ("Enable") Password Security

Make sure you turn on "enable" password security. This is really your "Backup Plan" to safeguard all your data should you happen to lose your BlackBerry. How to enable your Password Security:

1. Click on your **Options** Icon on your Home Screen. If you don't see it, then press the Menu key to get to the Applications menu and locate it.
2. Hit the letter "**S**" to jump down to "**Security Options**" and click on it..
3. Select "**General Settings**".

4. Click on the "Disabled" setting next to "**Password**" and change it to "**Enabled**".

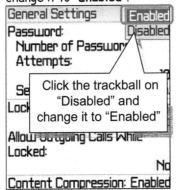

5. Press the **Menu key** and "**Save**" your settings.
6. You will now be asked to enter your password. On your Pearl you will notice the little "ABC" in the upper right corner that shows you are now in **Multitap** mode (instead of **SureType™**). Whenever you need to enter a password you are in Multitap mode. In Multitap, when you press a key once you see the first letter on that key, press it a 2nd time to see the next letter. This allows you to be precise with your passwords.

TIP: Use a sequence of key strokes for your password, rather than a specific password itself. For instance, you may choose pressing the number keys - even though your password is really showing up as the letters.

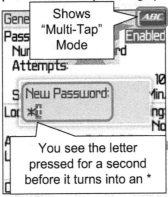

7. You will need to re-enter your password to make sure you've entered it correctly.

IMPORTANT: If you cannot remember your password, then you will lose all the data (Email, Addresses, Calendar, Tasks, everything) from your BlackBerry. Once you enter more than the set number of "Password Attempts" shown on this screen, the BlackBerry will automatically "Wipe" or erase all data.

Step 3: Set your "Owner Information"

We recommend including something to the effect of "Reward offered for safe return" in your owner information which would show up when someone found your BlackBerry in a "locked" mode. You may have already set your owner information in the Setup Wizard, however you can also set it by going to the Options Icon and selecting Owner Information.

To set your owner information:

1. Click on your **Options** Icon on your Home Screen. If you don't see it, then press the Menu key to get to the Applications menu and locate it.
2. Hit the letter "O" to jump down to "Owner" in the list of Options Settings, click the trackball to open it.
3. In the **Owner Information** settings screen, put yourself into the mind of the person who might find your BlackBerry and give them both the information and an incentive to return your

> **TIP**
> You can also enter your Owner Information from the **Setup Wizard** icon.

BlackBerry safely to you.

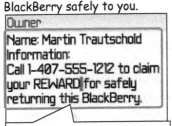

Enter information (and an incentive) to help the person who finds your BlackBerry return it to you.

4. Press the **Menu key** and "**Save**" your settings.

5. Test what you've entered by locking your BlackBerry. Locate and click on the "**Keyboard Lock**" icon:

To test your "Owner Information" locate and click on the Keyboard Lock Icon.

TIP

Keyboard Shortcut: From your Home Screen, pressing and holding the

SYM key to the left of the SPACE key will also "LOCK" your BlackBerry.

6. Now you will see your owner information:

Here is your Owner Info. displayed while locked.

Other Security Options

1. Now, you may adjust other settings depending on your preferences. You may want to leave the number of password attempts at 10 (Default) before your BlackBerry erases or "WIPES" all the data on the device.

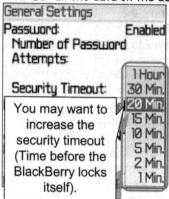

2. Security timeout of 2 minutes (default) might be a little too short for you. You might be able to change it up to 1 hour. But remember, the longer you set it the more your BlackBerry is left "unlocked" when it is lost/stolen. So weight the consequences before you make this too long.

3. NOTE: If your BlackBerry was issued by your organization, it is very likely that the organization has limited your options on the "Timeout" and possibly other settings on this Security page. For example, most organizations force you to "Enable" your Password, and do not allow you to "Disable" it.

4. You may also set your BlackBerry to automatically lock itself when you put it into the "holster" the leather or plastic carrier designed to hold your BlackBerry.

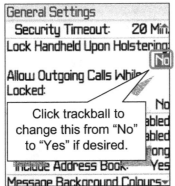

General Settings
Security Timeout: 20 Min.
Lock Handheld Upon Holstering: No

Allow Outgoing Calls While Locked:

Click trackball to change this from "No" to "Yes" if desired.

Include Address Book: Yes
Message Background Colours

NOTE: For this setting to work, your holster must have a magnet strategically placed so that when you insert your BlackBerry the screen goes off and it recognizes that it is "In the Holster." Some after-market holsters may not have this required magnet, the easiest way to test this is to hold the bottom of your BlackBerry next to the bottom of holster and see if the screen goes off when it gets close to the holster.

5. The next setting is to allow or disallow outgoing phone calls when your BlackBerry is locked.

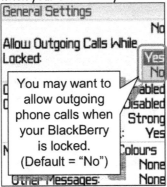

General Settings

Allow Outgoing Calls While Locked: Yes / No

You may want to allow outgoing phone calls when your BlackBerry is locked. (Default = "No")

6. **Content Compression:** This compresses all the information stored on your BlackBerry. We recommend leaving this set to "Enabled" to conserve memory space on your BlackBerry.

7. **Content Protection:** This encrypts all information on your BlackBerry and may slow down your BlackBerry. The default is "Disabled" or "Off". Considerations if you "Enable"

Content Protection: (1) When you receive a phone call from a contact in your BlackBerry Address Book, while your BlackBerry is locked, you will not see the caller's name, only their number. (2) Sometimes you may see a message "Organizing Address Book" when trying to open your Address book. (3) If you decide to "Wipe" or erase all data on your device, (Security Options > Menu Key > Wipe Handheld) it may take 2 hours or more if Content Protection is "Enabled."

8. Since the Address Book, if it has a great deal of information in it, may be slow to open when "Content Protection" is Enabled, you may choose to set it to "No"

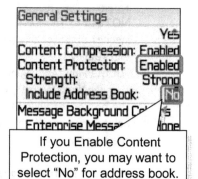

If you Enable Content Protection, you may want to select "No" for address book.

9. **Message Background Colors:** This option only applies to users who have a BlackBerry connected to a BlackBerry Enterprise Server. This may already be set (and cannot be changed) by your BlackBerry Administrator. Because of the different level of security / encryption of email that comes from your BlackBerry Enterprise Server (Strong Encryption) vs. BlackBerry Internet Service (Weaker Encryption). You may want to use a color to easily and immediately identify email messages sent through your BlackBerry Enterprise Server and "other" messages not sent through the server. The underlying message is those "other" messages are not as

secure compared to the Enterprise Server messages.

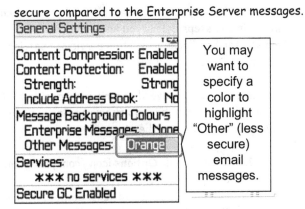

General Settings

Content Compression: Enabled
Content Protection: Enabled
  Strength: Strong
  Include Address Book: No
Message Background Colours
  Enterprise Messages: None
  Other Messages: [Orange]
Services:
  *** no services ***
Secure GC Enabled

You may want to specify a color to highlight "Other" (less secure) email messages.

If you Lose Your BlackBerry

If you work at an organization with a BlackBerry Enterprise Server or use a Hosted BlackBerry Enterprise Server, immediately call the help desk and let them know what has happened. Most Help Desks can send an immediate command to "Wipe" or erase all data stored on your BlackBerry device. The help desk should also contact the cell phone company to disable the BlackBerry phone.

If you are not at an organization that has a BlackBerry Enterprise Server, then hopefully you have followed the steps above to Enable your Password Security and put in Owner Information with an incentive to return your BlackBerry.

You should immediately contact the cell phone company that supplied your BlackBerry and let them know what happened.

Now, you may want to wait a day or two to see if someone finds your BlackBerry and calls you to return it.

How to Turn Off ("Disable") Password Security

NOTE: If you work at an organization with a BlackBerry Enterprise Server, it is quite likely that you will not be allowed to turn off (disable) password security. If you are unable to set "Disable" in the steps below, you know your BlackBerry Administrator has "locked out" this particular setting - forcing you to keep your password turned on.

If you have enabled password security and decide to disable it, then you will need to go back to the same Security Options screen to do it. Here are the steps.

1. Click on your **Options** icon from your Home Screen or Applications menu.
2. Hit the letter "S" to jump down to "**Security Options**", click the trackball to open it.
3. Select "**General Settings**" at the top of the list by clicking the trackball on it.
4. Click on the "**Enabled**" setting next to "**Password**" and change it to "**Disabled**".

5. If you have turned on Content Protection, then you will see a message similar to the one below, you must select "**Yes**" to continue with disabling your

password security.

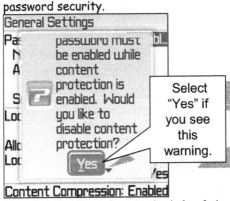

Select "Yes" if you see this warning.

6. Now, hit the **Menu key** to the left of the trackball and select "**Save**"
7. After you select "**Save**" then you will be asked to enter your password one last time – this is for your protection to make sure no one is allowed to disable your security without knowing your password.

Finally, to finish disabling your password, you need to enter it one last time.

Password Keeper Program

A useful program on your BlackBerry is the Password Keeper program; it allows you to store an unlimited number of usernames and passwords. These could be bank, shopping web sites, PIN numbers, anything that requires you to memorize a username and password combination.

Starting Password Keeper and Adding a New Password

1. Locate and click on the **Password Keeper** icon. If you don't see it from your Home Screen, then click the **Menu key** to the left of the trackball to list all your icons.

2. Now enter your main password used to get into the Password Keeper. Enter it twice to confirm it.

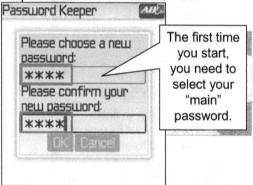

3. **IMPORTANT:** Make sure to remember this password, because if you forget it, there is no way to recover any information stored in the Password Keeper.

4. Once you have selected your "main" password to enter the program, you may add new passwords by clicking the trackball or **Menu key** and selecting "**New**"

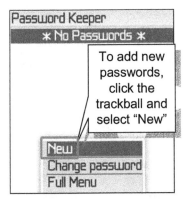

5. Now enter all information for this username / password combination.

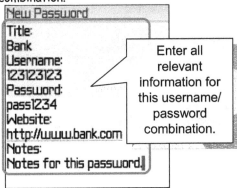

6. Click the trackball and select **"Save"**

7. Now you will see a list of your **Password Keeper** entries:

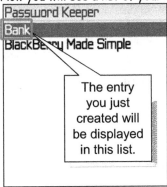

Using Password Keeper with Offline Locations

With offline locations like banks, ATMs, other passwords, you can just lookup your password entries read them and use them.

1. To use Password Keeper, click on the icon from your Home Screen.

2. Enter your "main" password to enter the program.

3. Roll down and highlight the entry you want to use and click on it, or if you have many entries, start typing a few letters of the entry you want to "**Find**" it (just like Address Book, Phone, and Web Bookmark Find: feature).

4. Now, click the trackball to view your password entry:

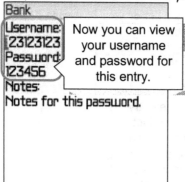

5. **IMPORTANT**: When you are finished using this password, make sure to press the **ESCAPE key** (to the right of the trackball) a few times to exit out of the program to keep your passwords safe.

Using Password Keeper with Web Sites

When you are storing passwords for web sites, you can do a few things to speed the login process right on your BlackBerry. (This assumes that the web site can be accessed by the BlackBerry Web Browser – some sites do not allow this.) You can copy and paste your username and password from the Password Keeper and even open up the web site listed right from Password Keeper.

Copy & Paste Usernames And Passwords

1. Select the entry with the username / password you want to copy. TIP: Type a few letters of the entry name to "Find:" it.

2. Click the **Menu key** and select "**Copy Username**" or "**Copy Password**"

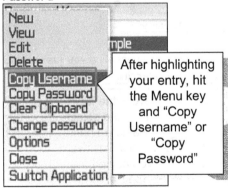

New
View
Edit — mple
Delete
Copy Username
Copy Password
Clear Clipboard
Change password
Options
Close
Switch Application

After highlighting your entry, hit the Menu key and "Copy Username" or "Copy Password"

3. Once you have your information copied, then click in the trackball to open the entry and see the web site link. Then highlight the Website link and click the trackball to "**Get**

Link" (go to the web site in your BlackBerry Browser)

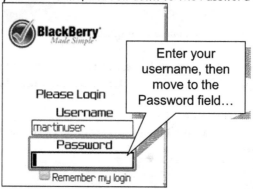

4. Once you are on the login page of the website, then enter your username, and roll down to the Password field.

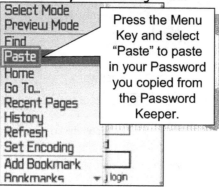

5. Now you can paste the password you just copied by pressing the **Menu key** and selecting "**Paste**"

6. Now you can simply press "Login"

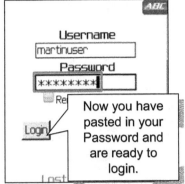

Now you have pasted in your Password and are ready to login.

7. You may see a "**Not Trusted**" message. You can view the site and if you feel it's trusted, then click the "Don't ask again" message.

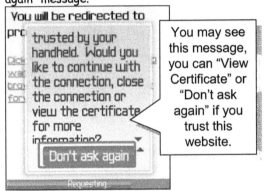

You may see this message, you can "View Certificate" or "Don't ask again" if you trust this website.

Help with Creating New "Hard to Guess" Random Passwords

Some people have trouble thinking of new passwords which are difficult to guess. Password Keeper has solved this problem with a feature called "**Random Password**" - it creates a new random password for you. You can even specify the length of the password, whether it contains only letters, only numbers or symbols or a combination of all types of characters.

In order to generate a Random Password for a specific entry, press the Menu key and select "Random Password" as shown below.

TIP: Some sites do not allow symbol characters or spaces in the password, you can restrict what is in your random passwords by pressing the Menu key and selecting "**Options**" inside the Password Keeper application. We show you how to do this below.

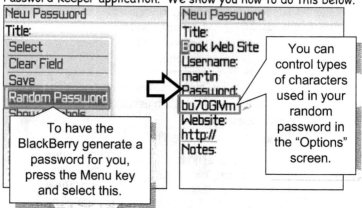

Password Keeper Options Screen

Most of the options in the Password Keeper are for the Random Password generator feature.

To access the Options screen in Password Keeper:
1. Start the Password Keeper Icon and enter your main password.

2. Click the **Menu key** and select "**Options**"

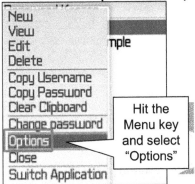

3. Many password systems do not allow symbols to be placed in the password, so you may want to switch the "**Random Includes Symbols**" to "**No**" by clicking the trackball, pressing the "**N**" key, or pressing **SPACE bar** when highlighting it. (All three methods work!)

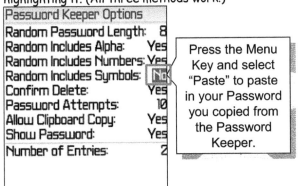

4. You can see the other options from the image above. The only other option you may want to change is the "**Show Password**" to "**No**"

5. When Show Password = "No" then all passwords are changed to the usual asterisks ("***********"). You can "**Copy**

Passwords" that are hidden, but obviously cannot read them.

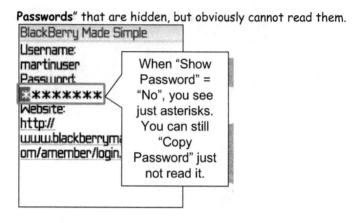

BlackBerry Made Simple

Username:
martinuser
Password:
****
Website:
http://
www.blackberrym
om/amember/login.

When "Show Password" = "No", you see just asterisks. You can still "Copy Password" just not read it.

Backup, Restore and Mass Delete

Chapter Contents:

Defining Backup

To "Backup your BlackBerry" is to transfer and save all the information, including all your email settings, third party applications, everything onto another location. The idea being if your BlackBerry was lost, stolen or damaged, you could acquire a new device, restore your data (from the backup) and be up and running with very little time and effort.

Worst Case Scenario

BlackBerries which are small mobile devices can sometimes become lost, damaged or dropped. One of the authors (Martin) even dropped his BlackBerry 8700 Model into the toilet! He quickly rescued it, took out the battery and SIM card and used a hair dryer to revive it. The speakerphone was never quite the same, it kept working for about 5 months and finally started rebooting when on phone calls. It was eventually retired to sit next to the other old BlackBerry models in the closet shelf: the original 957 Model and 7230 Model.

Why Backup? - My Organization Does It

MEDIA BACKUP

Even if your organization backs up the main data from your BlackBerry, usually they **do not back up** pictures or other media files, especially when they are stored on your Media Card.

Many organizations that issue BlackBerries to their employees will have BlackBerry Enterprise Servers which automatically synchronize or share all the Email, Calendar, Address Book, Task and Memo Pad data from your BlackBerry with your work computer. And most organizations will also have an automated backup procedure for the information stored on the server and sometimes even from your individual computer at work.

If you work at an organization that issued you the BlackBerry, then your data is probably already backed up. You may want to check with your Technology Support group to verify exactly what **is** and **is not** included in the normal back up.

The other thing to consider is what happens when you leave the organization?

Many people with BlackBerries end up putting both personal and work contacts and information on the BlackBerry. If you left the organization without any backup of your BlackBerry data, you would lose all that personal information. And, if you are in profession where your work contacts are very important to your career, then you may also want a backup of your BlackBerry data.

Why Backup? - I Already Sync to My Computer.

Sync
**Desktop or
Wireless**

Backup
**Connect to
Your Computer**

**The Sync
Only Includes
the four icons
shown.**

**The Backup
Includes every
icon, email settings,
new icons added,
everything.**

The main reason why you want to backup is that is captures all the information, email setup, Third Party applications and settings on your BlackBerry, not just addresses, calendar, tasks, email and notes. If you performed the email setup, added new software and otherwise fine-tuned your BlackBerry since you received it, you know how much work it would be to re-create all your settings.

Some of the things that do not get stored on your computer during a regular synchronization process are: email setup, other settings and preferences, fonts, profiles, alarms, password keeper data, web browser settings & bookmarks, third party applications installed or any pictures, videos, or songs stored on your media card. If you lost your BlackBerry, then you would have to manually re-setup, restore, and re-create all that information.

Where to Backup the BlackBerry?

Before one of the author's (again Martin's) laptop hard disk crashed, he would have answered "on my PC of course!" But now, the answer is "on one of my two my external USB hard disks, which I swap out every two weeks."

If you only synchronize information or backup to your computer's hard disk – you are at risk of losing all that data if your computer hard disk crashes.

Martin Trautschold experienced a total loss of his laptop hard disk: "It just didn't turn on one day – all I saw was a black screen" It turns out that the hard disk had crashed, not uncommon for a laptop that gets lots of use and transportation.

So our recommendation is to backup your BlackBerry (and your entire computer's hard disk) to an external source such as an external hard disk that can be connected to your computer using a USB cable. Hard disk prices keep coming down and (at publishing time) it was possible to buy a 250 gigabyte ("GB"), or larger, external hard disk for under US $100.00. By the time you read this, it is likely that the costs have come down even further.

Buy Two External Disks and Swap Them Out

For a truly secure backup procedure, we recommend buying two identical external hard disks together with some good backup software. Backup all data in a full "image" which includes your applications and data. Then setup your backup software to automatically backup your changed data files every time your computer goes idle for a few minutes. Finally, set up a schedule so that you swapping the two disks out every couple weeks and remove them from your premises and stored them somewhere else.

With a fairly recent backup (2 weeks or less) stored offsite, if disaster strikes at your office, you can still recover most of your work by buying a new laptop and restoring all the data from the offsite hard disk.

<u>Author's Note:</u> There are many fine backup/restore software tools available today. A quick web search for "Windows or Mac backup software" will show you lots of options. Martin happens to use the backup program from Acronis called "Acronis True Image" (www.acronis.com) which backs up all software programs and data from our entire computer hard disk.

What about online Backup Options? At the time of writing this book in mid-late 2007, several trials of different online backup services did not prove successful. One of the authors had a significant amount of data on his hard disk and the online backup sources could not seem to complete a single backup process without "time out" or "connection lost" or "failure." So he instead decided on the more reliable external USB hard disk solution. The added bonus is that it's less expensive too!

Backup and Restore Your BlackBerry (Windows™ Computer)

If you have an Apple Mac™ computer, please go to page 468.

On a Windows™ computer, you will need to use the **BlackBerry Desktop Manager** software, which you can download for free from www.blackberry.com. For detailed instructions on how to download and install this software please see page 95.

Now that you've finished installing the software, go ahead and start it up by double clicking on the Desktop Manager icon.

If you don't see the icon, then go to Start > All Programs > BlackBerry > Desktop Manager.

Once you've started it, you should see a screen similar to the ones below (either version 4.2 or version 4.3). Depending on how you installed it, you may see fewer or more icons than shown here.

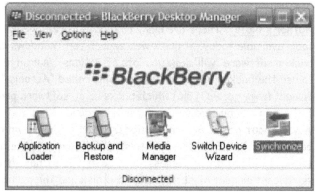

Desktop Manager v4.2 main screen

If you have installed version 4.3 then you will see a screen similar to this one.

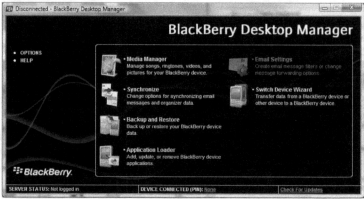

Desktop Manager v4.3 main screen
(v4.3 Images courtesy of Jibi at the "Boy Genius Report" -
http://www.boygeniusreport.com)

Differences between 4.2 and 4.3: You will notice that all the icons of the Desktop Manager are the same between 4.2 and 4.3. The grayed out Email Settings shown in the v4.3 image only appears "active" when you are using the Desktop Redirector or are in using your BlackBerry with a BlackBerry Enterprise Server. This is the same for v4.2.

To start setting up your Backup function:

1. Connect your BlackBerry to your computer (either with USB cable or Bluetooth connection).

2. For v4.2 Desktop Manager, then you must ensure you see your device PIN number and the word "**Connected**" in the bottom of the Desktop Manager main screen as shown, then on the "Backup and Restore" icon.

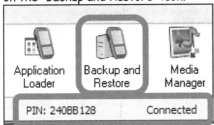

v4.2 screen

For v4.3 Desktop Manager, you need to see your device "PIN" number next to the words "**DEVICE CONNECTED (PIN:**)" at the bottom of the screen, then on the "Backup and Restore" icon.

v4.3 screen

3. If you are having trouble seeing the word "**Connected**" or your Device PIN number, then check out our troubleshooting tips on page 108.

4. After you have double-clicked on the **"Backup and Restore"** icon. You should see a screen similar to this one. The v4.3 screen may look a little different.

5. After clicking **"Backup"** you will be shown a pop-up window asking you where to save your backup file. As we described above, we **strongly recommend** saving your backup file to an external hard disk. (Just in case your main hard disk crashes). So you see in the image below, we have selected the drive letter "F:" for the external USB hard disk.

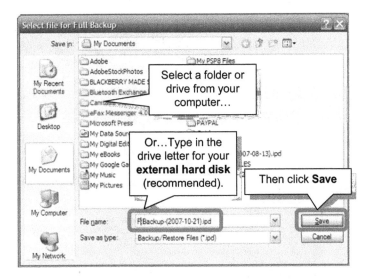

6.   After you have selected a location and clicked "**Save**" then
     the backup process will start. You should see a status
     screen similar to the one below.

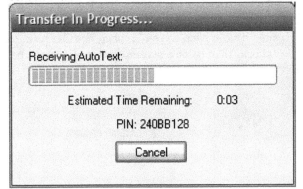

7.   When this screen goes away, your backup is complete and you will then be shown this screen:

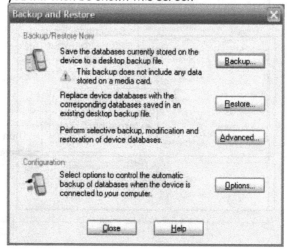

How to Restore Your BlackBerry Data (Windows™)

1.   Follow the directions in the "**Backup**" section above to start Desktop Manager, connect your BlackBerry to your computer and double-click on the "**Backup and Restore**" icon. You should then be on a screen similar to the one below.

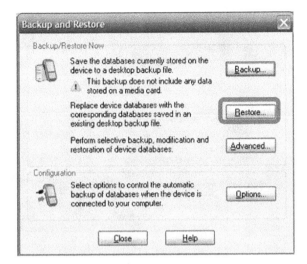

2. Click on the **"Restore"** button and you will be presented with a pop-up window similar to the one after you click Backup.

    IMPORTANT: Now you need to locate your most recent **"Backup"** or **"AutoBackup"** file. Notice from the picture below, you might be tempted to select the 2007-10-17 AutoBackup file, but if you scroll down to the **"Backup"** files, you will notice a more recent file from 2007-10-21 (October 21, 2007).

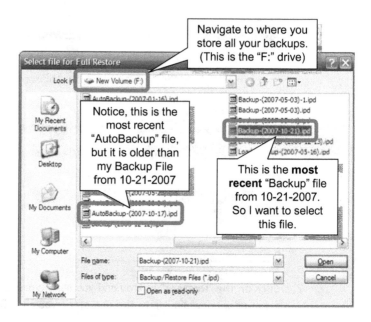

3. Once you click on the file to select it and click "**Open**" you
    will see a window similar to this one that is helping you
    confirm whether or not you want to restore this file to your
    BlackBerry.

    WARNING: Restoring this Backup file will erase everything
    currently on your BlackBerry and replace it with the data
    contained in this restore file, so you want to make sure it is
    the most recent copy as well as verify numbers of Address

Book entries. (Which you see every time you synchronize).

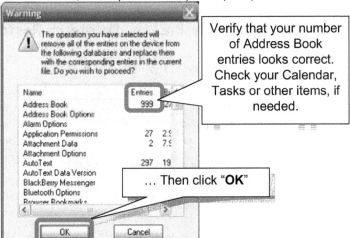

Verify that your number of Address Book entries looks correct. Check your Calendar, Tasks or other items, if needed.

... Then click "**OK**"

4. Now your BlackBerry will be restored with all data from the Backup file.

    NOTE: Any database that has been setup for wireless synchronization or wireless backup cannot be restored or deleted "Cleared." If you BlackBerry is connected to a BlackBerry Enterprise Server, then this will be your Address Book, Tasks, Calendar and MemoPad. Also, some third party applications use wireless synchronization. Examples are "SalesNOW™" and "Handheld Contact™" which wirelessly synchronize your sales-related data in the Sales Force Automation Section of our Software Guide on page 520.

How to Selectively Backup, Delete or Restore Data (Windows™)

1. Follow the directions in the **Backup section** above to start Desktop Manager, connect your BlackBerry to your computer and double-click on the "**Backup and Restore**" icon. You should then be on a screen similar to the one below.

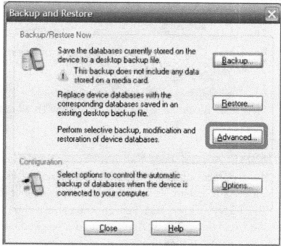

2. Click on the "**Advanced...**" button. Then you will see a screen similar to the one below with two windows. The window on the left is the currently open Desktop Backup file.

    If this window is blank, then you need to click on the "File >

Open" command at the top of the window as shown:

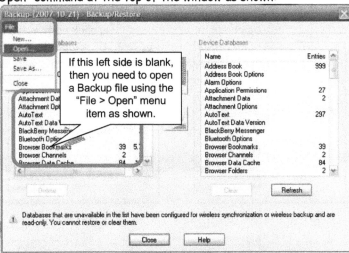

3. **To delete or clear just your Address Book, Tasks, Calendar or other database** from your BlackBerry – for example the Address Book, Calendar or Tasks – you would click on that database in the window on the right "Device Databases" and then click on the "**Clear**" button at the bottom as shown. You will then be warned that all data will be deleted from the selected database, do you want to continue. Indicate "**Yes**" or "**OK**" to delete that database.

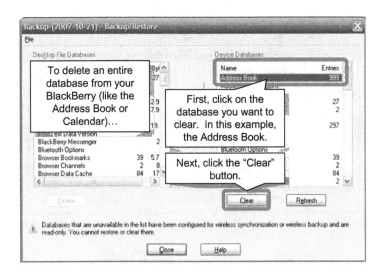

To selectively restore your Address Book, Tasks, Calendar or other database, click on the database in the **LEFT-HAND** window (your "**Desktop File Database**" window) and then click the arrow pointing to the right-hand window. This will copy the entire Address Book (or other selected file) you're your Backup file on your computer to your BlackBerry. Again, you will receive a warning message asking if you want to continue. Click "**OK**" or "**Yes**" to complete the process.

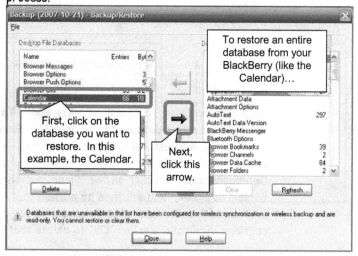

Now, the selected data file (Calendar, Address Book, etc.) will be restored from the backup file on your computer to your BlackBerry.

Automating the Backup Process (Windows™)

1. Follow the directions in the "**Backup**" section above to start Desktop Manager, connect your BlackBerry to your computer and double-click on the "**Backup and Restore**" icon. You should then be on a screen similar to the one below.

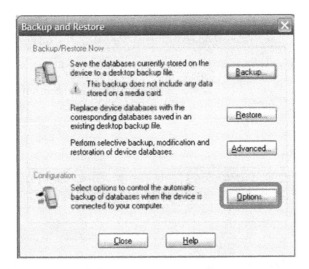

2. This time, click on the "**Options...**" button to see the screen
    similar to the one below. We highly recommend checking the
    box that says "**Automatically backup my device every..**"
    and set it to "**1**" (one) days. Also click on the "**Backup all my
    device application data, except for:**" and then click on the
    checkbox next to "**Messages**" as shown.

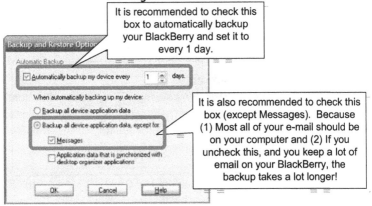

It is recommended to check this box to automatically backup your BlackBerry and set it to every 1 day.

It is also recommended to check this box (except Messages). Because (1) Most all of your e-mail should be on your computer and (2) If you uncheck this, and you keep a lot of email on your BlackBerry, the backup takes a lot longer!

3. If you set your options as shown above to every 1 day, then
    once a day, the first time you connect your BlackBerry to
    your computer, it will pop up a screen that tells you
    "**Automatic Backup**" is ready to start. Click on "**OK**" or "**Yes**"

to start it.   Then pick the location of the backup file – again we recommend an external hard disk for safest storage.

TIP: If you follow the above recommendations, you should rest a little easier knowing that your important BlackBerry data is backed up every single day.

Backup and Restore Your BlackBerry (Mac™ Computer)

If you have a Windows™ computer, please go to page 455.

IMPORTANT: The instructions below apply to **PocketMac for BlackBerry™ software version 4.0**. If you are using a different version of the software, or a different software altogether – e.g. **Missing Sync for BlackBerry™**, then please follow the current instructions provided to you by the software vendor.

NOTE: The information in this book related to PocketMac for the BlackBerry™ is from the **PocketMac for BlackBerry™ v4.0** guide © 2001-2006, Information Appliance Associates.

Backup is Automatic:
The **PocketMac SyncManager™** automatically creates backups of every single data item (called a 'record') it reads from the Mac before it writes it to the BlackBerry. This file is the one that you can use to restore your BlackBerry.

CAUTION: Since the restore function built into PocketMac for BlackBerry™ is non-selective, it will overwrite all information in your BlackBerry. You should be sure you want to do this before you proceed.

Where you backup data is stored (by default):

On your Mac hard disk in this folder:
/Users/[yourname]/Library/Application Support/PocketMac/Backup.

In that folder you will find one or more folders named for the applications that you are syncing to your BlackBerry. For example you may see **"Entourage Appointments," "Entourage Contacts,"** and **"Entourage Notes,"** if you are syncing with Entourage as shown below.

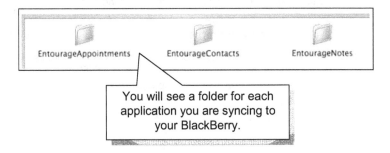

EntourageAppointments   EntourageContacts   EntourageNotes

You will see a folder for each application you are syncing to your BlackBerry.

How to Restore Data to Your BlackBerry:

WARNING: This process will "Add" all the data from your backup file to your BlackBerry Address Book, it will not first erase the Address Book then restore the data. This means if any of the names currently in your BlackBerry Address Book are the same as names in the backup file, you will end up with duplicate entries on your BlackBerry.

So... to avoid this 'duplicate entry' problem, you will need to delete all data from your BlackBerry Address Book before doing the restore.

You have two options to delete all Address Book data if you own a Mac computer:

Option 1: Find a friend or family member who has not yet "Seen the Light" and still uses a Windows™ computer. You'll need to install Desktop Manager and follow the instructions found above on page 464.

Option 2: You could "Wipe" your entire BlackBerry from the BlackBerry itself. This will clear out **ALL DATA** from your BlackBerry (Address Book, Calendar, Email, Email Settings, everything), so you will want to use it sparingly. To "Wipe" your BlackBerry, go into the **Options** Icon. Select "**Security Options**," then select "**General Settings**." Now, press the Menu key and select "**Wipe Handheld**." You will be asked a series of confirmation questions and be asked to type the word "**blackberry**" to confirm this drastic function.

To restore data from these backup folders you must do the following:

1. Quit PocketMac SyncManager, if it's running.
2. Double-click on the backup.SyncManagerRestoreAction file icon.

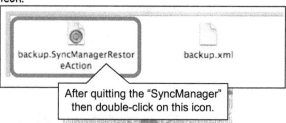

After quitting the "SyncManager" then double-click on this icon.

3. Then you will see the SyncManager RestoreTool and look something like this:

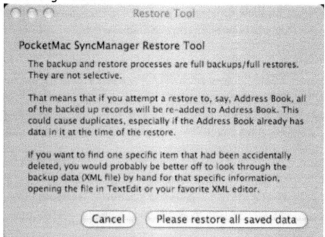

Note the strong warning from the screen shot above, it repeats what was said at the beginning of the section. Make sure you clear out or delete your BlackBerry Address Book (or other icon) before starting this restore process.

4. Click on the "**Please restore all saved data**" button to begin the restore process. You will then see a status pop-up window from the PocketMac Synchronizer. When the window closes, the restore process is complete.

5. Disconnect your BlackBerry and verify the restore worked correctly before you repeat the process for any other databases.

Automating the Backup Process (Mac™)

Since PocketMac for BlackBerry™ automatically backs up all your information before each sync, you do not need to turn this feature "on." The backup is always running.

Battery and
Power Options

Chapter Contents:

As everyone knows, your Battery is critical to the operation of your BlackBerry Pearl. But what you may not know is what happens when it gets too low, how often you should charge it, if there are extended life batteries available, or even what things that cause it to be drained more quickly. In this chapter we will give you an overview of battery-related information.

How often should you charge your Pearl?

We recommend charging the battery every night. Using your phone is the fastest way to consume your battery life, so if you talk a lot on your BlackBerry, you definitely want to charge it every night. Another big drain on your battery is using the speaker to play music or video sound – especially at higher volumes.

TIP: Just plug in your BlackBerry charger cable where you set your BlackBerry every night. Before setting the BlackBerry down, just plug it into the charging cable.

22
Battery
& Power

What happens when the battery gets low?

Low Battery Warning: If the battery gets to only 15% of its full charge, you will hear a beep and see a warning message saying "Low Battery" and the battery indicator will usually change red. At this point, you will want to start looking for a way to get your BlackBerry charged – either by connecting it to your computer with a USB cable, or the regular power charger.

You will hear a "beep" and see the battery indicator turn red and say "Low Battery"

Very Low Battery: When the battery gets down to 5% of its full charge you are in a "Very Low Battery" condition. At this point, in order to conserve what little remaining power there is, the BlackBerry will automatically turn off your wireless radio. This will prevent you from making any calls, browsing the web, sending/receiving email or any messages at all. You should try to charge it immediately or turn it off.

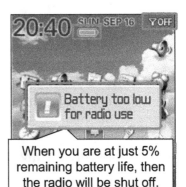

When you are at just 5% remaining battery life, then the radio will be shut off.

(Almost) Dead Battery: When the BlackBerry senses the battery is just about to run out altogether, then it will automatically shut off the BlackBerry itself. This is a preventative measure, to make sure your data remains safe on the device. However, we recommend getting the BlackBerry charged as quickly as possible after you are in this condition.

When your battery is just about to die, then the BlackBerry will shut itself off.

Can I re-charge my BlackBerry in the car?

Yes, the easiest way to do this is to purchase a car charger from a BlackBerry Accessory Store. To find a car charger; type in "blackberry car charger" in your favorite web search engine.

The other way to charge your BlackBerry is to use what is called a "vehicle power inverter" that converts your vehicle's 12V direct current (DC) into Alternating Current (AC) to which you can plugin your BlackBerry charger. The other option with a power inverter is to plug your laptop into it then connect your BlackBerry with the USB cable to the laptop (a true "mobile office" setup).

Can I re-charge my BlackBerry from my computer?

Yes, as long as your computer is plugged into a power outlet (or vehicle power inverter) and your BlackBerry is connected to your computer with a USB cable.

Tips and tricks to Extend my Battery Life

8. If you are in an area with very poor (or no) wireless coverage, turn off your radio with the "Turn Wireless Off"

22
Battery
& Power

icon. When the radio is searching for the network, it uses a lot of battery.

9. Use your headphones instead of the speaker to listen to music or watch videos.

10. Use your speakerphone sparingly; it uses much more energy than either the regular speaker or your earphones / headset.

11. Decrease the backlight brightness or reduce the timeout. You can do this in your Options icon > Screen/Keyboard as shown below.

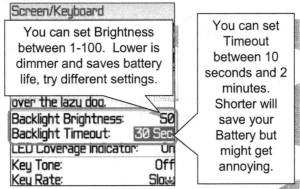

Screen/Keyboard

You can set Brightness between 1-100. Lower is dimmer and saves battery life, try different settings.

You can set Timeout between 10 seconds and 2 minutes. Shorter will save your Battery but might get annoying.

over the lazy dog.
Backlight Brightness: 50
Backlight Timeout: 30 Sec
LED Coverage Indicator: On
Key Tone: Off
Key Rate: Slow

12. Make sure to power down your BlackBerry every night. If you are forgetful about this or would just like it done automatically, then use the Auto On/Off settings. This is also found in the Options icon under "Auto On/Off". Adjust your settings for weekday and weekends as shown.

Auto On/Off

Weekday: Disabled
Turn On At: 07:00
Turn Off At: 22:00
Weekend: Disabled
Turn On At: 08:00
Turn Off At: 22:00

Set the Weekday and Weekend auto on / off settings.

13. If possible, set your profiles (see page 67) to ring and/or vibrate less often.

14. Use data intensive applications sparingly. Such applications make a lot of use of the radio transmit/receive and will use up the battery more quickly. Examples are mapping programs which transmit large amounts of data to show the map moving or satellite imagery.

15. Send email or text instead of talking on the phone. The phone is probably the most intensive user of the battery life. If possible, send an email or SMS text message instead of making a call. Lots of time this is less intrusive for the recipient and you may be able to get an answer when a phone call might not be possible – e.g. in a meeting, etc.

Can I buy a longer life battery for my Pearl?

For those of you who really need to use your Pearl to its fullest extent, yes, there are extended life batteries that will give you almost 200% of the capacity of the original battery. However, since many of these batteries are twice the size of the old battery, you will need to use a door that lets the battery stick out the back of the Pearl. NOTE: At publishing time, these extended life batteries and extra battery door covers were not available for every single model Pearl on every carrier. Just make sure that the battery and new door are compatible with your particular BlackBerry Pearl.

Section 8:
Adding Capabilities
to Your BlackBerry

Adding & Removing Software

Chapter Contents:
- Ways to Install New Software
- Installing Software Wirelessly on Your BlackBerry
- Installing using Desktop Manager (Windows™)
- Upgrading Your BlackBerry Device Software
- Installing using PocketMac for BlackBerry™ (Mac™)
- Removing Software directly from your BlackBerry
- Removing Software using Desktop Manager (Windows™)
- Removing Software using PocketMac for BlackBerry™ (Mac™)

Check out the next chapter – our "Mini" Software and Services Guide for answers to questions like:

"What is good software for my BlackBerry?"
"Where can I find it?"
"Is any of it free?"
"How much does it cost?"

Today there are hundreds of software applications and services to help extend the capabilities of your BlackBerry.

Ways to Install New Software

There are several ways to install software on your BlackBerry.

Option 1: Click on a link and download wirelessly or "Over the Air" also called "OTA". You may have the link emailed to you after entering your address into a web form on the software vendor's or web store's site. (See #1 below). Another way is to type a web address directly into your BlackBerry web browser (See #2 below). TIP: You will need to use the "**Go To...**" menu command in your Browser to type any web address.

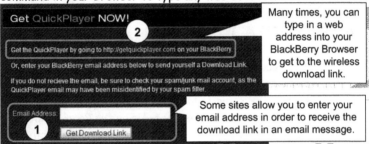

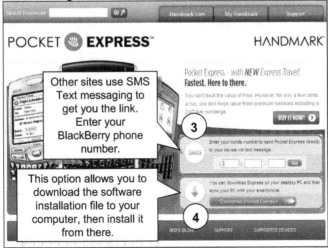

Some sites ask you to enter your "Mobile Phone Number" – this is your BlackBerry phone number – in order to send you an SMS Text Message with the download link. (See #3 below)

Option 2: Download a file to your computer then connect your BlackBerry to your computer and install it via USB cable connection. (See #4 above)

Option 3: (Only if your BlackBerry is connected to a BlackBerry Enterprise Server.) Your BlackBerry Server Administrator can "push" new software directly to your BlackBerry device. Using this option is both wireless and automatic from the user's perspective.

We will describe options 1 and 2 in this book.

Installing Software from Your BlackBerry Over-the-Air ("OTA")

The beauty of the wireless "Over-the-Air" ("OTA") software installation process is that you do not need a computer or CD, or even a USB cable to install new software. It is really quite easy to install software Over-the-Air on the Pearl. (Author's Note: Software installation used to be a much more painful process in older BlackBerry models, thank goodness for Research In Motion's continuous technical advances!)

To Install Software OTA:
1. To install software from your BlackBerry, as we described above, you need to either click a link you received in your email or SMS text message or start the Web Browser and "**Go To...**" a web address where the software download files are located. In this example, we will use www.mobile.blackberry.com
2. Navigate around the web site and click on a link for the software title you want to install.

3. Usually, a license agreement screen pops up. You must click "Accept" to continue with the download.

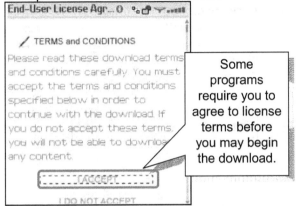

Some programs require you to agree to license terms before you may begin the download.

4. The next screen to appear is the standard "**Download**" screen. This screen shows the name, version, the "**Vendor**" (software company), and size of the program. Below all this information you see a "**Download**" button to click on.

Once you get to this screen, click on "Download"

5. The progress of the download will be displayed in the center of the screen.

6. NOTE: You may see a warning message that says something like:
    "**WARNING: Application is not digitally signed. Do you want to continue? Yes or No**"
    You must click "Yes" to continue, but make sure this is

software from a vendor that you recognize or have confidence that it is not malicious.

7. Once the application is completely downloaded, a dialogue box pops up notifying you the download was successful. You may be given an option to "Run" the program.

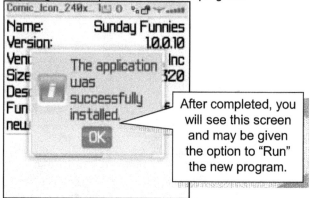

After completed, you will see this screen and may be given the option to "Run" the new program.

8. Finally, if you clicked on "**Run**" you would start the newly installed software; clicking "**OK**" brings you back to the original web page where you downloaded the file. To exit to your Home Screen, press the ESCAPE key a few times.

9. You will then see the new icon either on your Home Screen of icons, in the Applications sub-folder, or after you press the Menu key to see all your icons.

TIP: Depending on the type of software you have downloaded, you may need to do some special network configuration and settings work. Please see our **Access Point / TCP Network Settings** section starting on page 427.

Installing Software - BlackBerry Desktop Manager (Windows™)

Apple Mac™ User? You may use either use the "Over-the-Air" installation process found on page 480 or use the PocketMac for BlackBerry™ process on page 492.

Where to find good BlackBerry Software? You can download both free and paid software from a variety of places. If you haven't already, please see page 479 for more details.

TIP: If you have the option of using the wireless over-the-air installation method, you should use it. Over-the-air installation is generally easier (fewer steps) than this desktop installation option.

How do I know if I have the Over-The-Air option?
If you see a request for your email address or phone number from the software download website, this means that you have the over-the-air option available. (See on page 479).

The instructions below show you how to install new software on your BlackBerry using a file that you have downloaded to your Windows™ computer. You will be using BlackBerry Desktop Manager software to install this software on your BlackBerry.

1. If you have not already done so, download the software installation file from the software vendor or Internet store web site.

You can download Express on your desktop PC and then sync your PC with your smartphone.

Download Pocket Express

(Image from www.handmark.com)

2. The software installation file you will download usually has either an "**.exe**" or "**.zip**" file extension.

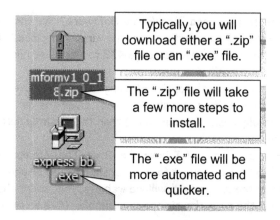

Typically, you will download either a ".zip" file or an ".exe" file.

The ".zip" file will take a few more steps to install.

The ".exe" file will be more automated and quicker.

".zip" extensions: This is a compressed file containing at least two files with these extensions: ".alx" and ".cod". If your download is a .zip file, then you will need to extract these files to a folder or to your Windows™ desktop.

(a) To do this, double-click on the .zip file to open it up.

(b) Right-click inside the folder that just opened and select "Extract All..."

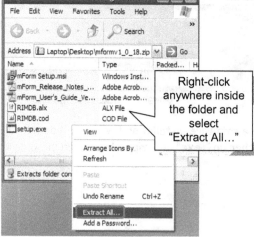

Right-click anywhere inside the folder and select "Extract All..."

(c) Follow the wizard to extract all the files. Usually, it will extract all the files into a folder on your Windows Desktop with the same name as the original .zip file.

(d) Remember the folder name or extraction location. You will need it later when you have to "Add" the ".alx" file from within the BlackBerry Desktop Manager Application Loader Icon.

".exe" extensions: This is a software installation file. When you double click on it, it will start a normal Windows software installation program. This method will be slightly easier for you, because a few of the manual steps with the '.zip' file are performed automatically by the .exe installation file. The .alx and .cod installation files are automatically placed in a location that is recognized by the Desktop Manager. Then the Desktop Manager is automatically started to complete the installation to your BlackBerry.

23
Adding
Software

WARNING: After you double-click on the .exe file, you may be asked to choose between several options. You will need to ensure that you are selecting the software option that is designed for your BlackBerry Pearl, also known as the **"BlackBerry 8100"** as shown below.

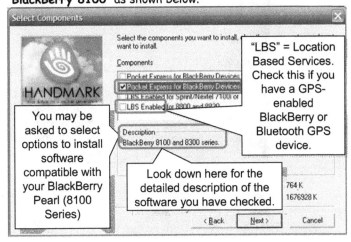

3. If the BlackBerry Desktop Manager has not started automatically at this point, go ahead and start it by clicking on the Desktop Manager icon on your desktop or going to "Start > All Programs > BlackBerry > Desktop Manager." Once started, you will then want to double-click on the "Application Loader" icon inside Desktop Manager.

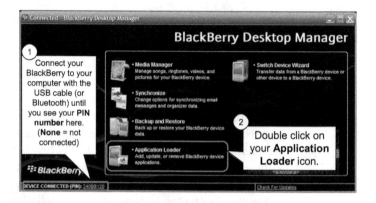

4. Now, make sure your BlackBerry is connected to your computer and then click the "Next" button.

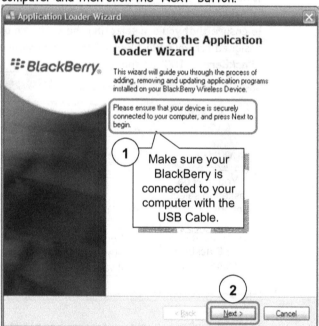

5. You will then see a screen similar to the one below. You will then need to make sure there is a checkmark next to the application you are trying to install.

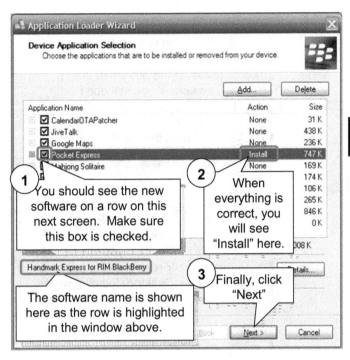

TIP: If you don't see the software you want to install in the list, first try scrolling to the bottom of the list. Sometimes it's just "off the bottom of the screen." If you still don't see it then click on the "Add" button as shown below. Locate the folder where the ".alx" file is located and double-click on that file. This will be where you 'unzipped' the files if you started this process with a '.zip' file.

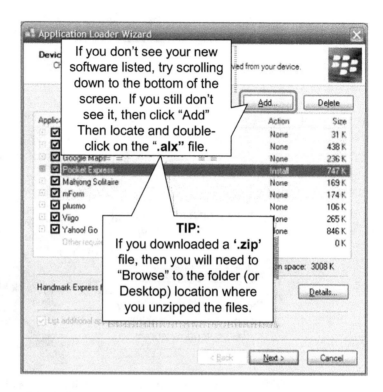

TROUBLESHOOTING: If you have just double-clicked on the ".alx" install file and you see this error message about "No additional applications..." (See below), then it is very likely that the application is already "checked" and on the list but off the bottom of the visible list of applications. Just scroll down to make sure it's there.

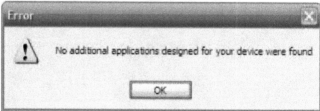

6. The next screen you will see will ask you to confirm your selections and then click "Finish" as shown:

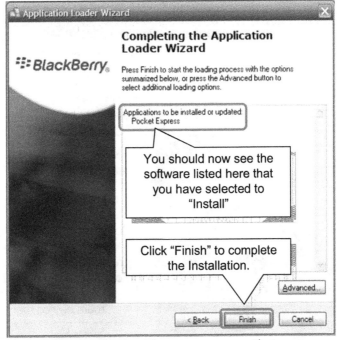

TROUBLESHOOTING: If you see an error that says something like **"The device file system is full"** as shown below, then you will need to either remove other applications (See page 495), media files (See the chapter in this book about working with Media files) or other data like old email (See page 228) from your BlackBerry main "Device Memory"

before you can install this program.

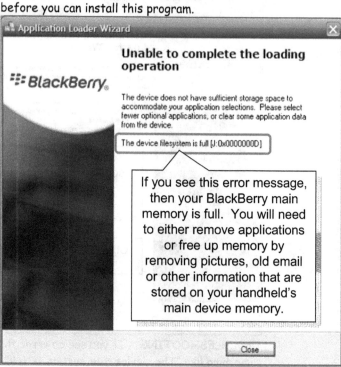

7. When you see a screen saying the loader has successfully completed, you may detach your BlackBerry from your computer and start to use the new application software. NOTE: In some cases, your BlackBerry may reboot itself to complete the installation. This is normal and may take a few minutes to complete.

Once your BlackBerry is done rebooting, you may need to press the Menu key in order to locate the new icon.

TIP: If your new software application requires a wireless connection to transfer data and it does not "auto-configure" its network settings, then you may want to check out the TCP Troubleshooting section on page 427. You may also need to contact the vendor for support.

Upgrading Your BlackBerry Device Software

The software running on your BlackBerry is called "Device Software," "Handheld Software," "System Software," or your "Operating System" software. From time-to-time, RIM together with your BlackBerry phone company will release new versions of this software for your handheld.

23
Adding
Software

WARNING: If you received your BlackBerry from work, then please check with your organization's Help Desk before doing any software upgrade procedure.

In order to upgrade your BlackBerry Device Software, you need to download the upgrade software from the phone company's web site or your phone company's section of the BlackBerry.com web site. Once you download and install this software on your Windows™ computer, then the next time you connect your BlackBerry to your computer, the Desktop Manager software will prompt you that an upgrade to your System Software is ready to be installed. The Application Loader inside Desktop Manager will guide you through the process which usually includes a backup and restore process. See our section on the Application Loader starting on page 482.

BLACKBERRY DEVICE SOFTWARE UPGRADE SITES:

Please visit:
http://na.blackberry.com/eng/support/downloads/download_site s.jsp

You will see a screen similar to the one below. Scroll down to find your BlackBerry phone company.

NOTE: If your phone company was not listed on this screen, please contact your phone company directly for the correct link.

Installing Software - PocketMac for BlackBerry™ (Apple Mac™)

Windows™ PC User? You may use either use the "Over-the-Air" installation process found on page 480 or use the BlackBerry Desktop Manager for Windows™ process on page 482.

Where to find good BlackBerry Software? You can download both free and paid software from a variety of places. If you haven't already, please see page 479 for more details.

Internet.lnk

TIP: If you have the option of using the wireless over-the-air installation method, you should use it. Over-the-air installation is generally easier (fewer steps) than the Mac-BlackBerry installation option.

How do I know if I have the Over-The-Air option?
If you see a request for your email address or phone number from the software download website, this means that you have the over-the-air option available. (See on page 479).

The instructions below show you how to install new software on your BlackBerry using a file that you have downloaded to your Apple Mac™ computer. You will be using PocketMac for BlackBerry™ program to install this software on your BlackBerry.

Source of the information in this section: *PocketMac for BlackBerry™ v4.0 User Guide* ©2001-2006 Information Appliance Associates. If you are using a newer version of the software, steps may have changes, please consult the user guide for the most up-to-date information.

1. Download the new BlackBerry software application to your Mac. If the file you have downloaded is in a compressed or zipped format, then you will need to "unzip" these files in order to install them on your BlackBerry. To "unzip" the files, double-click on the file you downloaded and follow the instructions to uncompress all the files. Sometimes, you can highlight all the files and just drag them to your desktop to extract them. If these files get extracted to a particular folder, then remember the folder name, you will need it later to install these files.

2. Start your PocketMac for BlackBerry™ software and Click on the BlackBerry icon at the top of the screen. Then click on the "Status" bar and verify you see the BlackBerry is

23
Adding
Software

shown next to "Device" and the Status is shown as "Available"

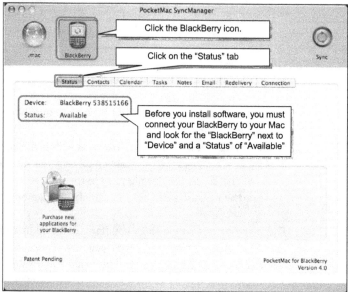

3. Now, click on the "Utilities" menu at the top of the screen and select "Install Software to Device"

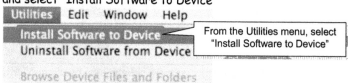

4. You will be asked to locate the ".alx" file to install the software to your BlackBerry. This is the software file you downloaded to your Mac from the web or copied from a CD/DVD. This might also be the software that you just unzipped. Once you locate the correct file, then you will see

a screen similar to the one below.

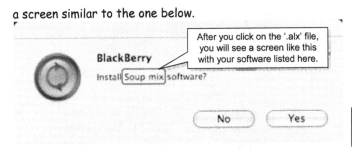

After you click on the '.alx' file, you will see a screen like this with your software listed here.

BlackBerry

Install Soup mix software?

No   Yes

5. Finally, if the software installs correctly, you will see a screen similar to the one above, but with the word "Done" instead of the question.

    TROUBLESHOOTING: If you see an error that says something like "**The device file system is full**", then you will need to either remove other applications (See page 495), media files (See the chapter in this book about working with Media files) or other data like old email (See page 228) from your BlackBerry main "Device Memory"

Removing Software Directly from your BlackBerry

There will be times when you wish to remove a software title from the BlackBerry and you are not connected to your computer. Fortunately, it is very easy and intuitive to remove programs from the Pearl itself.

To remove software directly from the BlackBerry, just do the following:

1. Press the Menu key and click on the "Options" icon.
2. Click on "Advanced Options"

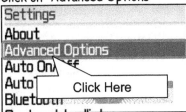

Settings
About
Advanced Options
Auto On/Off
Auto   Click Here
Bluetooth

3. Scroll to the top of the list and click on "Applications."

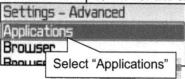

4. The screen will now display all the programs installed on your BlackBerry. Scroll to the application you want to delete to highlight it, then press the Menu key and select "Delete"

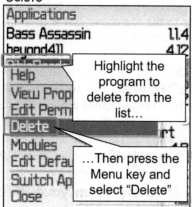

5. Then you will need to confirm that you want to delete the program and it will be removed.

    NOTE: Sometimes you BlackBerry will need to reboot itself in order to complete the program deletion process. It will tell you if it needs to reboot and ask you to confirm.

    TROUBLESHOOTING: If the software is not completely removed from your BlackBerry after following the above steps, then try this:
    1. Go back into the **Options** icon.
    2. Select "**Advanced Options**"
    3. Select "**Applications**"
    4. Press the Menu key and select "**Modules**"
    5. Now scroll down the list of modules and make sure to delete every module with a name that is related to the software you are trying to remove. (You highlight a module, press the

Menu key and select "Delete" from the menu).

Removing Software - BlackBerry Desktop Manager (Windows)

While it is possible to remove most software titles from the BlackBerry itself, there may be times when you prefer to remove a particular software title using the Desktop Manager Program.

23
Adding
Software

One of the key benefits to using this method instead of deleting programs directly from your BlackBerry is that you can delete many programs at once.

To remove software using Desktop Manager, perform the following steps:

1. Start the BlackBerry Desktop Manager software on your Windows™ computer. You may either click on the Desktop Manager icon on your desktop or go to "**Start > All Programs > BlackBerry > Desktop Manager.**" Once started, you will then want to double-click on the "**Application Loader**" icon inside Desktop Manager.

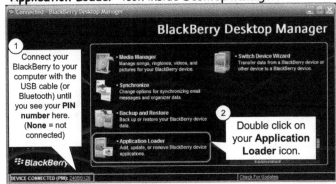

2. Now, make sure your BlackBerry is connected to your computer and then click the "**Next**" button.

3. The next screen will show a list of all programs installed on your BlackBerry with check boxes to the left of each one. Simply uncheck the box next to all the programs you wish to

un-install and then click "**Next**."

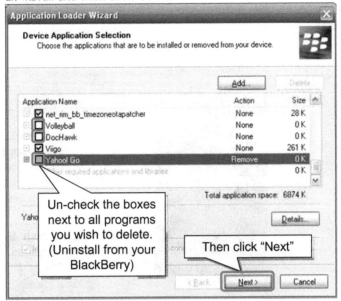

4. The final screen confirms the application to be deleted. Just click "**Finish**" and the selected application will be

removed from the BlackBerry.

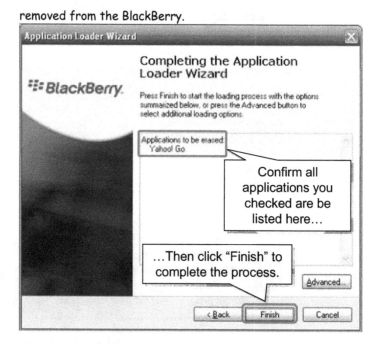

5. When the process is complete, you will see a "**Success**" screen and it is likely your BlackBerry will be rebooting itself. The reboot process takes several minutes, during which you will see the spinning hourglass. When the BlackBerry is done rebooting, all the programs you deleted should be removed.

   TROUBLESHOOTING: If certain programs are not being removed, or you encounter errors when you try to remove programs, then try doing a "Hard Reset" and then repeat the above program deletion steps. The "Hard Reset" is when you remove the battery from your BlackBerry, wait 10-15 seconds and replace it.

Removing Software - PocketMac for BlackBerry™ (Mac™)

IMPORTANT: Only software that has been installed using your Mac computer on your BlackBerry can be removed using this procedure. If you have installed software using the wireless 'Over-the-Air' method on your BlackBerry, then you must also remove that software directly from your BlackBerry. See page 495 for details.

23
Adding
Software

Source of the information in this section: *PocketMac for BlackBerry™ v4.0 User Guide* ©2001-2006 Information Appliance Associates. If you are using a newer version of the software, steps may have changes, please consult the user guide for the most up-to-date information.

1. Start your PocketMac for BlackBerry™ software and Click on the BlackBerry icon at the top of the screen. Then click on the "Status" bar and verify you see the BlackBerry is shown next to "Device" and the Status is shown as "Available"

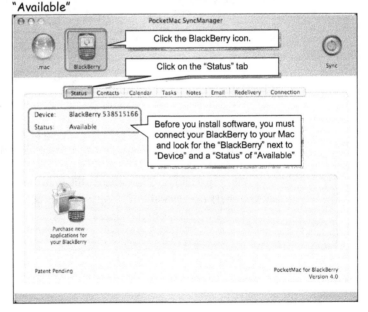

2. Now, click on the "Utilities" menu at the top of the screen and select "Uninstall Software to Device"

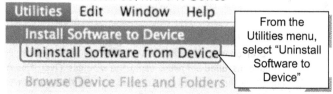

From the Utilities menu, select "Uninstall Software to Device"

3. You will be shown a list of software that was installed using this Mac computer. Click on the software title you want to remove and then click the "Uninstall" button. (Note: If you did not install the software using this Mac, you can still remove it using the process on page 495)

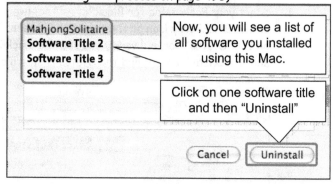

Now, you will see a list of all software you installed using this Mac.

Click on one software title and then "Uninstall"

TROUBLESHOOTING: If you have some problems with the uninstall process, then try doing a "Hard Reset" of your BlackBerry by removing the battery, waiting 10-15 seconds and then replacing it. Sometimes this helps to remove some of the software 'locking' of programs that could cause trouble with the uninstall process.

A Brief Software and Services Guide

Chapter Contents:

Purpose of this Brief Guide

We have included this "**brief**" software and services guide to help you begin to understand the scope of cool and amazing things you can do with your BlackBerry. It is not meant to be a 'definitive' software guide. (We may put one together in the future if there is enough popular demand. Please email us at info@blackberrymadesimple.com and let us know your thoughts!)

Some of these Third Party Software and Services apply equally to users with BlackBerry Enterprise Servers as well as small office/home office or individual users. In this guide we make an effort to stay focused on products that have the widest applicability.

The software we cover in this guide tends to be "fairly" easy to download, install and configure and (most often) does not require you to have your BlackBerry connected to a BlackBerry Enterprise Server.

What follows is a brief sampling of the many thousands of software and services you can use to add capabilities to your BlackBerry. **Enjoy!**

Overview of Third Party Software and Services

We all know the BlackBerry can do some amazing things by itself, but what you may not know are all the cool, helpful and productivity boosting things that can be done when you add-on new software and services.

Any software or services that you add to your BlackBerry after you take it out of the box are sometimes called "**Third Party Software and Services**" or "**Add-On Software.**" .

Research In Motion, BlackBerry's maker calls them "Independent Software Vendors" ("ISV" for short) and has setup an "Alliance Program" for vendors who want to work more closely with RIM. Some of the vendors listed in this guide are "RIM ISV Alliance Members" and others are not, you should be able to tell by visiting the software vendor's web site. The complete list of all RIM Independent Software Vendors Alliance Members can be found by going to BlackBerry's web site and looking at their **Solutions Guide**. (See page 507).

The Third Party software and services market has grown almost as fast as BlackBerry sales themselves. Today there are hundreds of software applications and services to help extend the capabilities of your BlackBerry.

Benefits of Software and Services

Some of the benefits of third party software and services are:
- Take a break with BlackBerry games
- Make changes to that Microsoft Word™ or Excel™ document right on your BlackBerry
- Re-book travel easily with 'All-in-one' services
- Drive more safely with your BlackBerry reading email and calendar events to you
- Keep up-to-the-minute track of sales efforts from your BlackBerry
- Project your BlackBerry on your computer for great training and sales applications
- Find just about anything, anywhere using great search tools
- Get help from a personal concierge service anywhere in the world
- Get up-to-the-minute news and radio broadcasts
- Send and receive faxes right from your BlackBerry
- Keep highly organized managing hundreds of tasks and get more done by effectively delegating to colleagues
- Track travel expenses and mileage right on your BlackBerry
- Have your voicemails converted to text for easy (and discrete) reading and acting upon (even during meetings).
- Stay in touch anywhere by receive voicemail as email audio attachments from your other phone numbers.
- Brush up on a new foreign language with dictionaries and audio phrase books.
- Get all your contacts, calendar, tasks and memo items wirelessly synchronized and get 'military grade' security
- Buy almost anything from your BlackBerry easily and securely.
- Convert BlackBerry pictures to clearer images and even editable text.
- Save money on international calls by using voice over IP (VOIP) technology from your BlackBerry.

24
Software
& Services

Changing Software & Companies

New software companies are springing up frequently and existing companies are expanding and improving their offerings. Software and Services companies tend to come and go frequently. Please be aware that some of the products and services listed in this book may no longer be available, or newer versions and companies may have emerged by the time you read this book. At the time of writing this book in late 2007, this was what we feel is a broad sampling of what was available.

On almost a weekly basis, if you do a web search for "BlackBerry Software" or "BlackBerry Services" you will find new software titles and companies appear or disappear.

Where to Find BlackBerry Software, Services & Technical Support

There are quite a few places to find Software and Services. The first place we recommend is the Partners section of www.blackberrymadesimple.com. You can get there directly by entering www.blackberrymadesimple.com/partners into your computer's web browser.

Web Stores
You can usually purchase software from these stores.
www.bberry.com
www.crackberry.com
www.eaccess.com
www.handango.com

Online Reviews of Software, Services, Accessories and other BlackBerry-related news and Technical Support.
www.allblackberry.com
www.bbhub.com
www.berryreview.com

www.blackberrycool.com
www.blackberryforums.com
www.boygeniusreport.com
www.howardforums.com (The RIM-Research In Motion Section)
www.pinstack.com
www.RIMarkable.com

BlackBerry Official Partners
BlackBerry Solutions Guide
https://www.blackberry.com/SolutionsGuide/index.do
Software and services you will find in the Solutions Guide will be
more focused toward business users than individuals.

24
**Software
& Services**

The "Built for BlackBerry" Software Site
http://na.blackberry.com/eng/builtforblackberry/

Each of the categories pages looks like this: *(At least at the time
of writing of this book – they may look different when you are viewing
them.)*

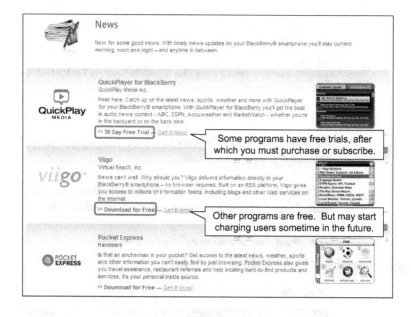

Fun Stuff: Games from Magmic

All of us have wanted to unwind and 'kill a little time' after a hard day's work – what better way than with a great game or two on our BlackBerry? The people at Magmic have quite an array of fun games for your BlackBerry. Watch out – some of these games have been known to be quite addictive!

How to find these games? Go to www.magmic.com from your BlackBerry web browser.

What is the pricing? US$5 - $20.

Below are a few of the game titles that were available at the time of publishing. They come out with new games every month, so check out their web site for more.

Fun Stuff: Customize Your Pearl Trackball Color

Pimp My Pearl for BlackBerry - This application allows you to customize your Pearl trackball color from seven choices and even add several effects such as (Solid, Disco, Rainbow, Dimmer and

Flash) **How do you get it?** Go to www.handmark.com, select the Pearl from the device list, click on the "Store" link at the top and scroll down until you find it. **How much does it cost?** $4.99 one-time.

Finding Things: Your Favorite Search Engines

All the big search engine sites such as **Google** (page 329) and **Yahoo!** (page 328) all have mobile sites, go ahead and visit them from your BlackBerry.

Google also has software called "**Google Maps**" (free) that is very useful to find addresses, businesses, directions and even traffic reports for major cities. We describe how to get the most out of Google Maps see page 382.

Finding Things: Semantic Search from AskMeNow

The service from AskMeKnow is known as 'semantic search' or 'natural language search'. What this means is that you just type in your question and hit "Send" – then the service will respond with the most likely answer via email or SMS text message. Examples might be trivia questions such as: "What year was bubble gum invented?" or "Which baseball team has won the most world series titles?" or "Who is the tallest person?" You can even ask for things

```
Aug 20, 2007 2:17:23 PM
1/2
MLB
8/19/2007
LA Angels 3 at Boston 1
FINAL
Next Game: 8/20/2007 7:10
PM Boston at Tampa BayGet
Brittanicas Daily Biography
free! Reply BIO
$0.0
```

like weather and the latest sports scores. You can use their "AskMeNow" application to send email messages about specific topics, or send an SMS text message with question to 27653 ("ASKME"). You will receive the answer back in a few moments. You may also access 411 listings, weather. Movies, sports, directions and more. If you like the service, you should download and install the AskMeNow application to your BlackBerry. With the application, you can choose a category such as Sports, Weather, News Headlines, Directions, Stocks and more. Once you ask your question, you will notice a new email sent by the application and soon receive an answer via email as well.

How to I get this application? To get it, go to www.askmenow.com from your computer and click on the "Applications" link to enter your BlackBerry phone number. Then you will receive a text SMS message with the download link. (See our instructions on wireless "OTA" downloads on page 480)
What is the pricing? US$0.25 for each question or $5 a month if you subscribe – all billed to your BlackBerry phone carrier bill.

All-In-One Services (Search, Travel, News, etc.)

There are several vendors, and more coming that tackle the problem of organizing search, travel, weather, news and other information on your small blackberry screen into an easier-to-navigate and digest package. Some of these products even alert you when there are changes to your flight or other travel-related issues.

All-In-One: PocketExpress

24
Software & Services

Pocket Express gives you an organized view of News, Sports, Weather, Stocks, Entertainment (Movies, Theater), Search (411), Flights and Hotels, Maps and an "Assist." The Assist function ties you into your own personal assistant for help with restaurants, reservations, tickets to events, ground transportation, movie, weather information. You can also get help resolving flight and hotel re-booking, resolving other transpiration and hotel problems while on the road and even translator / interpreter services. They also offer emergency assistance including road-side assistance, help outside regular business hours and help contacting friends and family with urgent news. The assistant can also connect you to medical professionals for help.

How do you get it? Visit http://express.handmark.com/ and download your free trial using your BlackBerry phone number.
How much does it cost? Free for the Travel, News, Sports and Weather channels. $6.99/month or $69.90/year for the Express Executive edition which gives you everything except the Concierge Assistant service. $9.99/month or $99.90/year for the Elite edition which includes the "MobileCierge" concierge service.

All-In-One: WorldMate Live

WorldMate Live from MobiMate provides a way to manage your full travel itinerary including your travel arrangements and business meetings. All details are available right on your BlackBerry. You receive alerts of upcoming events and when certain items status change such as a airline flight status. You synchronize information from your organizer calendar on your computer (e.g. Microsoft™ Outlook™) to your account on the WorldMate Live web server. They do have a special "plug-in" to more easily synchronize data from your Microsoft™ Outlook™ calendar. Then you can view, edit and update the information on your BlackBerry. You can synchronize flight, hotel, car, meeting, and public transportation. You also then receive real-time access to flight details and on-time status, gate changes, maps and directions, critical phone numbers, and all your e-ticket and confirmation numbers. You also receive live updates of changes to your itinerary (e.g. flight status, arrival notices, etc.) so you can make real-time alternate arrangements and contact people for help. You can also access all the same information on a live web application and even view your itinerary on a map. Get flight details and verify addresses. You can even share your itinerary with your colleagues or have an assistant manage it for you. Your itinerary is always kept up-to-date wirelessly on your BlackBerry.
How do you get it? Visit www.worldmatelive.com from your computer. **How much does it cost?** Free for the basic edition. They also offer a premium edition.

All-In-One: Yahoo Go!

Recently Yahoo! Has launched a free new software and service called "Yahoo! Go" which is an application that installs right on your BlackBerry. If you have a Yahoo! User ID, then you can read and reply to email and more fully integrate to your Yahoo! Account. (But you don't need a Yahoo! ID to use this software.) The idea is to make it much simpler to browse information and find answers.

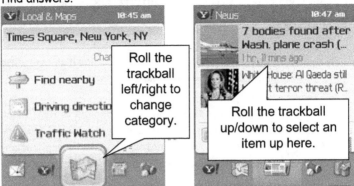

The search screen is the main screen and looks like this image below. NOTE: At time of publishing, this search screen required you to use 'Multitap' to enter your search text (a little cumbersome compared to SureType™). This may be changed by the time you read this book.

24
Software & Services

How to get access? Go to www.yahoo.com from your BlackBerry web browser and click on the "Upgrade to Yahoo! Go" or "Y! Go" links.

What is the pricing? Free

Productivity Booster: Document Management with MasterDoc™

MasterDoc™ is an application has that has many very useful capabilities bundled into a single software package:

- ✓ Store and access any file types on your BlackBerry main memory or expansion MicroSD memory card (not limited to media files, like in the native BlackBerry applications).
- ✓ Store and access files from an online storage system wirelessly.
- ✓ Store, search for, and access files stored on your home or office computer. (NOTE: Your home/office computer needs to be turned on, connected to the Internet and running software called "eFile Desktop" from DynoPlex).
- ✓ View email attachments in a way that offers improved functionality over the native BlackBerry email attachment viewer.
- ✓ Receive and send faxes right from your BlackBerry.
- ✓ You can even print documents and faxes directly to a Bluetooth-compatible printer.

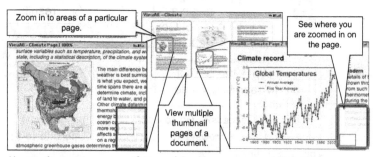

MasterDoc appears as if it could make a great addition to your BlackBerry. **How to get access?** Go to www.dynoplex.com from your BlackBerry web browser and navigate to the "Mobile" site, then the "Downloads" page and finally click on the "Install" link next to "MasterDoc". **What is the pricing?** US$50 (They also offer a free trial.)

Productivity Booster: Microsoft™ Office™ Documents

As we all know, Microsoft™ Office™ is a very powerful and full-featured tool for our desktop or laptop computers. When you try to 'squeeze' a good deal of the core functionality of Office™ onto the small BlackBerry screen, without a mouse, you should expect a different 'user experience' than on your powerful desktop or laptop computer. One of the key differences you will experience is that things seem much slower on your BlackBerry than you are used to on your desktop. This is because the BlackBerry has a much less powerful processor than your desktop. With all those 'caveats' you have one option today and will have a second option by early 2008. The goal of these software packages is to increase your productivity by giving you the ability to access, edit, store and send important business documents anywhere on your BlackBerry.

24
Software
& Services

Productivity Booster: eOffice™ from DynoPlex

DynoPlex has been offering their Microsoft Office™ product for several years and is already in version 4.0.

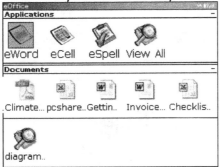

eOffice™ provides full-featured MS Word and MS Excel viewing and editing capabilities. It also has many of the same capabilities of MasterDoc™ listed above. There is also a built-in spell checking application. You can access or store documents on the BlackBerry main memory, media card (MicroSD), on a secure Internet site, or even your home or office computer (if it's turned on and 'on-line'). Print documents to a local or network printer and even send documents as faxes from your BlackBerry.

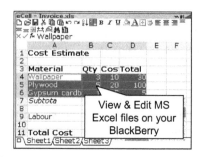

View & Edit MS Excel files on your BlackBerry

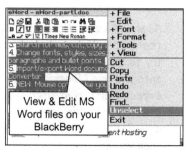

View & Edit MS Word files on your BlackBerry

Productivity Booster: Documents to Go® from DataViz, Inc.

(Estimated Release Date: 1st Quarter 2008)

Those of you coming from the Palm OS world will already be familiar with "Documents to Go®" software from DataViz, Inc. This software maker is now preparing a BlackBerry version that will allow you to view and edit Microsoft™ Office™ documents on your BlackBerry. DataViz, Inc. says they will allow you to edit Word, Excel® and PowerPoint® files on your BlackBerry. Below are some 'pre-release' screen shots of the application running on a BlackBerry Pearl.

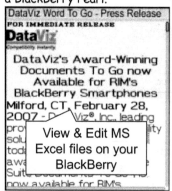

View & Edit MS Excel files on your BlackBerry

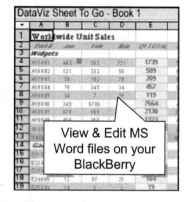

View & Edit MS Word files on your BlackBerry

Productivity Booster: High-Powered Task List

ToDoMatrix Professional from REXwireless software is a very powerful and feature-rich to-do / task management application designed just for the BlackBerry. This is the task list to end all task lists! With ToDoMatrix, you can manage an unlimited number of tasks organized by project and folder. You can also delegate your tasks to anyone in your BlackBerry address book. And what's even better, your tasks are sorted by delegate – so you can instantly pull up all tasks delegated to a particular person and check status with them while on a phone call.

24
Software & Services

You can set up to three alarms for each task – which can be extremely useful if you need to remember to do something (Alarm-1) the night before (remind your son/daughter about tomorrow's dentist appointment), (Alarm-2) the morning of (make sure your child has a note about the dentist to take to school) and (Alarm-3) right before the event itself (make sure to leave enough time to pick up your child from school).

If you, or a colleague or family member wants to view or update your tasks, they can do so on a secure web site (as long as you give them your username and password) from any internet connected computer. ToDoMatrix is provides a great tool for the busy professional who juggles multiple projects simultaneously at work and home.

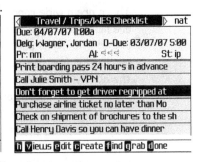

In the screens below, we see the ability to "Inject" or create a task in ToDoMatrix directly from an email message received on your BlackBerry. We also see the ability to delegate a task to anyone in your BlackBerry address book – after we delegate, we have the option of sending an email directly to that delegate –

saving the time required to make a phone call. (Works best if your delegate already knows the task may be coming...)

Message Stat	Inject into todoMatrix	To–Do Edit	Choose delegate
Sent: Dec 20,	Inject into ideaMatrix	Folder: Travel / T	Add from contacts
From: BlackBer	Select	Due:	Save
Subject: Top 10	Mark Unopened	Delg:	Close
, To open the	Save	Delg Due:	not set
selected phone	Delete	Status:	not started
Send key. To e	Previous Item	Priority:	normal
End key.	Next Item	Alert 1:	not set
2. To dial a pho	Next Unopened Item	Call Julie Smith – VPN	
Home screen,	Close		
prevent dialing	from the Home		

How much does it cost? $59.95 which includes 6 months of REXDesktop. After that period, REXDesktop is $24.00 / year. **Where to get it?** On your computer's web browser, go to www.rexwireless.com

Other BlackBerry software from REXWireless include: IdeaMatrix (great for developing new ideas and notes in a freeform database); and for teams: ReferenceMatrix delivers always-fresh information to a team's BlackBerry smartphones. KnowledgeMatrix supplies a collaborative workspace for teams.

Productivity Booster: Faxing On Your BlackBerry

There are a wide range of vendors in this area. Some vendors are more 'pure' fax companies (e.g. eFax), other companies provide faxing as part of a more full-featured BlackBerry application (e.g. MasterDoc™ from DynoPlex). Needless to say, the ability to send and receive / view faxes directly on your BlackBerry is a great productivity booster. You save trips to your office to retrieve and send faxes and can be much more responsive while you're away from your desk.

eFax – Send and Receive Faxes. TIP: With this service, you can also use any local fax machine as a printer to print most common email attachments (Word, Excel, PowerPoint, PDF, etc.). **NOTE:** In order to be able to view faxes on your BlackBerry, you need to make sure you set the fax image attachment format to Adobe PDF, the default image format is not readable on your

BlackBerry. **How do you get it?** Go to the partners section on www.blackberrymadesimple.com and click on the link or, on your computer web browser go to: www.efax.com **How much does it cost?** $129.95/year.

MasterDoc™ from DynoPlex. This is a full-featured application that packs many of the top requirements into a single application. We describe it on page 277.

Productivity Booster: Mobile Forms

The ability to create customized forms to allow BlackBerry users to collect information while out in the field on a sales call, service call or simple survey is a great productivity booster. Like all the other applications areas, this is one which has a growing number of vendors. However, because of the custom nature of the forms, you will likely want to find a consulting company that has already successfully implemented a BlackBerry forms solution.

24
Software & Services

At publishing time, here are a few vendors who said they have ability to put custom forms on BlackBerry devices:
mBiz Tech – www.mbiztech.com
Pronto – www.prontoforms.com
Rovenet Portable Forms – www.portableforms.com
Flowfinity Forms – www.flowfinity.com

Here are a few consulting companies that have worked with BlackBerry devices:
AVID Wireless – www.avidwireless.com
Integrated Mobile – www.integratedmobile.com

Productivity Booster: Mobile Sales Tracking Software

A powerful way to boost productivity is by providing your highly mobile sales force access to their key information: contacts, sales opportunities, schedule, tasks and other resources. There are a wide variety of applications in this market and typically fall into two major groups:

(1) "Tied Into Other Software" BlackBerry software that ties into a specific desktop or web-based sales force package or service (For these, you are required to purchase the desktop or web-based sales force package in addition to the BlackBerry application), and,

(2) "Complete / Web Based" Software that is 'independent' and does not require you to already own or purchase a specific sales force package. This option works well if you or your organization does not already use a specific sales force automation system.

SalesNOW™ from Interchange Solutions Inc. falls into the 'Complete / Web Based' group (It does not require you to own or purchase a separate sales force system to get access to the data while not on your BlackBerry). SalesNOW provides a complete solution for both on-BlackBerry and off-BlackBerry access to sales contacts, companies, sales opportunities ("deals") and activities. The SalesNOW Team Edition provides team collaboration and visibility on all sales activities and team forecasts. With this solution, there is no software to purchase, you are subscribing to the service for both BlackBerry and web access available from any Internet-connected computer.

The SalesNOW™ BlackBerry application is fully integrated into the core BlackBerry applications. Just work as you normally would in BlackBerry email, phone, tasks or calendar. You will see the "Add to SalesNOW" menu item to allow you to attach that phone call log, meeting, or task to a contact or 'deal' in SalesNOW. You can even see up-to-the-minute sales reports such as the 'sales funnel', 'sales history' and 'sales forecast by month' right on your BlackBerry. Since the information is kept up-to-date wirelessly with the SalesNOW web interface, you or your entire team can stay in touch anywhere.

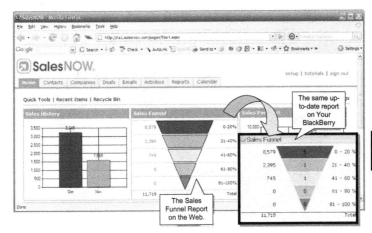

How do you get access? Visit www.salesnow.com from your computer's web browser.

How much does it cost? $25/month for an individual or $40/month for a team member (Enterprise Edition).

Handheld Contact from J2X Technologies, Inc. falls into the "Tied Into Other Software" category as it requires you to own or purchase ACT!® Contact Management software from Sage Software company. Just like in ACT! you can view your Contact List, Calendar and Task List. Delegate using the "Schedule For" field in the Calendar and Task list. See your familiar "Calls," "Meetings," and "To-Do's" all in separate colors on your calendar.

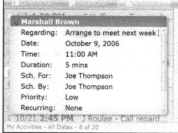

It enables you to wirelessly access and manage your Sage ACT! contacts, tasks, calendar, and notes from your BlackBerry handheld. **How do you get access?** Visit www.handheldcontact.com from your computer's web browser. **How much does it cost?** $24.95/month or $239/year.

Other large sales force automation software or service providers such as Salesforce.com and SAP do have BlackBerry versions to access key data while on the go. If you have a particular sales force automation system, probably the best way is to start with a web search which includes your software name and 'blackberry' or 'blackberry access' to see what might be available today.

Productivity Booster: Track Expenses and Mileage

ExpenseLog Pro from J2X Technologies, Inc. is a complete expense tracking and reporting hosted solution. It lets you manage and report your expenses wirelessly on your BlackBerry. It also includes unlimited access to the ExpenseLog Pro website to archive expenses and reports from your computer. You can even email your expense reports to colleagues.

ExpenseLog Pro has many features including currency conversion, colleague collaboration, expense categories, and more. **How do you get access?** Visit www.expenselog.net from your computer's web browser. **How much does it cost?** $29.90/year.

24
Software & Services

MileageTracker Pro from J2X Technologies, Inc. is a complete mileage tracking and reporting hosted solution. It lets you manage and report your mileage wirelessly on your BlackBerry. It also includes unlimited access to the MileageTracker Pro website to archive trips and reports. You can email mileage reports to colleagues.

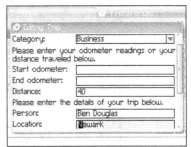

MileageTracker Pro has many features including mileage rate and currency customization, colleague collaboration, trip categories, and more. **How do you get access?** Visit www.mileagetrackerpro.net from your computer's web browser. **How much does it cost?** $29.90/year.

Safety: Use Your BlackBerry (More) Safely in Your Car

In addition to always using a Bluetooth Headset or Car Kit, we also recommend one of the many programs that will read your voice mail or text messages or email to you in the car. These services allow you both 'hands free' and 'eyes free' access to your BlackBerry email, phone, calendar, contacts and other functions.

Our first recommendation is that when you are driving – you drive and leave the email or calendar for when you are not driving. If you find your self unable to do this, you may want to check out our upcoming "BlackBerry Addiction / CrackBerry" book from BlackBerry Made Simple!

Nuance – (Available Now) Nuance Voice Control allows you to make phone calls, work with your calendar and dictate short email messages by speaking instead of typing.

How do you get it? Go to www.handmark.com, select the Pearl from the device list, click on the "Store" link at the top and scroll down until you find it. **How much does it cost?** $5.99/month.

Voice on the Go – (Available Now) (www.voiceonthego.com) Voice on the Go provides hands and eyes-free access to email,

contacts and calendar while driving. There is a In locations where using the BlackBerry with your hands is either unsafe or prohibited by law, Voice on the Go provides access and control of your BlackBerry. (See the review from www.blackberrycool.com at http://blackberrycool.com/2007/07/18/005150)
How do you get it? Visit www.voiceonthego.com from your computer's web browser. **How much does it cost?** $5.99/month for the Individual version. You need to contact them for pricing on their Business version.

iLane – (Not yet available at publishing time) from Intelligent Mechatronic Systems Inc. (www.ilane.com). This is a product seen by one of the authors at the 2007 BlackBerry Wireless Enterprise Symposium show in Orlando, Florida. Their web site at time of publishing says "coming soon," however, by the time you are reading this it may be fully available. This product reads your emails to you, allows you to speak responses for replies or forwarding the message. You can do the same with SMS text messaging, access your calendar, receive the latest news, stocks and sports updates, and open text-based attachments, all without typing, scrolling or pressing any buttons.

24
Software
& Services

Anti-SPAM: Spam Prevention from SpamArrest®

As soon as you start using your BlackBerry, you become even more sensitive to SPAM email messages. There is no SPAM checker built into the BlackBerry itself, like you might find on your work or desktop email application. Unless you have effective SPAM protection at work or elsewhere, you will need to invest in a service. The authors have tried a number of different Anti-SPAM services or software. The one that seems to work well with the BlackBerry handheld is one called SpamArrest. The reason it works well is that all email sent to your account (unless you put an 'approved sender' on the list) is "challenged." In other words, spammers will receive a email reply from your SpamArrest account asking them to verify they are a real person by typing in a code that is visible on the screen to a human, but not a computer. This seems to eliminate virtually all your SPAM email messages.

How do you get it? On your computer web browser go to: http://www.spamarrest.com/affl?4004399

How much does it cost? $5.95/month, $24.95/6 months, $44.95/year.

Voicemail Tools: Voicemail to Text Services

These vendors will convert your voicemail messages into text and email that text to your BlackBerry. The key benefits of voicemail-to-test services are:

✓ **Save time listening to lots of voice mail messages -** reading the short text email messages are much faster

✓ **Delegate tasks by quickly forwarding the transcribed voicemail** message as an email to a colleague or assistant.

✓ **Respond quickly and accurately via email** by replying to the caller via email. (Especially helpful if the caller was looking for a name, email, street address, phone, fax number or other written information.)

Be much more responsive from almost anywhere - there are times – in meetings, waiting in public places, etc. – when reading and replying to an email message (transcribed from a voice mail) is more socially acceptable and private than dialing-in to check voicemail and then calling people back.

Do Your Own Research

There are also a lot of vendors in this market, and the companies come and go... so the best thing to do is to use the list below as just a 'starting point', but do your own research when you are ready to start moving forward. As always, a web search with relevant terms ("voicemail to text" or "blackberry voicemail to text") seems like a good way to find the current vendors.

Line1 (www.viewyourvoicemail.com) – this provider seems to be re-packaging SpinVox services. See SpinVox write-up.

SimulScribe™ (www.simulscribe.com) – From their web site: SimulScribe utilizes voice recognition technology to convert your voicemail messages into text. SimulScribe delivers the transcribed voicemail, along with the original audio, to your BlackBerry. **How much does this cost?** $9.95/month for up to 40 messages. ($0.25 for each additional message) $29.95/month for unlimited messages.

SpinVox (www.spinvox.com) This provider even takes the idea a few steps further with "SpinMyBlog" (Speak you Blog posting into your BlackBerry and it gets converted to text and posted on your Blog), "SpinMyBroadcast" (Speak your text message – it is converted into text and broadcast to a group of people), "SpinMyMemo" (Speak a memo into your BlackBerry and SpinVox sends it as text to your email inbox).

24
Software & Services

Vonage (www.vonage.com) If you have Vonage phone services, they are now offering this voicemail-to-text option as part of a premium service.

Voicemail Tools: Voicemail from Other Phones

One thing that is useful is to hear voicemail messages as email attachments from your phone numbers that are not your BlackBerry phone. What happens is this: (1) A caller leaves a message for you on another phone number. (2) The phone company/service provider creates an audio file (e.g. .wav format) and sends it to you as an attachment to an email message. (3) You see the email arrive on your BlackBerry and open the audio attachment which has the voice mail message.
Benefits:
- Never had to dial-in to check messages
- Be much more responsive by seeing voice mail messages instantly when they are left (rather than having to check your messages).

Most regular phone companies do not offer this service, but we have found a few companies that do offer it today: AT&T

CallVantage (www.attcallvantage.com) and Vonage (www.vonage.com). We are certain there are other services that provide this voicemail as email attachment, you just need to research their service offering very carefully. NOTE: We strongly recommend you do a test message, or verify that the format of the audio attachment is one that can be read by your BlackBerry device as an email attachment. (".wav" is a good format.)

News and RSS Readers

Many web sites, especially those with content that changes frequently like news, weather, sports, forums, blogs, etc. will have "RSS" or "Really Simple Syndication" feeds. These are feeds that package their top information into "always updated" and "bite size" chunks. Usually each news article will be sent out in an "Abstract," "Summary," and give a link to "Read More" or "Full Story". The "Abstract" is usually just the headline. The "Summary" is normally a 1-2 sentence summary of the story. And the "Read More / Full Story" usually takes you to the web site to read the full story.

There are a number of players in this market. We have just listed a couple in the book. Again, to find the most current list, try entering "blackberry rss reader" into your favorite internet search engine.

News: FreeRange WebReader from FreeRange Communications

This reader was just updated in late summer 2007 and has many features: organize feeds into folders, mark stories to read later, zoom into images (a good tool for small BlackBerry screens), their own 'slimmed-down' browser to easily perform the 'read full story' function, "Mark for later," email articles, post to "Del.icio.us," shortcut keys, and a "Flight Mode" which allows you virtually 'full use' while on an airplane. They also provide some short video tutorials on their web site: www.freerangeinc.com to help you learn the basics and advanced features.

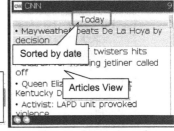

"Flight Mode" which allows you to view the reader and perform features even with your BlackBerry wireless radio "OFF" (as when you are on an airplane). You can still use the features that normally require a wireless network connection like "View Full Article" or "Email Article". All these requests are queued until you turn off Flight Mode and then automatically performed.

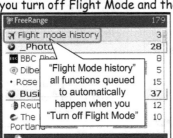
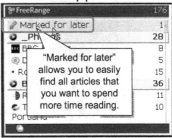

How to get it? Visit http://mwap.at from your BlackBerry Browser. **How much does it cost?** Free for up to 10 feeds or $39.95/year for unlimited feeds.

News: Viigo RSS Reader from Virtual Reach

This RSS reader is also designed to work perfectly on the BlackBerry. You can setup an number of "Channels" (RSS Feeds) in your Viigo reader. It is packed with features: View abstract or full articles, view in you BlackBerry web browser, or in Viigo's web browser, Email an Article, save interesting articles, and post to Del.icio.us. It is fast and works well, and it's free.

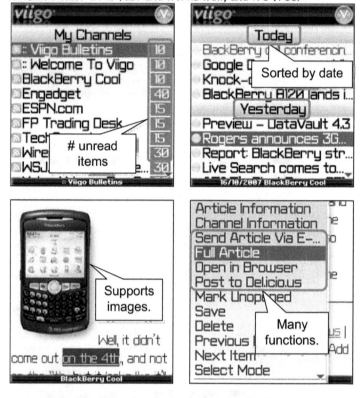

How to get it? Visit http://mobile.virtualreach.com from your BlackBerry Browser. **How much does it cost?** Free for the Standard Edition with over 1,000 channels.

News: QuickPlayer Streaming Radio Broadcasts

QuickPlayer provides access to over 100 'channels' of short broadcasts for your BlackBerry. At publishing time, the content categories included: News, Business, Sports, Entertainment, Opinion, Health and Wellness, Inspirational, Local News and Local Sports. This makes your BlackBerry act and sound like a mini-satellite radio. Popular channels include: ABC News, ESPN, Accuweather and MarketWatch.

Select your channel and listen to your favorite information right on your BlackBerry. WARNING: This service is quite data intensive and may require about 20 MB (mega bytes) of data per month just for itself. It is recommended to have an unlimited data plan for this service. Check with your BlackBerry carrier before you subscribe. **How do you get it?** On your BlackBerry, go to: www.getquickplayer.com and follow the instructions to download the software. **How much does it cost?** There is a 30-day free trial. After that it is $7.95/month.

24
Software
& Services

Reference: Translators, Phrase Books and other Dictionaries

Since your BlackBerry is always with you, it's a great place to put a foreign language translator. You can also use it to look up medical, legal or other terms.

BEIKS provides a full range of spell checkers, translators, phrase books (including pronunciation guides) and other language tools such as the Medical, Legal or Christian dictionaries. Languages available at publishing time are Arabic, Bulgarian, Dutch, English, French, German, Greek, Hebrew, Italian, Japanese, Latin, Portuguese, Russian, Spanish and Turkish.

How to get this software? Visit http://mobile.beiks.com from your BlackBerry Browser. Then select "RIM BlackBerry." Then click on "Dictionaries" or whatever else you might be interested in. **How much does it cost?** The software ranges in price. The LexSpell checker is free. Dictionaries are $29.95. Phrase books are $19.95.

Wireless Sync: Hosted Email and Enterprise Server

Small offices and individuals, who do not have the technical or financial resources to have an email server and BlackBerry Enterprise Server in-house, can 'rent' access to a hosted environment. Why would you want to do this? Added security, wireless updates (never plug in to sync again) of address book, calendar, tasks and memo pad, shared calendaring, and reduce fixed expenses of buying servers and hiring extra technology staff to maintain them. (See page 80 for a more complete list of benefits.)

There are several companies out there today that offer hosted Microsoft Exchange email accounts as well as access to those accounts via a BlackBerry Enterprise Server which connects to your BlackBerry. Such companies usually charge you a monthly or annual subscription fee.

TYPICAL PRICING: Most of these providers give you access to a Microsoft Exchange™ mail box for about $10 / month then you need to buy access to the BlackBerry Enterprise Server for another $10 / month and there may be some one-time setup fees (of US $30-$50).

ASP-ONE - Visit: http://www.asp-one.com
Mi8 Hosted Exchange - Visit: http://www.mi8.com
MailStreet - Visit: http://www.mailstreet.com

Cool: Buy Things from Your BlackBerry

Digby is a way to shop instantly and easily right from your BlackBerry. Many popular stores are already available, with more being added frequently. At publishing time, some of the stores available were: FTD.com,

Barnes & Noble, Best Buy, Chefs, Fossil, Godiva, Cooking.com, QuickGifts, OfficeMax, Wine.com, Sephora and RedEnvelope. Your credit card information is stored on your BlackBerry and is secured by a password. It is sent over a secure web link as part of orders you make on Digby. Imagine sitting in an airport and buying some great Godiva chocolates or FTD flowers for her or a new BestBuy digital toy or Barnes & Noble new book for him before your long business trip. **How to get it?** On your BlackBerry go to: http://www.digby.com/download **How much does it cost?** It's free.

Cool: BlackBerry Viewer from Rove Wireless

24
Software
& Services

The products in this section are ideal for any application where you need to display a "live" BlackBerry screen onto your Windows™ computer. Typical applications might be:
- Training people on the BlackBerry
- Doing a sales demonstration of your BlackBerry software (either live or via web-conferencing tool).
- Capturing evidence from a BlackBerry device
- Displaying evidence from a BlackBerry in a courtroom
- Displaying your BlackBerry screen at a large convention or trade show
- Creating some of the screen shots shown in this book.

NOTE: Not all of the applications below are both Mac and Windows™ compatible.

BlackBerry Viewer from Rove Wireless (formerly **Idokorro**): Although the BlackBerry Viewer is not software you install on your BlackBerry, it is quite useful if you ever have to train a group of people or demonstrate something on your BlackBerry to a group of people. What it does is take your BlackBerry screen and give you an "almost live" version of the

BlackBerry screen on your desktop or laptop computer. ("Almost live" because the image 'lags' a little and sometimes key-clicks and trackball-clicks on the BlackBerry are missed – you just need to repeat them.)

With the BlackBerry Viewer you can then project that image on a large screen or even share it via the web for remote training, sales or support applications. For years, this application was made by a company called "Idokorro", but recently they changed their name to "Rove Mobile" www.rovemobile.com. Rove provides many other cool software tools including their flagship "Mobile Admin" that allows people to remotely manage servers, databases or networks from their BlackBerry handhelds. **How do you get this software?** Go to http://www.rovemobile.com/products/bbviewer/ from your computer. **What is the pricing?** US$25.00.

NOTE: At publishing time, this did not work on a Mac. If you use a Mac, then check out the **Project-a-Phone product** in this section.

Cool: Video Your BlackBerry Screen with Project-a-Phone

This is a product that includes a setup where the BlackBerry (or any mobile phone) is held on a stand with a clamp and a computer-connected video camera is trained on the device itself.

24
Software
& Services

Author's Note: That is not a BlackBerry Pearl in the image... just use your imagination! (Source: www.projectaphone.com)
It is essentially taking a video image of the screen of your BlackBerry and displaying that video image on your computer. It is quite flexible as a training or sales tool and is also used to take screen shots and record audio video clips for documentation, marketing, or evidence collection purposes. There are two models the ICD-1300 (lower resolution) and the ICD-5000 a high-resolution product. The ICD-5000 can take screen shots up to 3.15 mega pixels and provide up to 30 frames per second at VGA video resolution (640 x 480). At the time of publishing, Project-a-Phone was planning to introduce a model that connects directly to a monitor or projector.
How do I buy this product? Go to www.projectaphone.com from your computer web browser.
How much does it cost? The ICD-5000 costs $395, the lower-resolution ICD-1300 costs $295. The ICD-1300 will work on a Mac™

Cool: Convert Document Pictures to Clearer Images & Text

scanR scanR – www.scanr.com – This is an innovative service that will take pictures of documents that are sent as email attachments, clean them up and, if possible, convert these images into usable text. For BlackBerry Pearl 8130 and devices with the 2.0 mega pixel or higher cameras – you can even take pictures of documents and whiteboards to convert them into very clear PDF files or send them to a fax machine.

How it works? Snap a picture of a white board or document. Then email the whiteboard image to wb@scanR.com, or the document to doc@scanR.com. The scanR service processes the image, creates an Adobe PDF file and attempts to turn it into a text file. NOTE: It can be difficult with the images you can get from your BlackBerry to convert documents into a text file. However, the PDF files look great and we believe that as the BlackBerry cameras continue to improve in quality, the text quality will also improve. scanR offers a business card service that turns pictures into electronic contacts (vCard). This requires a 2 mega pixel camera with auto-focus. Hopefully, RIM will create a model with such a camera soon!

How do I get this service? Just snap a picture and email it to the address indicated above. (See how to do this on page 336).
How much does it cost? The service is free to try and costs $3 per month for unlimited storage, scanning and faxing.

Cool: Voice Over IP (VOIP) from Your BlackBerry

This is the same technology that allows people today to make voice calls using their high-speed internet connections with services such as AT&T CallVantage, JAJAH, Skype, and Vonage. Now, with higher speed wireless data networks, this Voice Over IP ("VOIP") technology is starting to be extended to BlackBerry devices. There are rumors that RIM, the maker of BlackBerry is exploring this as well. Since this is such a fast growing and changing area, please take the list below with an understanding that some of these companies will no longer be in existence and in there may be new players with better service, better pricing or both. The safest way to check the current market is type in "VOIP and BlackBerry" into your favorite Web Search Engine and see what pops up.

24
Software & Services

Author's Note: Some of these BlackBerry - VOIP technologies are in their 'infancy' and may prove to be slightly difficult to setup or use compared to just dialing the BlackBerry phone. Therefore, we strongly suggest you 'try before you buy' with any of these services.

A few companies that were providing this service at the time of publishing are listed in alphabetical order:

BBCalls & JAJAH (www.bbcalls.com and www.jajah.com) To use this combination, you will need to download and install the BBCalls software on your BlackBerry and sign up for a free JAJAH calling account. Once setup, you can call any other JAJAH subscriber for free and other callers at reduced rates. **How to get this software?** Visit http://bbcalls.com/ota/bbcalls.jad from your BlackBerry web browser. (See page 314 for Web Browser help.)

Gizmo Project (www.gizmoproject.com) This software allows you to place a free voice call to any of the following instant messenger ("IM") contacts: Gizmo Project, Yahoo! Messenger, Google Talk, or Windows Live users. If you want to call anyone else in the world, then you need to buy "Call Out" credits. There

are relatively low rates to call international numbers. **How to get this software?** Visit www.gizmo5.com from your BlackBerry web browser. (See page 314 for Web Browser help.)
TIP: You can even use this software on your Windows™, Mac™ or Linux™ computer.

Mino Wireless (www.minowireless.com) allows you to place international phone calls at a lower rate than you normally are charged. Mino allows you to dial directly from your BlackBerry Phone or Address Book by selecting a "Call with MINO" from the menu before you start the call. After installed, you will see a new icon from which you can follow the setup instructions. **How to get this software?** Visit http://getmino.com from your BlackBerry Web Browser.

Where to Go
for More Information

Chapter Contents:
- Resources Available From the BlackBerry
- Forums and Discussion Groups
- BlackBerry.com
- BlackBerry Made Simple Videos

One of the great things about owning a BlackBerry is that you immediately become a part of a large, worldwide camaraderie of BlackBerry owners.

Many BlackBerry owners would be classified as "Enthusiasts" and are part of any number of BlackBerry user groups. These user groups along with various forums and web sites serve as a great resource for BlackBerry users.

Many of these resources are available right from your BlackBerry and others are web sites that you might want to visit on your Computer.

Resources to Access from the Pearl Itself

The first place to start is the "Help" item found on most of the menus. Learn all about how to use BlackBerry built-in help on page 51.

Some of the resources actually have software icons to install right on your BlackBerry Home Screen. Others, you will want to set as bookmarks in your BlackBerry web browser (Learn about bookmarks on page 317).

The official BlackBerry mobile website:
1.   Start your BlackBerry Web Browser.
2.   Press the Menu key and select "**Go To…**"
3.   Type in mobile.blackberry.com
4.   The Page is organized with a Help Directory, a "What's Hot" section, Fun and Games, Great Sites, Messaging, Maps & GPS and a BlackBerry page.

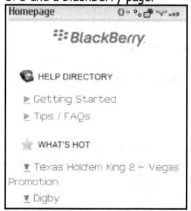

5.   Click on any link to download software or visit the linked Web site.

Forums and Discussion Groups such as "Pinstack" and "BlackBerry Forums." A forum is an organized discussion about anything and everything BlackBerry. On each of these sites, you can discuss your Pearl, find tips and tricks as well as post questions and read answers to other user's questions.

At time of publishing, here are a few of these more popular forums.
www.boygeniusreport.com
www.blackberrycool.com
www.blackberryforums.com
www.crackberry.com

www.pinstack.com

Some sites, like Pinstack, even provide you a way to install an icon in your BlackBerry application menu for one-click access.

1. Like you did previously, open your Web Browser and use the "Go to" menu command to go to www.pinstack.com

2. Complete the registration process and your screen will reflect your user name.

3. Use the trackball and navigate to the Forums, Downloads, FAQ or Shop. For our purposes, we will go to "BB Forums" and click.

4. Navigate through the Forums or use the Search tool to find a particular topic of interest. One of the forums will be specific to the BlackBerry Pearl – usually entitled BlackBerry Pearl 8100.

25
Other
Resources

5. Various discussion threads on topics related to the Pearl will then be listed like those below. TIP: Try your best to enter your question under the 'correct' forum topic – you are much more likely to find people answering you if you are in the correct topic area.

There are many, many other web sites to visit for more information and helpful resources such as www.blackberryforums.com, www.blackberrycool.com, www.crackberry.com and others offer news, information and discussion forums.

BlackBerry Made Simple Short Video Training for Individuals

Our videos are all short and to-the-point – most are just 3 minutes long.

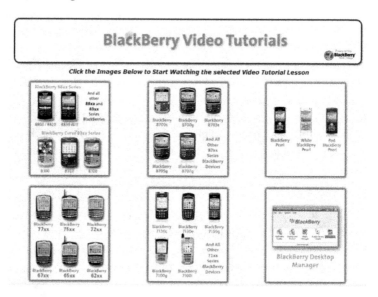

With these videos, you can learn a new thing in just a few minutes.

Gone are the days of trying to puzzle out how to do something. You can just watch and learn by seeing the expert do it on their BlackBerry.

At publishing time, these videos were organized into five easy-to-use lessons: (We continuously improve the user interface, so you may soon see them organized in a different way.)

Video Home Page > **BlackBerry Pearl™ / 8100 Series Videos**

 Click here for Click here for Click here for Click here for

Getting Around	Phone	Voice Dialing	Pictures	Troubleshooting
Stand By	Email	Bluetooth Headset	Security	Settings
Typing Tips	Fax	Address Book	Web Browser	Google Maps
Email Setup	Calendar			Modem

How to Turn On and Off Your Pearl

Learning Your Way Around

Stand By Mode (put in pocket)

Organizing Your Icons (Move / Hide)

Changing Side Convenience Keys

Changing the Theme (Look & Feel)

Typing: SureType vs. Multi-Tap

Typing: SureType Tips

Typing: Save Time with AutoText

BlackBerry Pearl / White BlackBerry Pearl / Red BlackBerry Pearl

Click Topic to view Video or PDF file.
Videos require Flash Player
PDF files require Adobe Reader.

Email Setup: Corporate (BlackBerry Enterprise Server)

Email Setup: Internet Email (BlackBerry Internet Service)

Email Setup: Create a New BlackBerry Email Account

Email Setup: Change or Remove Internet Email Account

Organize Top 5 Icons (Zen Theme)

  Feedback Keyword Search Lesson Quiz Next Lesson

25
Other
Resources

Video Home Page > **BlackBerry Pearl™ / 8100 Series Videos**

Click here for   Click here for Click here for Click here for

Getting Around	Phone	Voice Dialing	Pictures	Troubleshooting
Stand By	Email	Bluetooth Headset	Security	Settings
Typing Tips	Fax	Address Book	Web Browser	Google Maps
Email Setup	Calendar			Modem

Phone: Typing & Sending Call Notes

Phone: Viewing Call Logs in Messages Inbox

Phone: Calling Voice Mail

Phone: Speed Dial

Phone: Check Calendar, Addresses, Email

Email: Setting Inbox Display & General Options

Email: Hotkeys - Short cuts (PDF)

BlackBerry Pearl / White BlackBerry Pearl / Red BlackBerry Pearl

Click Topic to view Video or PDF file.
Videos require Flash Player
PDF files require Adobe Reader.

Email: Opening Attachments (Word,Excel,PDF,Picture)

Fax: Receiving and Viewing a Fax

Calendar: Hot Keys (PDF)

 Back Lesson Feedback Keyword Search Lesson Quiz Next Lesson

Video Home Page > **BlackBerry Pearl™ / 8100 Series Videos**

| Getting Around Stand By Typing Tips Email Setup | Phone Email Fax Calendar | Voice Dialing Bluetooth Headset Address Book | Pictures Security Web Browser | Troubleshooting Settings Google Maps Modem |

BlackBerry Pearl   White BlackBerry Pearl   Red BlackBerry Pearl

Click Topic to view Video or PDF file.
Videos require Flash Player
PDF files require Adobe Reader.

Voice Dialing: Basics
Voice Dialing: Prompts and My Number
Bluetooth Headset - Setup
Bluetooth Headset - Accept Connection
Bluetooth Headset - Using It
Address: Introduction & Finding Addresses
Address: Add New, Add Picture, Editing
Address: New Address from Email Message
Address: New Address from Phone Call Log

Video Home Page > **BlackBerry Pearl™ / 8100 Series Videos**

| Getting Around Stand By Typing Tips Email Setup | Phone Email Fax Calendar | Voice Dialing Bluetooth Headset Address Book | Pictures Security Web Browser | Troubleshooting Settings Google Maps Modem |

BlackBerry Pearl   White BlackBerry Pearl   Red BlackBerry Pearl

Click Topic to view Video or PDF file.
Videos require Flash Player
PDF files require Adobe Reader.

Pictures: Put Your Picture On The Home Screen
Pictures: Select New Home Screen Image
Pictures: Picture for Caller ID
Security: Turn on Password
Security: Turn off Password
Security: Erase All Data from BlackBerry
Web Browser: Hot Keys (PDF)

New Videos are Added Frequently

25
Other
Resources

We listen to our customers and watch development with new BlackBerry models to add new videos frequently. When you check out the site, it's quite likely there will be a number of new videos on the Pearl and other devices.

Test your Skills with our Video Lesson Quizzes

At the bottom of each of the lessons, you will see a quiz button that brings up a 10-question multiple choice test. Tests questions are drawn at random from a database of over 500 questions. Even the answers are put in a random order each time you see the questions. What's even better is that you receive instant feedback at the end of the quiz showing you exactly which questions you answered correctly. You can even see the answers to the questions you missed!

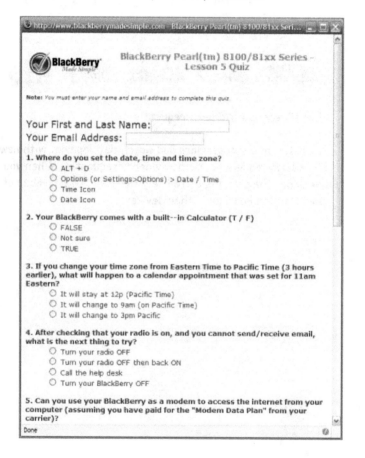

BlackBerry Made Simple Video Training for Organizations

We also offer the Video Tutorials in affordable site licenses which allow teams, departments or even entire organizations to deploy the videos on their internal servers or learning systems.

Organizations or teams buy a site license, receive a DVD which they can copy, customize and install quickly on their internal servers for use of the videos for an unlimited time.

Learn more about this by visiting our web site at www.blackberrymadesimple.com or emailing us at info@blackberrymadesimple.com.

A Range of Clients:
BlackBerry Made Simple's video tutorial clients range across most types of organizations:

25
Other
Resources

Commercial Organizations:
Auto and Truck Manufacturing
Clothing Fashion Design
Scientific Companies
Electric Power Distribution
Stone and Aggregate Manufacturing
Large Financial Services Companies
Other Fortune 500 Companies

Non-Profit Organizations
Inner-city school day care management
Regional offices of large charitable organizations
Global providers of food and assistance

Educational Institutions:
School Districts (Public and Private)
Colleges and Universities

Government/Military:
State Governments
Federal Government Institutions
Military Bases

Upcoming Books from BlackBerry Made Simple

Keep your eyes on www.blackberrymadesimple.com and on www.amazon.com for our two new books; "BlackBerry Made Simple's Definitive Guide to the Blackberry 8800/8300" and "CrackBerry; True Stories of BlackBerry Use and Abuse." (Titles may change slightly by publishing time) To be notified when each of these books is available for purchase, just sign up on our web site here:
http://www.blackberrymadesimple.com/bbms_booknotify_signup.shtml

Thanks Again!

Again, we sincerely thank you for purchasing this book and hope it has helped you really learn how to get every last drop of productivity and fun out of your BlackBerry Pearl™!

If you have any suggestions or ideas for improvements, we welcome them any time. You may even email them to us directly from your BlackBerry at info@blackberrymadesimple.com.

25
Other
Resources

www.ingramcontent.com/pod-product-compliance
Lightning Source LLC
Chambersburg PA
CBHW071354050326
40689CB00010B/1643